**DO NOT REMOVE
CARDS FROM POCKET**

The Political
and Socioeconomic
Transformation of Turkey

The Political
and Socioeconomic
Transformation of Turkey

Edited by
Atila Eralp, Muharrem Tünay,
and Birol Yeşilada

PRAEGER

Westport, Connecticut
London

Library of Congress Cataloging-in-Publication Data

The political and socioeconomic transformation of Turkey / edited by
  Atila Eralp, Muharrem Tünay, and Birol Yeşilada.
      p. cm.
   Includes bibliographical references and index.
   ISBN 0-275-93204-4
   1. Turkey–Economic policy. 2. Turkey–Economic conditions–1960-
3. Turkey–Politics and government–1980- I. Eralp, Atila.
II. Tünay, Muharrem. III. Yeşilada, Birol A.
HC492.P67 1993
338.9561–dc20   92-46638

British Library Cataloguing in Publication Data is available.

Library of Congress Catalog Card Number: 92-46638
ISBN: 0-275-93204-4

First published in 1993

Praeger Publishers, 88 Post Road West, Westport, CT 06881
An imprint of Greenwood Publishing Group, Inc.

Printed in the United States of America

The paper used in this book complies with the
Permanent Paper Standard issued by the National
Information Standards Organization (Z39.48-1984).

10 9 8 7 6 5 4 3 2 1

Contents

Acknowledgments

This volume is a product of a project that started in the spring of 1988 during a discussion between the coeditors. At that time, we were amazed by the fact that there were no published works in the Western literature that systematically examined the socioeconomic and political consequences of economic restructuring in Turkey that began with the January 24, 1980 austerity measures. This was a remarkable vacuum in the literature, because the Turkish experience with austerity and economic restructuring was hailed by international organizations like the World Bank and International Monetary Fund as a miracle model for other developing countries to follow. Furthermore, hardly anyone discussed the politics of austerity in Turkey. We believed that if we pooled together the knowledge and experiences of the young Turkish scholars in Turkey, we could compile a volume that would be a significant contribution to the literature in this field. The editing process, however, took more time than we had originally anticipated. The distance between Ankara, Turkey, and Columbia, Missouri and other logistical problems contributed to this delay. Despite the delay, we believe that the final product is a significant contribution to our understanding of the socioeconomic and political transformation of Turkey that began with the adoption of the January 24, 1980 austerity package by the Demirel government.

This project was assisted by a grant from the Research Council of the Middle East Technical University in Ankara, Turkey. Many individuals have contributed to this book, the most significant group being the authors whose works are included here. To them we extend our heartfelt thanks. We are grateful to Susan Yeşilada, who spent endless hours editing the manuscript. We also thank John Green, Linda Eikmeier, and DeAnna Walkenbach for their help with the typing of the chapters. Finally, we would like to thank Dan Eades at Praeger for his patience and encouraging comments and Julie Cullen, our production editor at Greenwood Publishing Group, for her attention to detail and invaluable suggestions during the preparation of this book.

Atila Eralp
Muharrem Tünay
Birol A. Yeşilada

The Political
and Socioeconomic
Transformation of Turkey

Introduction

Atila Eralp, Muharrem Tünay, and Birol A. Yeşilada

The decade of the 1980s marked a crucial turning point in Turkey's socioeconomic structure and polity. At the heart of the socioeconomic transformation lay the January 24, 1980 economic austerity package and the September 12, 1980 coup d'état that altered not only the Turkish economy and societal structure but the political system and external relations as well. The meanings of right and left, of modernity and backwardness, and of Turkishness were completely revised. This book attempts to show some of the economic and political processes that characterized this transformation. The authors' intent is to contextualize the 1980s both in time (to locate the 1980s in terms of what happened immediately before and after 1980) and space (in terms of relations in the international arena).

During the 1970s Turkey faced what was perhaps the worst political and socioeconomic crises of its republican history: social unrest, political violence, paralysis of the state bureaucracy and other institutions, foreign exchange problems, growing foreign debt, negative economic growth, high inflation and unemployment, a series of shortages, and alarming trade and balance of payments deficits. The economic basis of these crises can be viewed as the "crisis of the import substitution industrialization," which Albert Hirschman (1968) called the "difficult phase." Industrialization based on production for the internal market reached its structural limits as it became increasingly more difficult to obtain foreign exchange to import intermediate and capital goods. Toward the end of the 1970s Turkey encountered a major debt problem and became the first major developing country to face a resulting debt payment crisis (Celasun and Rodrik, 1989:193).

Confronted with growing socioeconomic and political problems, the last civilian government of the 1970s, headed by Süleyman Demirel, adopted a policy package on January 24, 1980, aimed at massive restructuring of the economy. The main thrust of the program was the implementation of export-oriented growth strategies. The US administration and international finance organizations like the IMF and World Bank supported these measures and the subsequent political order achieved by the military government (Yeşilada and Fisunoğlu, 1992:184). Nevertheless, these measures proved extremely difficult to implement and it was not until after the September 12, 1980 coup that officials were able to enact these policies. The military government, known as the National Security Council (NSC) and headed by General Kenan Evren, delegated the running of the new economic strategy to Turgut Özal, the then under secretary of the State Planning Organization. In this role, and later as prime minister, Özal embarked on a mission to thoroughly integrate Turkey into the world capitalist market. Thus, we define the decade of the 1980s as the period of economic austerity and restructuring in Turkey.

According to Miles Kahler (1990:3), the decade of the 1980s was the time when orthodox policies of the industrialized countries were also reflected, especially following the debt crisis, in the policies of the less developed countries (LDCs). However, policies adopted for economic stabilization and balance of payments adjustments in these countries varied greatly. While neoorthodoxy characterized stabilization policies in most LDCs, a few such countries, namely Argentina, Brazil, Israel, and Peru, adopted heterodox policies (Nelson, 1990). As Yeşilada and Fisunoğlu explain:

the neoorthodox policies were a reaction to the stagnation and crisis conditions that resulted from the difficulties associated with completion of the first and second phases of import substitution industrialization and the subsequent transition to the much needed export–led growth strategies. During the ensuing crises, authoritarian regimes or conservative governments came to power determined to undo their predecessors' inward-looking policies. (1992:184)

The neoorthodox policies that followed in most LDCs which adopted stabilization programs contained a common factor in that they linked stabilization (the short-term goal), structural adjustment (the medium-term objective), and economic strategy (the long-term goal) together. In addition, they required strict social and political order for the implementation of the necessary measures. The stabilization program that the government adopted on January 24, 1980, emphasized the following points (OECD, 1980; as cited in Yeşilada and Fisunoğlu, 1992:187):

1. Institutional changes aimed at making policy formulation and implementation more effective.
2. A devaluation of the Turkish lira vis-à-vis the US dollar by 33 percent, followed by continuous mini-devaluations, and the limitation of multiple exchange rate policies.

3. Greater liberalization of the trade and payment regulations.
4. Additional promotional measures for exports.
5. Substantial price increases for state traded goods and abolition of price controls.
6. Increased competition for State Economic Enterprises (SEEs) by eliminating state subsidies and abolition of price controls on their products.
7. Higher rates of interest.
8. Promotion of foreign investments.
9. Arrangements for consolidating Turkey's private commercial debt.
10. Draft legislation for tax reform.

In addition, the implementation of these policies required the restoration of sociopolitical order through an authoritarian political system. This, unwritten requirement received the quiet support of the IMF. Thus, as Yeşilada and Fisunoğlu explain (1992:187) "Turkey embarked on a new policy designed not only as a comprehensive program of economic stabilization but also as a basic reorientation of economic programs away from detailed government regulation and control toward greater reliance on market forces, foreign competition, and foreign investments." In reality, however, state regulation of the economy did not decrease after 1980. Rather, there were important changes in its form and direction. Now, state support focused on exporters who had the potential to integrate the Turkish economy with the world market. The abolition of the quota system and import licensing, the main pillars of import substitution industrialization, kept alive the rhetoric of liberalization. At the same time, import surcharges, tax exemptions, and rebates became the main mechanisms through which the government regulated the economy (Eralp, 1990). It is crucial to note that these policies closely resemble the neoorthodox adjustment programs that are discussed by Joan Nelson (1990:321-361). The relative success of such programs depends on five sets of causal variables for decision-making and policy implementation: (1) the type of crisis, (2) the capacity of the state, (3) political structures, (4) political circumstances, and (5) the role of external agencies like the IMF.

Economic restructuring in Turkey also benefited from changes in the international climate at the end of the 1970s. The Soviet invasion of Afghanistan in 1979, the Iranian Revolution, and the conflict in Lebanon undermined the process of detente, and both the United States and Turkey became extremely suspicious of Soviet expansionist intentions. Under these circumstances, Turkey's strategic position became very important for the American administration. Thus, in a repeat of Turkish-American relations of the 1950s, the strategic location of Turkey helped in the Turkish-American rapprochement during the 1980s. This rapprochement affected international lending agencies, resulting in funds beginning to flow to Turkey from the World Bank, the IMF, and the OECD. 1979-1981 is rather exceptional in terms of the flow of external resources when compared to the earlier period of 1975-1978

(Celasun and Rodrik, 1989). We maintain that these external financial resources were rather significant in alleviating the chronic foreign exchange problems. Furthermore, the new economic strategy of export promotion was able to develop in this propitious international climate.

The strategic alliance with the US at the turn of the 1980s marked the beginning of a new trend in Turkish foreign relations–a trend which culminated in the establishment of closer links between Turkey and the Middle East and a souring of relations with Europe. This resulted from a number of international problems faced by Turkey, both in economic and political terms. Despite efforts to integrate Turkey into the world market, the 1980s witnessed a serious deterioration of Turkey's trade links with Europe. Not only were European aid and credits curtailed as a result of the 1980 coup, Turkey's exports to the European Community, which had always constituted a significant portion of her foreign exchange earnings, suffered a serious setback. Thus, Turkey had to look for new markets in order to implement its new growth strategy. The Middle East, especially Iran, Iraq, and Saudi Arabia, began to fill the gap.

The crucial factors behind worsening of relations with the European Community were Turkey's military rule and its human rights record. As Europe increasingly distanced itself from Turkey, the US took on a more supportive position. This situation constituted a major turning point not only in terms of Turkey's foreign policy but also in its identity. Since the founding of the republic in 1923, Turkey has maintained the political goal to become part of the West. This desire also related to Turkey's identity; the leaders of the new republic opted for development in line with the Western model of modernization. Europe's decision to distance itself from Turkey enabled those anti-Western forces in Turkey to use this to challenge the vitality of Westernization. Ironically, the domestic policies of the military government helped to strengthen the position of the anti-Western forces. Efforts by the military to use religion as a buffer against socialism allowed a hitherto suppressed Muslim identity a voice. This is ironic, because the military was one institution in Turkey that had always opposed religious and other anti-Western groups. In any case, closer economic ties with the Middle East and disenchantment with Westernization-modernization policies at home prompted a search for new methods of development, a new identity, and a new utopia. With this shift, Islamic identity became more visible not only because of increased veiling and prayer practices in the streets and in the universities, but most importantly in the educational and cultural policies of the Özal governments.

World events in 1989 only served to exacerbate these trends. The removal of the Soviet threat meant that Turkey would no longer be able to occupy a strategic position in the traditional meaning of the East-West rivalry. However, the Gulf War, regional problems in the Middle East, and the rise of Turkic republics in Central Asia provided Turkey with a new form of strategic significance in the West–"new" Middle East relations. We argue that this new significance of Turkey is a product of international and domestic processes that began a decade earlier. Therefore, a careful analysis of the structural changes of the 1980s is crucial to our understanding of present developments. The 1980s set the stage for even greater regional involvement for Turkey, both in the Middle East and the Turkic republics of the former Soviet Union. In conjunction with this outcome, questions of religious and ethnic identity now occupy a greater place in the domestic politics of Turkey.

This book treats the separate but related aspects of Turkey's domestic and international affairs in an attempt to aid our understanding of the country's responses to the changing environment of the 1990s. The time period of analysis is between January 24, 1980, and 1989, during which the military government of General Kenan Evren and the post-1983 civilian governments of Turgut Özal embarked on a mission of fully integrating Turkey into the world capitalist market via the implementation of the basic policy reforms of the January 24, 1980 package.

The topics examined in this book can be divided into two broad subject areas. The first six chapters focus on transformation in the domestic domain, covering areas of domestic politics, religion, industrialization, labor relations, and agriculture. In chapter 1 Muharrem Tünay examines how the political right, concentrated around the Motherland party of Turgut Özal, attempted to establish its hegemony, in the Gramscian sense, in Turkish politics. This analysis shows that the new right has been unable to succeed in establishing a new hegemonic bloc. It did not have the capacity to merge different interests into a national-popular program. Furthermore, Tünay maintains that the Motherland party bloc has been incapable of overcoming its internal contradiction: the ideological conflict between "Americanophile liberalism" and Islamic fundamentalism.

In chapter 2, Ayşe Ayata analyzes the ideology, social bases, and organiza-tional structures of the post-1980 political parties. She demonstrates that, in general terms, the organized working class and the new middle classes (professionals, civil servants, and the like) tend to vote predominantly left, while the traditional urban middle classes (small businessmen, shopkeepers, artisans) and the peasants are inclined to vote for the rightist parties. A similar division occurs along religious lines. The Alevis vote for the leftist parties, while the Sunni voters prefer the rightist parties. In essence, Ayata shows that the new political parties inherited some of the old social cleavages of pre-1980 Turkey, although they tried to introduce new ideas and represented new interests and cleavages. Furthermore, since the new political system did not permit the smaller parties to enter the National Assembly, due to the new elections law, only those parties which could appeal for mass support were able to muster the necessary votes for representation. Along with Tünay, Ayata concludes that the Motherland party faces the problem of the durability and stability of its support base. Also, she argues that the party lacks a core of permanent and loyal voters who identify themselves with the organization. Thus, in terms of organizational strength, the True Path party (successor to the Justice party) and the Social Democratic Populist party (successor to the Republican People's party), have a clear advantage over the Motherland party with regard to voter support base.

On a different level of analysis, Sencer Ayata examines the rise of Islamic fundamentalism and its institutional framework in chapter 3. He analyzes Islamic perspectives in the mass media, the different religious orders (*tarikat*), their ties to political and economic organizations, Sufism versus radicalism, and religion and education in Turkey. Ayata argues that Islam appeals increasingly to all social classes and sections of the population, whether educated or not, and urban as well as rural. Its influence is pervasive in traditional small communities, in the economy, and in education; and almost everywhere it is becoming increasingly politicized. In the face of uneven economic development, rapid urbanization, and poor income distribution, Ayata maintains that Islamic fundamentalism will become a greater force in Turkish social and political life and contribute to the most serious crisis of legitimacy ever witnessed since the early days of the republic.

In chapter 4 the focus of analysis moves into the economic domain. Here, Oktar Türel examines the development of the manufacturing sector in Turkey. He evaluates changes in the composition of gross output, international trade orientation, factor use, changes in productivity, and trends in fixed capital formation. Türel shows that the Turkish economic administration preferred to leave industrial development to its "natural" course with the assumption that eventually the profit motive would stimulate the manufacturing industries. The lack of any rational and conscious industrial policy during the 1980s demonstrated that this "natural" course has transferred profits away from industrial pursuits to rentiers and traders (domestic or international) and hampered capital formation. He finally cautions that the future growth of the Turkish economy might rapidly be strangled either by capacity constraints in, or by rising import dependence of, the manufacturing sector.

In chapter 5 Fikret Şenses examines the labor market policies of the 1980 Stabilization Program. He reviews collective bargaining, administrative controls over trade union activities, and policies of employment and wages. His analysis demonstrates that the tight controls over trade union activities and wages were direct products of the Stabilization Program. All of these policies strengthened the hand of the state over its working-class citizens. In fact, Şenses's findings support our argument about the unwritten requirements of the stabilization program: domestic social and political order.

Chapter 6 examines a different spect of the transformation of the Turkish economy. This time, the causal factor is an external agent, the World Bank. In this chapter, Zülküf Aydın analyzes how the World Bank helped transform Turkish agriculture during the 1980s. He suggests that the predominance of small producers in the Turkish countryside is a conjunctural one and that the process unleashed since 1980 will prove to be very powerful in destroying the viability of petty commodity producers. In the wake of stabilization policies, social differentiation in rural Turkey has unprecedentedly accelerated. These outcomes closely follow the strategies of international agencies like the World Bank for the Third World in general.

The last four chapters of this book examine transformation in Turkey's external affairs. Chapter 7, by Canan Balkır, examines the infamous trade strategy of the stabilization program. This is one of the most crucial aspects of these policies, because it marks a fundamental change in Turkish economic growth strategy from the inward-oriented import substitution model to an outward–oriented export led growth model. Balkır provides a thorough examination of the government's export incentive mechanisms and assesses the reality behind these ventures. She argues that rapid export growth occurred primarily as a result of exporting available stock of idle capacity rather than through additional investments in export industries. Balkır also establishes a link between the export policies and worsening position of laborers, particularly those employed by small firms oriented toward internal markets. In essence, Balkır questions the so-called success of Turkey's export explosion during the 1980s and disputes the vitality of this sector, as characterized by the policies of the government, for future economic development and social equity.

In chapter 8 Birol Yeşilada analyzes changes in Turkey's foreign policy towards the Middle East. He argues that during the 1980s Turkey's foreign policy became increasingly personalized. Both President Kenan Evren and President Turgut Özal personally shaped their country's foreign policy profile and tried to balance the interests of their NATO allies, primarily the Americans, with their Islamic friends in the region. In the first area, Turkish and US relations entered a new age of cooperation characterized by joint ventures in defense industries, joint military maneuvers in the area, and the adoption of a defense strategy that provided a staging point for Western military campaigns in the Middle East. At the same time, Turkey tried to maintain its neutrality in the Iran-Iraq war and sold materials to both sides. However, relations with Iraq began to sour as the Kurdish guerrillas intensified their campaign against Turkey from bases within that country. Finally, for the first time since the establishment of the republic, Turkish officials began to improve their country's ties to oil-rich Islamic states of the region. The most significant improvement is observed in relations with Saudi Arabia. Yeşilada argues that there exists a personal and economic reason behind this development. In essence, Saudi Arabian finance houses maintain economic partnership with President Turgut Özal's brother and his firms in Turkey.

In chapter 9 Atila Eralp analyzes relations between Turkey and the European Community. He examines the factors behind Turkey's application for membership in the Community in 1987 and assesses the Europeans' response to this development. Eralp explains that two traditional concerns have determined Turkish efforts to become part of Europe. The first factor is Westernization, though it has become more problematic during the 1980s as result of the proliferation of diverse attitudes in Turkey and tensions in European-American relations. The second factor is the Greek issue. Eralp argues that the present inclusion of Greece in the Community acts as a powerful catalyst that reinforces Turkey's determination to become a member of the EC. He further maintains that Turkish policymakers turn to Europe when economic and political problems at home urge them to look for new policy alternatives abroad. In contrast, when events at home are calm, relations with the EC seem to be given secondary importance, while efforts to reinforce relations with the US gain more significance. This pattern, Eralp argues, was observed in the last years of both the Democrat party and Motherland party rule. In view of his findings, Eralp asks whether this Turkish habit of turning to Europe only at times of need has an important cost: that of losing sight of the dynamics of European development. This habit seems to preclude the formation of a longer and more sustained policy toward the EC as well as the capacity to find viable policy strategies at the right moment.

In the final chapter Duygu Sezer examines Turkey in the Western alliance during the 1980s in light of the dramatic changes in East-West relations. She argues that against the evolving configuration of power relations, the most likely scenario for Turkey seems to be one in which it would continue to be tied to Western Europe, but with looser security ties embodied in bilateral agreements of military assistance, improved commercial relations, and a bilateral defense partnership with the US in the context of America's shifting Middle East policies and interests. This, however, is least favorable for a large portion of the Turkish political and business elites because it would make Turkey an American outpost. It would also strengthen the hands of the Islamic fundamentalists. Sezer states that the fear of being reduced to a non-European country on the fringes of Europe pressures the Turkish policymakers to push for membership in the EC, the Western European Union, or any other European institution. However, the signals from Europe do not seem promising.

Since the analysis of the above chapters ended in 1989, the editors felt it necessary to include an epilogue that would attempt to bridge the findings of the contributors with developments that have taken place since 1990. The final chapter, written by the editors, establishes this tie and asks: (1) whether or not socioeconomic and political transformation has been successful? and (2) if economic stabilization was worth the price?

REFERENCES

Celasun, M. and D. Rodrik (1989). "Turkish Experience with Debt: Macroeconomic Policy and Performance." In Jeffrey D. Sachs, ed., *Developing Country Debt and the World Economy*. Chicago: University of Chicago Press.

Eralp, A. (1990). "The Politics of Turkish Development Strategies." In A. Finkel and N. Sirman, eds., *Turkish State, Turkish Society*. London: Routledge.

Hirschman, A. O. (1968). "The Political Economy of Import Substituting Industrialization in Latin America." *Quarterly Journal of Economics*. (February).

Kahler, M. (1990). "Orthodoxy and Its Alternatives: Explaining Approaches to Stabilization and Adjustment." In J. M. Nelson, ed., *Economic Crisis and Policy Choice: The Politics of Adjustment in the Third World*. Princeton: Princeton University Press.

Nelson, J. M. (1990). *Economic Crisis and Policy Choices: The Politics of Adjustment in the Third World*. Princeton: Princeton University Press.

OECD (1980). *Economic Surveys: Turkey*. Paris: OECD Publications.

Yeşilada, B. A. (1988). "Problems of Political Development in the Third Turkish Republic." *Polity*. Vol. 21. No. 2 (Winter):345-372.

Yeşilada, B. A. and M. Fisunoğlu (1992). "Assessing the January 24 1980 Economic Stabilization Program in Turkey." In H. J. Barkey, ed., *The Political Economy of Stabilization Measures in the Middle East*. New York: St. Martin's Press.

1

The Turkish New Right's Attempt at Hegemony

Muharrem Tünay

INTRODUCTION

Turkey's continuing economic and political distress has intensified particularly after 1980 due to the interplay of various factors. The shift to an export promotion development strategy, the reconstitution of law and order, the progressively worsening income distribution, the emergence of a new type of individualism, and above all, the formation of a new right movement are among the most striking developments leading to the new equilibrium. On the one hand, IMF–directed policies have secured Turkey's further integration into the world capitalist system, while on the other, a new right political alliance has formed showing great similarities in its ideological stance and specific strategies to those of Reaganism and Thatcherism.

What is unduly surprising in this symbiosis is that although immense differences exist among these countries with respect to their social structures, more or less the same political and economic policies have been implemented within the new right ideological framework. As I shall try to show in this study, the new right in Turkey certainly maintains various traditional elements in its ideological appeal, but at the same time it incorporates into its national-popular agenda several new assets such as anti-statism, privatization, the two nations project, a liberal-competitive individualism, and apparently contradictory Islamic capitalist free enterprise. There are, however, so many discrepancies (inconsistencies) not only within the elements of this ideological framework but also between the new right's attempt at social transformation and the balance of forces in society that any simplistic approach to the problem fails theoretically. Consequently, the main objective of this paper is to examine the Turkish new right with respect to its structure, ideology, and attempt at hegemony.

In this chapter, I intend to evaluate the Turkish situation with the aid of certain Gramscian concepts which current literature has refined within the same tradition, since it is next to impossible to investigate such a complex phenomenon with too many different ideologies. This necessitates a reexamination of these crucial concepts such as hegemony, ideology in the Gramscian context, hegemonic projects, accumulation strategy, and passive revolution. However, some of these concepts, such as hegemony and ideology, are very problematic theoretical categories, and therefore, they need to be reworked to make them operational in the study of a specific case. It is precisely this complexity of the Gramscian thought that prompts many thinkers to revise these crucial concepts in order to study politics in the Western world. Moreover, the rise of new right movements, particularly in the US and England, has provoked the reexamination of our previous forms of understanding political analysis.

There is therefore good reason for revisiting Gramsci, "the theoretician of superstructures," who spent a great part of his life in the study of the balance of forces in society, and the ideological and hegemonic successes of the Western dominant classes. Nonetheless, in my view, there is no reason to restrict this theoretical approach to advanced capitalist countries alone. After all, a country like Turkey is perhaps far more advanced than the Italy of "Risorgimento," which occupied a central place in Gramsci's political analysis. In a later section of this chapter I investigate the rise of the Turkish new right and its present features. This new right clearly tried to establish a new hegemony after the 1980 military takeover. This attempt centered not only on the acquisition of governmental power but also extended to the capture of crucial hegemonic fields such as schools, religious behavior, individuality, media, and above all, the restoration of the necessary exploitation relation between capital and labor. In a way, the new right struggled for the reinforcement of its political power, essentially the state, with the creation of a new collective will in civil society. Also of importance, the same movement accomplished its projects within a Thatcherite form. This not only demonstrates a crucial aspect of Turkey's further integration into the world capitalist system, but also conforms with the present accumulation strategy determined both by indigenous factors and the division of labor imposed by advanced capitalist centers. Conclusively, this rather complicated phenomenon must be studied at a certain level of abstraction going beyond a narration of the history of the country since 1980.

REVIEW OF THE RELEVANT CONCEPTS

This section examines Gramsci's writings and several recent works that aim at the refinement and concretization of the Gramscian system of thought. This system has contributed considerably to our understanding of Reaganism, and more specifically Thatcherism, through both Gramsci's works and the newer formulations of more explanatory theoretical categories. At the highest level of abstraction, hegemony and ideology seem to be the broadest and most central concepts. Furthermore, *hegemony* can be identified with consent as opposed to coercion, or physical force.[1] In other words, hegemony refers to domination by the creation of a collective will, or general interest, which articulates the interests of all other classes and groups to that of the hegemonic class. This articulation process is mediated through a variety of cultural institutions, such as the church or corresponding institutions in other religions, schools, media, architecture, and value systems, which even include the names of the streets (Mouffe, 1979:187).

Therefore, hegemony is not only the maintenance of a political alliance, or unity, within the sections of the dominant class, but also a moral and intellectual leadership of the dominant class, or a section of that class, over the subordinate classes or groups. In this respect, it is a pedagogical relationship (Entwistle, 1979:12) encompassing processes of integration, assimilation, articulation, and at times, neutralization of particular interests in society. Only in this way can a hegemonic class "nationalize" itself, and thus extend its power beyond the seizure of governmental institutions and the assertion of specific class interests. At the center of hegemony lies the essential domination relationship exercised "in the decisive nucleus of economic activity" (Mouffe, 1979:10). Hence, the unity of the base and superstructure, and the formation of a sound historical bloc (Jessop, 1983:92) distinguish economic hegemony from economic domination, in that whereas the latter can be reduced to the imposition of the economic-corporate interest of a specific fraction of capital on other fractions, the former denotes an articulation of different interests to that of the leading group. In my view such an approach is misleading, since the concept of hegemony necessarily relies on economic domination together with the establishment of a unity between the economic, political, and cultural levels.[2]

Hegemony may assume two forms: passive revolution and expansive hegemony. In passive revolution (for this concept, see Gramsci, 1973:106-114; Mouffe, 1979:11-13; Jessop, 1983:105; and Jessop et al., 1984:36) no mass mobilization is required. A new hegemony is founded upon the basis of the containment, or the neutralization, of the interests, political activities and ideological struggles of subordinate classes and groups. Here, the important point for the dominant class is not the creation of a new collective will by articulating other interests to its own, or even by sacrificing its short-term economic-corporate benefits for the sake of establishing a stable equilibrium, but rather the preemption of the political drive of all oppositional forces. Therefore, it is of the utmost importance for the dominant class to mobilize only the key sections of society under the rubric of its ideological advance. Apparently, this form is an extremity and a very uncomfortable situation in the conceptualization of hegemony, for it rests more upon direct political action plus a certain degree of integration among the sections of the dominant class than on the absorption of civil society as a whole.

Expansive hegemony, however, dissolves all class lines on a nationwide basis and manages to create almost a consensus in society. The hegemonic class founds this form of hegemony through the adoption of the interests of the popular classes, paving the way for the creation of a "national-popular will" (Jessop, 1983:101). In this case, the specific demands of subordinate forces are neither repressed nor neutralized to prevent their independent development; they are instead assimilated into an organic whole which corresponds to the kernel of each demand. This is a direct and active consensus advancing the whole society toward a predetermined goal, and it creates, at a lower level of abstraction, a new common sense, or the rearticulation and reorganization of the elements of the old one. However, Gramsci indicates that this form of hegemony frequently encounters risks and problems, since it is based on the exploitation relation of the hegemonic class. Consequently, it generally results in a resort to compulsion, or outright police measures such as "coups d'etat" (Gramsci, 1973:60-61).

What is, then, the role of ideology in this context? According to Gramsci, ideology is a worldview geared to social practice and action having a material basis (Mouffe, 1979:186). In other words, it is a way of life attached to and organized by a social bloc; but the daily practice, or the common sense, of the individual does not stem from his/her own creativity, since the former is necessarily linked to the higher philosophies of a social collectivity, that is, the social class. Only through this process does the individual acquire a sort of consciousness. However, ideological elements do not acquire their class character spontaneously, or by a direct correspondence to the relations of production, but through the articulation of the values of several groups forming a unified ideological system imprinted characteristically by a fundamental class. The role of ideology in a hegemonic system is, then, to cement different worldviews, or value systems, to assure the exercise of the political and social hegemony of a specific class (Mouffe, 1979:191-193). This cement functions not only to articulate the interests of subordinate groups or classes to those of the hegemonic class, but to secure unity between the factions of the latter as well. If hegemony is a general apparatus of domination encompassing the whole of the civil society beyond the monopolization of solely the governmental power, then ideology is the most important mediator, or even the guarantor of this domination, without which the system cannot possibly reproduce itself. As Mouffe puts it:

The importance of intellectual and moral reform lies in the fact that the hegemony of a fundamental class consists in the creation of a "collective will" (on the basis of a common world-view which will serve as a unifying principle) in which this class and its allies will fuse to form a "collective man." . . . The creation of a new hegemony, therefore, implies the transformation of the previous ideological terrain and the creation of a new world-view which will serve as a unifying principle for a new collective will. This is the process of ideological transformation which Gramsci designates with the term "intellectual and moral reform." (1979:191)

These assessments are still too abstract and need to become more operational and concrete for specific case analyses. Jessop developed two useful concept within the Gramscian line of thought that may well fulfill this requirement. The first one is the hegemonic project, which is a precondition for the hegemonic class to carry out its moral and intellectual leadership. In other words, it is a nationwide project welding together at least the majority of particular interests in society around a specific goal.

In abstract terms, this conflict (between particular interests and the general interest) is probably insoluble because of the potentially infinite range of particular interests that could oppose any definition of the general interest. Nonetheless, the hegemonic leadership should resolve this conflict on a less abstract plane through specific political, intellectual, and moral practices. This involves the mobilization of support behind a concrete, national-popular program of action which asserts a general interest in the pursuit of objectives that explicitly or implicitly advance the long-term interests of the hegemonic class (faction) and which also privilege particular economic-corporate interests compatible with this program. According to Jessop (1983:100 and Hall, 1985:118), hegemonic projects may include military success, social reform, political stability, or moral regeneration, each possessing the capability of mobilizing popular groups toward a definite end which ultimately evades apparent contradictions and thus benefits mainly the hegemonic class.

Jessop's second concept is the accumulation strategy, which "defines a specific economic growth model" (1983:91). It is by and large promoted by one faction of capital, but to be successful it has to unite the interests of other factions, or in other words, it has to secure the smooth operation of the circuit of capital. This does not eliminate competition among the factions of capital: rather, they compete with each other to establish a definite course of accumulation. Just as the hegemonic project unites particular interests with that of the hegemonic class, so an accumulation strategy creates a collective will, or general interest of all capitals, of course under the domination of one particular faction. Finally, accumulation strategies may vary from "Fordism" to "Keynesianism" with more explicit examples of "import substitution" and "export promotion" development strategies (Jessop, 1983:94). To complete the picture, I must note that an already–established hegemony may, at a certain point, face a crisis. In other words, the question is not only the entrenchment of hegemony by a specific class, but also its collapse, which necessarily causes a "crisis of authority."

Gramsci defines the nature and the conditions of such a hegemonic crisis as follows:

In every country the process is different, although the content is the same, and the content is the crisis of the ruling class's hegemony, which occurs either because the ruling class has failed in some major political undertaking for which it has requested, or forcibly extracted, the consent of the broad masses (war, for example), or because huge masses . . . have passed suddenly from a state of political passivity to a certain activity, and put forward demands which taken together, albeit not organically formulated, add up to a revolution. A "crisis of authority" is spoken of: this is precisely the crisis of hegemony, or general crisis of the state. (1973:210)

The theoretical scheme mentioned above has been employed for some time in the analysis of the new right movements in the US, and more specifically in England, although there is no consensus among the authors as far as those concepts are concerned.[3] Particularly in the latter case, Thatcherism is clearly designated as a passive revolution carrying out a two nations hegemonic project. It means that there is no national-popular consensus, hence no expansive hegemony, integrating the interests of the popular groups, but rather a process of neutralizing or containing them under massive political propaganda. The new right divides the nation into two parts, one of which–unions, the unemployed, the disabled, pensioners, and so on–is deprived of the benefits of the Keynesian welfare state and subjected to wage cuts, political repression, and so forth. Rhetorical themes such as anti-statism, or "future benefits will follow from present suffering" (Jessop et al., 1984:47), reinforce the general ventriloquism of the new right to outflank social democracy, which has long been identified with statism, socialism, and welfare policies (Hall, 1979:18 and 1984:25). The accumulation strategy in this context is export promotion, which generally results in the decline of manufacturing and construction while benefiting mostly sectors such as oil, communications, agriculture, finance, and electrical engineering (Jessop et al., 1984:54). This post-Fordist model, however, does not seem to be a remedy for the crisis of capitalism.

The new right ideology both in the US and England consists of old elements, such as the family, religious fundamentalism, moral regeneration, racial discrimination, and anticommunism, as well as neo-liberal issues of anti-statism, free competitive markets, productivism, and selective welfarism favoring only one nation (Davis, 1981:12-19 and Jessop et al., 1984:51). However, these elements combine in such a way that the contradictory old ones are rearticulated into the new ideological principles, or they are refined to express the new situation. The advocacy of a strong, centralized state, for example, is presented as the political *cordon sanitaire* for the free functioning of the market economy. Moreover, the liberal principle of providing incentives for the skilled workers, aiming at the creation of divisions within the workingclass, has so far succeeded in justifying reprisal against unions, in the name of rewarding the productive and taming the unproductive and undisciplined (Leonard, 1979:10-11; Gamble, 1985:23; and Jessop et al., 1987:105).

The conceptual framework developed in the Gramscian line of thought has been very helpful in understanding the complex phenomenon of the new right in terms of its structure, rhetoric, ideology, strategy, and policies. Now we can at least locate the real intentions behind the new right's project, as well as the form of hegemony it tries to accomplish, and the stage of the hegemonic struggle within the context of the crisis of world capitalism. The next section uses the analytic tools of this theoretical construction to explore recent developments and the rise of the new rightist movement in Turkey. However, Turkey cannot immediately be compared to Western capitalist countries, since there are immense differences with respect to their histories, national characteristics, and the degree of their capitalist development. Nonetheless, many striking similarities exist with regard to their new right projects for hegemony, so that one cannot dispense with the hypothesis pointing to the progressive integration between the center and the periphery. This will necessarily take us to a comparative theoretical inquiry into the Turkish new right movement.

THE NEW RIGHT AND ITS STRUGGLE FOR HEGEMONY

The November 1983 general elections in Turkey marked the beginning of a very significant era in the history of the country, because the new right, under the political leadership of the Motherland party (MP), initiated a campaign to solve the ongoing hegemonic crisis. In fact, this crisis can be traced back to as early as the 1970s, and probably even to the 1960s, during which time rapid capitalist development occurred. This development, however, induced great social transformations and revealed many of the structural contradictions intrinsic to the capitalist mode of production.

By 1980 the transition from an agricultural to a semi-industrial society had already ended with millions of agricultural producers separated from their means of production, resulting in a mass migration movement to cities and industrial zones. The extremely low level of wages, problems of unemployment, and the lack of organized labor had progressively impoverished the majority within this sector. In addition, the process of social stratification in rural areas, as a result of capitalist development, had accelerated the breakdown of the traditional form of economic organization in agriculture and thereby had unleashed serious social discontent with respect to value systems, social behavior, and political orientation (Tünay, 1978:ch. 4). Islam, which had been controlled and never permitted to become an organized movement in the Kemalist period, represented a form of reaction to rapid social transformation in the 1960s. However, it would be misleading to say that Islam became a political force at that time, since certain political parties manipulated religious sentiments only to enlarge the electorate at the polls. In other words, Islam did not constitute an ideological cement ensuring hegemony in civil society, nor did it represent the spearhead of opposition to the rule of the bourgeoisie. It only signaled a reaction to the development of capitalism although, paradoxically, it was manipulated by bourgeois political parties to maintain popular support.

As for as the position of the bourgeoisie in society, this class tried to promote a Western way of life and the bourgeois worldview in the 1960s, but it was still incapable of asserting competitive individualism instead of traditional collectivism and the corresponding social behavior. Its hegemonic project was one of rejecting all class-based issues and movements, but was more democratic in political orientation and organization than in the subsequent periods. However, this one nation project did not identify itself strictly with nationalism as an ideology until the mid-1970s; rather, the Turkish left monopolized nationalism, forwarding it as a synonym for anti-imperialism. In this context, anti-imperialism targeted more specifically the American imperialism that had gradually been establishing dependency ties with Turkey since the Marshall Plan. Turkey's integration into the world capitalist system and the construction of assembly industries through close trade links with the US assumed the form of import substitution as the accumulation strategy of the 1960s (Eralp, 1990:222-224).

However, a strong political rule and grip over civil society did not reinforce economic domination of the bourgeoisie, since the early organization of the opposition forces shook the very foundations of the whole system and resulted in the military takeover of 1971. The progressive deterioration of income distribution, rapid but inequitable process of growth, rejection of co-optation policies of the government by a number of radical unions, students' protests, social grievances in the countryside, dislike of the new rich, due to their extravagance, and the dramatic juxtaposition of old and new values, as well as the parliamentary struggle carried out by one section of the revolutionary left, all merged into a form of social discontent. This was the beginning of the hegemonic crisis which has lasted until today.

A crucial cause of the failure to sustain hegemony, or the creation of a new hegemony, was the ideological feebleness of the bourgeoisie, which could not find relevant ideological elements to unite the interests of subordinate groups around a national-popular program, let alone those of factions of capital. Industrial capital seemed to be the most energetic and leading section, yet a smooth transformation of merchant capital to industrial capital could not be accomplished. This required either the "Bismarckian road to industrialization" (Kemp, 1976:90-118 and Kemp, 1978), which squeezed all the stages of capitalist development to only thirty-forty years, or a more relaxed development strategy capable of absorbing social tensions in due time. However, Turkey's economic development was characteristically a dependent capitalist one, constantly undermining the formation of ideological coherence, and thus preventing the establishment of hegemony. Attempts at even a passive revolution were successful only in the short run, since the interests of different groups and classes could not be neutralized except when military regimes subjected the whole society to severe political repression during limited periods.

The 1971 military takeover did not even try to install any form of hegemony and restricted itself solely to police measures in order to cope with the extreme left and terroristic organizations (Yeşilada, 1988a:345-346). The late 1970s, on the other hand, witnessed one of the most illustrative cases of a hegemonic crisis: the collapse of political order, the decay of parliamentary democracy, labor militancy, student revolts, armed struggle between extreme right and extreme left organizations, the unprecedented growth of social democracy, and above all, the incompetence of the right-wing political parties in constituting the political expression of the economic-corporate interests of the dominant class. Apparently bringing the country to the verge of a civil war, terrorism was of the utmost importance, as later declared by the officials of the 1980 takeover (for the actual figures on terroristic activities see, Yeşilada, 1988a:351).

However, terrorism was not the only basis for military intervention. What is important is that the country faced a real impasse. On the one hand, balance of payment difficulties, inflation, and the sharp confrontation between labor and capital, blocking the accumulation strategy of the latter, led the economy to a complete collapse; while on the other, no political solution was able to stabilize conditions in the chaotic atmosphere of those days. Since the import substitution strategy depended on the abundance of foreign currency, the Turkish economy experienced serious financial bottlenecks and resulting large deficits. Various attempts to acquire foreign loans to compensate for the dwindling foreign currency reserves were doomed to fail due to the lack of credibility abroad.[4] This was the peak of the hegemonic crisis, or the forcible unfolding of the structural contradictions of the past decades. Gramsci had drawn attention to the dissociation of the link between the dominant class and its political representation as the prominent manifestation of the hegemonic crisis; a similar phenomenon occurred in Turkey during that period. No right-wing political party could stabilize economic and political conditions; thus, they failed to serve the interests of the dominant class, let alone resolve interclass conflicts. Accordingly, by the late 1970s prospects for a military intervention were already visible.

Unlike the previous ones, the 1980 military takeover ambitiously aimed at inducing societal transformations. This can also be viewed as an attempt to establish a new hegemony, but obviously with no specific hegemonic project or ideological system. Its failure could be foreseen from the beginning, but like all Caesarist solutions, it was bound to lead up eventually to either a historically reactionary or a progressive movement, that is, giving support to either conservative or popular forces. Between 1980 and 1983 the military regime repressed terrorist organizations, banned political parties, and implemented certain reforms, such as the reorganization of the political system, the establishment of new labor relations based on the restriction of wage increases, and the strengthening of the security forces for the purpose of maintaining law and order. An authoritarian constitution in 1982 replaced the liberal-democratic constitution of 1961, encompassing general policies, as well as more particular ones like the imposition of tight controls over universities (Yeşilada, 1988a:353-355). Far from being a revolution from above, and more likely a police measure apparatus, these policies stabilized political conditions over and above a silenced majority that could neither attach itself to a specific goal nor get organized in opposition.

The crucial aspect of the same period, however, is that the Caesarism of the early 1980s paved the way for a very significant change in the balance of political forces. This was the grand strategy of the military regime, despite all its rhetoric about the maintenance and further development of the secular Kemalist ideology, to counterbalance the revolutionary left forces by providing support to Islamic movements. Of course, this operation was not overt but carried out insidiously with the idea that a right-wing social force, outside the boundaries of the state, had to be activated to provide security for conservative forces in the long run. The pan-Turkist extreme right-wing party, the Nationalist Action party and its paramilitary organizations, had already discredited themselves by the end of the 1970s through terrorist activities, and now the military broke their backbone. So was the case with the left-wing organizations; at the same time social democracy weakened considerably. However, officials anticipated that both moderate and revolutionary left-wing movements would reincarnate once a civilian regime was instituted. I would argue that even the top leaders of the military regime at the time were incapable of predicting the implications of this strategy. In actuality it would soon prepare the ground for the revival of militant Islamic fundamentalism,[5] a real threat posed against the very existence of the republic. Of course, one cannot take this argument too far, since there was only a modicum of evidence to substantiate it. Nonetheless, history showed in the following years that this line of thought was not at all on the wrong track. As we shall see below, Islamic fundamentalist movements, uniting their forces with the remnants of pan-Turkist nationalist elements, occupied a central position not only in the new right formation but in its ideology as well. This outcome owes much to toleration by the military regime, which did not target Islamic forces.

The November 1983 general election was held under such circumstances. Most prominently, military officials restricted the number of political parties and even vetoed some parties and party candidates. In a word, it was hardly a democratic election process and forcibly oriented the electorate toward only specific political choices. The party that emerged victorious from the elections was Turgut Özal's Motherland party.

The new right campaign throughout the election process and even after the new government came to power clearly demonstrated an attempt to form an expansive type of hegemony. Pinpointing the long lasting economic and political crisis, the new right leaders claimed that Turkey needed a completely new approach to her worsening conditions. Accordingly, before anything else, national unity was required, since all the evils of the past supposedly stemmed basically from the political divisions in society. Therefore, the maintenance of law and order was of the utmost importance, for any return to pre-1980 political orientations and patterns of behavior would bring back the vicissitudes of the past. The MP clearly stated that its popularity and its success in the elections were based upon its inclusive structure, which encompassed four different political orientations (ANAP, 1983:153 and Özal, 1987:23-24). Those orientations were, namely, the liberals, pan-Turkist extreme right-wing elements, Islamic fundamentalists, and the social democrats.

Of course, there were apparent contradictions in this structure, such as those between the liberals and the extreme right and also those between the social democrats and the rest. In any case, the new right tried to capitalize on the developments of the military regime period. Its assessment was that the social democrats had already been disillusioned by the beginning of the 1980s, while the traditional liberals had long been looking for an integrating leadership to take them out of ideological crisis. However, probably more important was the ideological fusion of the pan-Turkist and Islamic fundamentalist forces, a unification which had partly taken place in the 1970s.[6] Social democracy, on the other hand, had witnessed its dramatic and short-lived heyday in the late 1970s and had suffered a devastating defeat with the military coup. As I mentioned above, the liberals too had experienced a series of ideological crises in the late 1960s and in the 1970s. In fact, in the latter period they had captured the nationalist ideology from the left and totally changed its meaning. Nationalism in the 1970s counterbalanced socialist internationalism, or simply was anticommunism. Thus, it was not a coincidence that all the right-wing coalition governments between the 1971 and 1980 military takeovers called themselves the "Nationalist Front." This monopolization of nationalism, however, had not brought a remedy, nor had it mobilized the masses.

The new right after 1983 tried to shape a new ideological system by harmonizing all the contradictory elements of the traditional ideologies, and strove for the formation of an "organic ideology," which would be at the heart of the constitution and provide an expansive hegemony that had never existed in Turkish society before. This ideology was called "conservative nationalism" (Özal, 1987:138), and it was a more refined and much more enriched form of the limited–appeal nationalism of the 1970s. Also, since conservative nationalism would discriminate against only the revolutionary left, it could articulate the interests of different groups into a compact whole. Obviously, this approach was expected to attract the disillusioned social democrats to a national-popular program. Other evidence supported the view that the new right was initially in search of the creation of an expansive hegemony to solve the crisis of bourgeoisie rule. For example, like Thatcherism, the Turkish new right asserted certain concepts, such as *ortadirek*, or literally the "central pole of the nomad's tent," to dissolve any mode of thinking based on class analysis. Here, *ortadirek* refers specifically to small agricultural producers, workers, government employees, craftsmen, and artisans, who symbolically constitute the center of Turkish society (ANAP, 1983:170-172). This persuasive concept was deliberately forwarded to absorb various sections of the popular masses within the framework of a societal movement. Furthermore, once again in a way quite similar to the Thatcherite discourse, anti-statism[7] was manipulated as a device to create a national consensus around this specific issue. Such arguments caused unrest among almost all sections of society, including the bourgeoisie itself.

The rightists were aware that the Ottoman statist tradition, together with the central role of the state in all corners of both the political and civil societies in the republican era, had been creating serious problems not only on critical issues but also in daily life. Therefore, the new right decided to carry out certain administrative reforms, such as the attenuation of bureaucratic red tape, more efficient means of getting passports and driver's licenses, and the reorganization of the security forces for the restoration of law and order. Such palliative measures could ease the tension exerted by the state apparatus over individuals without enacting structural reforms. Finally, the bias shown in favor of religion and nationalism, as expressed in the party program, in congress reports, and by the new right leaders, attempted to mobilize different sections of society around a one nation hegemonic project, particularly with the power of Islam (ANAP, 1987:89-98, *The Programme of the Motherland Party*, 1983:8-11; *Petek*, September 1, 1988 and May 9, 1988). The special emphasis on the role of religion in education and the liberation of sectarian activities from state control marked a turningpoint in the history of republican Turkey, even though the new right acted solely to cement different, and often contradictory, ideological elements and end the crisis of hegemony once and for all.

Beyond the social and political issues, the economic policy of the new right was central. Both Özal and the party program repeatedly declared that the economy should be understood in its technical content, meaning no economic policy could be conducted with welfarism, egalitarian income distribution, political considerations, and so forth. Therefore, the economy had its own laws: If these laws were improperly implemented, as during the past governments, it would be impossible to cope with inflation, unemployment, low productivity, balance of payments difficulties, and so on. In fact, this marked a change in the attitude of the Turkish right, which in the past had always stressed the primacy of political, moral, and cultural factors over economic matters. This new approach implied that once the economy was considered as the most important variable with its independent laws, then the recognition of certain inequalities necessary in the functioning and development of capitalism became inevitable. For instance, the productivist ideology as a lever for industrialization meant to reward productive sectors, services, and persons while penalizing the unemployed, pensioners, unskilled and semiskilled workers, and a large section of government employees (ANAP, 1987:81-82 and Özal, 1987:101). Moreover, restrictions on collective bargaining, the right to strike, and salary increases revealed as early as 1983 that there would be a two nations hegemonic project in spite of an all-encompassing national-popular campaign. Of course, the Thatcherite rhetoric that "future benefits will follow from present suffering" or "we are only obeying the dictates of the science of economics," merely covered the misfortunes to come. In reality, only one section of society would suffer in expectation of future benefits and be subject to the unchangeable and autonomous laws of the economy. This apparent contradiction between the attempt at the formation of an expansive hegemony, or national consensus, and a two nations hegemonic project was based on the mobilization of the social democrat masses, dispersed and lacking in leadership during the military regime.

The accumulation strategy of the new right was the export promotion development model. All party documents and Özal himself indicated, "Despite all agitation on the necessity to restrict state intervention and thus promote the free functioning of the market mechanisms, this model obviously rested upon the state direction of those sectors which were ready for international competition." Anti-statism, in this sense, is the elimination of the notorious bureaucratic red tape while continuing state intervention in the economy as before except for a change in its direction (Eralp, 1985:14). Within the context of export promotion, the new right planned to provide financial privileges and encouraging tax benefits for export-oriented industries. Obviously, this development strategy would benefit only a section of capital, but the Turkish bourgeoisie initially welcomed Özal, since the famous and well-articulated British formula TINA (There Is No Alternative) forced it to do so. Thinking that the economic-corporate interests of different sections of capital were not complementary to the export promotion model, which necessitates a certain degree of development, quality, and productivity for international competition, the bourgeoisie hoped for the foundation of a loyal government that would serve its political interests in the long run while guaranteeing its short-term profits through strict control over wage increases. Also, official IMF policy orientations and standby agreements prominently aided the actual success of this project. Within the same framework, the struggle against inflation was key. Thus, a reduction of inflationary pressure would ensure political support from the impoverished masses, the *ortadirek*, in particular. In short, the new right government completely identified itself with the fight against inflation, which would soon account to a great extent for its economic failure.

The two basic mechanisms for the functioning of this economic model were monetarism and the tools of supply-side economics (ANAP, 1983:71 and

ANAP, 1987:38-39). The Özal government tried to control the money supply with the former mechanism in order to press inflation downward while, paradoxically, increasing the supply of commodities, specifically through product diversification. Pursuing contradictory economic policies, Özal often failed to fulfill the requirements of the IMF agreements. Once again it appeared that he received the necessary messages from abroad for Turkey's further integration into the world capitalist system, but faced insurmountable barriers in adapting such policies to the structure and specific conditions of the country.

Next, an analysis follows of the most significant factors that have prepared the ground for the failure of the new right in its attempt to create an expansive hegemony. First of all, during Özal's first term in office between 1983 and 1987, none of his promises came true. The export promotion accumulation strategy turned out to be an illusion, since the seeming increase in the volume of exports could be related to "paper exports." This discredited the government in political as well as economic terms (Eralp, 1985:17-18). The apparent change in the structure of exports in favor of industrial products is equally unreliable, because even exported figs, light textile goods, and canned vegetables are registered as manufactures, or industrial exports, in this tabulation. Also, world oil prices did not rise and even declined within the same period. A general decline in manufacturing resulted in losses for many giant corporations as well as small firms (Türel, in this volume). In summary, the attempt to promote Islamic capitalism with the purpose of founding an "Islamic Peace Line" (Özal, 1987:221-222) in the Middle East tried to utilize an export–oriented accumulation strategy, but it brought a halt to industrialization and benefited only a limited number of enterprises.

As mentioned earlier in this study, the new right immediately after its ascendancy to power saw inflation as a central problem. The fight against this enemy of the masses, and specifically the fixed-income groups, has turned out to be a complete failure, for the rate of inflation after 1983 did not decrease below 40 percent annually. In fact, it showed a marked increase above 80 percent in 1988 (*Milliyet*, November 7, 1988). Since a major commitment of Özal and his party to the people was controlling inflationary pressures, inability to do so accounted for much of Özal's loss of popularity.

The military regime's tight grip on labor between 1980 and 1983 was allowed to continue after 1983 for the regime's legislation on labor relations remained untouched during the Özal administration. Although the right to strike was not prohibited in line with the international agreements made with ILO, it became an ineffective right with legal restrictions.[8] Also, different pieces of legislation placed other restrictions on labor relations, such as the requirement to work in one specific industrial branch for at least ten years in order to become eligible for union leadership, and the prohibition of union membership for those workers who at the same time had a student status. Another aspect of labor relations clearly showing the intentions of both the dominant class and its political organ is the attempt to discourage and thus limit union membership. For example, terms like the acceptance or rejection of one's union membership by the union administration at will, and the condition that only those unions that had signed a collective contract could benefit from the checkoff system, were in reality antidemocratic measures to attenuate union activity in general. Of course, an extension of the two nations hegemonic project could be observed in this field, since those measures and restrictions mentioned above could be manipulated as a carrot-and-stick policy depending on the degree of co-optation or dissidence of the concerned union.

This lack of social and economic success occurred while major political defeats led to the decline of the MP's share of votes from 45.1 percent in 1983 to 36.3 percent in the 1987 general election.[9] During the first term of the Özal administration, the new right movement did not manage to attract the social democrat masses, which generally held around 30 percent of the vote even when divided between two social democratic parties. Thus, the expectation of leading a considerable section of the disorganized social democratic movement remained an illusion. In my view, the major reason for the failure of this project is the inability of the Turkish new right to provide benefits for the first nation. The literature on neoconservatism, for example, especially emphasizes the success of the British new right in providing privileges for the City and skilled labor in return for their political support, and that of Reagan in having a similar relationship with the Sunbelt states, in spite of all the defeats suffered in the economic field.

This new right formula of economic failure but political success did not materialize in Turkey because even the two nations hegemonic project could not be carried out consistently in its logic. A crucial reason for this failure was the limited size of the first nation in Turkey, which was composed of a few monopolies, interest-bearing capital, a group of rentiers, and speculators. In contrast to England, for example, the Turkish new right political power failed to divide the working class according to levels of skill and degrees of productivity. This necessarily enlarged the size of the second nation to an unprecedented degree so that it encompassed the whole of the working class, the majority of agricultural producers, government employees, millions of the unemployed, professionals, artisans, tradesmen, pensioners, and so on. If we add to that a part of the liberals and those of the Islamic fundamentalists who have remained out of the new right bloc and followed other political parties, the dimensions and the depth of the collapse of the hegemonic attack become quite clear.

Since the 1987 general election the new right has made a significant change in its strategy toward a transition from an expansive hegemony to a passive revolution. Now that the former strategy has been proved to be next to impossible, more adherence to the two nations project appears as a last resort. However, this attempt is equally futile, because a passive revolution requires, before anything else, the neutralization of the interests and demands of the subordinate classes and groups, and the formation of a unity, or at least a temporary fusion of interests, within the sections of the dominant class. Neither of these seems to be possible at the moment.

The neutralization or containment of interests without active mobilization in society presupposes the prior existence of a coherent, cementing ideology to secure moral and intellectual leadership of at least one faction of the dominant class. None of the ideological elements, such as nationalism, Islamic fundamentalism, or productivism, seem to have sufficient power to succeed. Also, a fusion of interests among the sections of capital under the political leadership of the new right seems to be a very remote possibility, since many of those sections have already shown both their economic and their political resentment toward the Özal administration.

Today, a good many industrial undertakings and their corresponding organizations clearly express that they are in search of an alternative political formation. Moreover, the recently founded "Holy Alliance"–a united front of pan-Turkists and Islamic fundamentalists within the MP–has been trying to take the party to a more conservative platform, and thus liquidate the liberal elements (*Nokta*, 1988:27-28 and *Milliyet*, June 21, 1988). Also, for some time the liberals too have been organizing their forces to retaliate against the "Holy Alliance," and capture the party leadership (*Milliyet*, August 8, 1988). All in all, irrevocable breaches between the economic-corporate interests of the sections of capital, the MP, and the bourgeoisie, and between the factions within the MP itself, signal nothing but a deepening hegemonic crisis, whose outcome may take the form of another Caesarist solution, if other alternative political solutions are not forthcoming.

CONCLUSIONS

Turkey presents an interesting case study for political economy in terms of the specific features of dependent capitalism, its corresponding state forms, and the struggle for hegemony. In this study, I have confined myself to a theoretical inquiry of solely the recent hegemonic crisis, which has a history of at least two decades. This attempt shows that there has been a chronic series of both economic and political crises, and only the new right after 1983 has tried to establish initially an expansive hegemony and later a passive revolution. The new right, owing its existence in part to the specific policies of the military regime striving to counterbalance the left by the liberation of the extreme right forces, has aimed at the mobilization of the popular sections of society under the banner of a national program. However, it had its own contradictions.

The initial attempt to create an expansive type of hegemony was doomed to fail, since no national consensus could form as a result of the conduct of a two nations project. Apart from this, the conformity that had to exist between the accumulation strategy and the hegemonic project had not been established from the beginning. In other words, the export promotion development strategy should have benefited at least the first nation, and it should have benefited a much larger part of the population. Had this been accomplished, then a passive revolution such as Reaganism or Thatcherism could have been unleashed, compensating economic weaknesses by political success. However, the Turkish new right has been far from instituting even a passive revolution. It has not had the cementing ideological system to rearticulate different interests to a national-popular program or at least neutralize the interests of the second nation. Moreover, this power bloc has been incapable of overcoming its internal contradictions, such as the ideological conflict between Americanophile liberalism and Islamic fundamentalism, a factor which has also contributed to complete economic and political setbacks.

In this chapter I have analyzed the theoretical nexus between the Turkish new right and its counterparts abroad without actually investigating external linkages and feedbacks giving shape to the Turkish phenomenon. There are in fact great similarities between those new right movements as far as their hegemonic projects, accumulation strategies, ideological elements, and rhetorics are concerned. However, two types of further research are necessary to complete the picture. The first one should look into the parallels with respect to outcomes, in spite of all those great differences in social structure, degree of capitalist development, and national histories. The second type of research should be oriented toward the unfolding of the center-periphery relationships within the same context, so as to find out the kernel of this international phenomenon. In my view, only in this way can we proceed to the examination of worldwide political formations under the conditions of crisis of the capitalist system.

NOTES

1. There is abundant literature on the concept of hegemony. Here I provide only some illustrative works: See Gramsci (1973), Mouffe (1979), Entwistle (1979), Jessop et al. (1985), Habermas (1979), and Hall (1985).

2. Here, I intend to focus only on specific concepts and debates relevant for the purpose of this study. It should be noted, however, that Gramsci frequently equated "the mode of economic behaviour" with civil society, which is the arena for the exertion of hegemony. See Gramsci (1973:208-209).

3. Selected readings on the analysis of and the debates concerning Thatcherism and Reaganism follow: Jessop et al. (1984, 1985, and 1987), Bulpitt (1986), Gamble (1985), Leonard (1979), Leys (1985), Wolfe (1981), Friedrich (1955), Hall (1979, 1984, and 1985), and Davis (1981, 1985, and 1987). For the relationships between the economic crisis and the rise of the new right, see Habermas (1979), Therborn (1985), O'Connor (1981), Bleaney (1985), and Arrighi (1978).

4. Various attempts to find foreign debt to compensate for the drainage of foreign currency failed due to the lack of credibility abroad.

5. For the inner structure of Islamic fundamentalism, see Sencer Ayata (this volume) and Yeşilada (1988b and 1989).

6. In fact, the origins of this fusion can be traced back to the 1970s, but it is important to note that the autonomous development and organizational structure of pan-Turkism predates its association with Islam. For details, see Ağaoğulları (1987).

7. A very significant component of anti-statism was expounded as privatization, which so far has not found a wide range of implementation at all. See, for example, Özmen (1987:57-82 and 181-186).

8. There has been debate on labor relations since 1980. For the debate and changes in legislation in this field, see Koç (1986a, 1986b, and 1987), Güzel (1987), and Geniş (1987).

9. The most significant sign of economic and social failure, which at the same time is a logical component of the two nations project, can be observed in the drastic changes in income distribution. Merih Celasun estimated that the proportion between the lowest and the highest income groups in terms of annual revenues increased from 42.01% in 1978 to 47.27% in 1983 (*Cumhuriyet*, September 9, 1986). According to Süleyman Özmucur, the share of the national income acquired by wage and salary earners decreased from 16.3% to 14.0% of total between 1987 and 1988 (*Cumhuriyet*, April 22, 1988). For a fuller analysis of income distribution in Turkey, see Celasun (1986), Özmucur (1987), and Pamuk (1986). For analysis of the 1983 and 1987 general election, see Çakmak (1990).

REFERENCES

Ağaoğulları, M. A. (1987). "The Ultranationalist Right." In Irvin Schick and Ahmet Tonak, eds., *Turkey in Transition*. Oxford: Oxford University Press.

ANAP (1987). *Anavatan Partisi Programı, 1987*. Ankara: ANAP Publication.

_____ (1983). *Anavatan Partisi Programı , 1983*. Ankara: ANAP Publication.

Anavatan Partisi I. Olağan Büyük Kongresi MKYK Faaliyet Raporu (1985). Ankara: ANAP Publication.

Arrighi, G. (1978). "Towards a Theory of Capitalist Crisis", *New Left Review*, No. 111.

Bleaney, M. (1985). "The Present Crisis in Historical Perspective." *Economy and Society*. Vol. 14. No. 4.

Bulpitt, J. (1986). "The Discipline of the New Democracy: Mrs. Thacher's Domestic Statecraft." *Political Studies*. No. 34.

Çakmak, C. (1990). "1987 Genel Seçimleri Üzerine Bazı Düşünceler." In Tuncer Bulutay, ed., *Sadun Aren'e Armağan*. Ankara: Mülkiyeliler Birliği Vakfı Yayınları, pp. 182-201.

Celasun, M. (1986). "A General Equilibrium Model of the Turkish Economy, SIMLOG-1." *METU Studies in Development*. Vol. 13. No. 102.

Cumhuriyet (Turkish daily, various issues).

Davis, M. (1981). "The New Right's Road to Power." *New Left Review*. No. 128, pp. 3-23.

_____ (1985). "Reagonomics' Magical Mystery Tour." *New Left Review.* No. 149, pp. 45-65.

_____ (1987). "From Fordism to Reaganism." In R. Bush and G. Johnston Coates, eds., *The World Order: Socialist Perspectives.* Cambridge: Polity Press.

Entwistle, H. (1970). *Antonio Gramsci.* London: Routledge and Kegan Paul.

Eralp, A. (1985). "İstikrar, Yabancı Sermaye ve Gerçekleşmeyen Beklentiler." *İktisat Dergisi.* No. 243.

_____ (1990). "The Politics of Turkish Development Strategies." In A. Finkel and N. Sirman, eds., *Turkish State, Turkish Society.* London: Routledge, pp. 219-258.

Friedrich, C. (1955). "The Political Thought of Neo-Liberalism." *American Political Science Review.* Vol. 49, pp. 509-525.

Gamble, A. (1985). "Smashing the State." *Marxism Today.* Vol. 29. No. 6, pp. 21-26.

Geniş, A. (1987). "İşçi Hakları ve Mücadele." *Onbirinci Tez.* No. 6, pp. 242-249.

Gramsci, A. (1973). *Selection from the Prison Notebooks.* New York: International Publishers.

Gülalp, H. (1985). "Patterns of Capital Accumulation and State-Society Relations in Turkey." *Journal of Contemporary Asia.* Vol.15. No. 5, pp. 76-91.

Güzel, S. (1987). "1980 Sonrasında İşçi Haklarında Gerilemeler." *Onbirinci Tez.* No. 5, pp. 76-91.

Habermas, J. (1979). "Conservatism and Capitalist Crisis." *New Left Review.* No. 115, pp. 73-84.

Hall, S. (1979). "The Great Moving Right Show." *Marxism Today.* (January):14-20.

_____ (1984). The State-Socialism's Old Caretaker." *Marxism Today.* (November): 24-29.

_____ (1985). "Authoritarian Populism: A Reply to Jessop et al." *New Left Review.* No. 151, pp. 115-123.

Işıklı, A. (1987). "Türkiye'de İşçi Hareketinin Batı İşçi Hareketi Karşısında Özgünlüğü." *Onbirinci Tez.* No. 5, pp. 10-31.

Jessop, B. (1983). "Accumulation Strategies, State Forms, and Hegemonic Projects." *Kapitalistate.* Nos. 10-11, pp. 89-111.

Jessop, B., K. Bonnet, S. Bromley, and T. Ling (1984). "Authoritarian Populism, Two Nations, and Thatcherism." *New Left Review.* No. 147, pp. 32-60.

_____ (1985). "Thatcherism and the Politics of Hegemony: A Reply to Stuart Hall." *New Left Review.* No. 153, pp. 87-101.

_____ (1987). "Popular Capitalism, Flexible Accumulation and Left Strategy." *New Left Review.* No. 165, pp. 104-122.

Kemp, T. (1976). *Industrialization in Nineteenth Century Europe.* London: Longman .

_____ (1978). *Historical Patterns of Industrialization.* New York: Longman.

Koç, Y. (1986a). "Sendikaların Bağımsızlığı, ABD ve Türk-İş." *Onbirinci Tez.* No. 3, pp. 249-257.

_____ (1986b). "Türkiye'de Sosyal Demokrasi ve Sendikacılık." *Onbirinci Tez.* No. 4, pp. 107-139.

_____ (1987). "İşçi Hakları ve Sendikacılık." *Onbirinci Tez*. No. 5, pp. 32-755.

Leonard, P. (1979). "Restructuring the Welfare State." *Marxism Today*. Vol. 19. No. 9, pp. 7-13.

Leys, C. (1985). "Thatcherism and British Manufacturing: A Question of Hegemony." *New Left Review*. No. 151, pp. 5-25.

Milliyet (Turkish daily, various issues).

Mouffe, C. (1979). *Gramsci and Marxist Theory*. London: Routledge and Kegan Paul.

Nokta (1988). No. 33.

O'connor, J. (1981). "The Fiscal Crisis of the State Revised: A Look at Economic Crisis and Reagan's Budget Policy." *Kapitalistate*. No. 9, pp. 41-61.

Özal, T. (1987). *Başbakan Turgut Özal'in Konuşma, Mesaj, Beyanat ve Mülakatları*. Ankara: ANAP.

Özmen, S. (1987). *KİTler'in Özelleştirilmesi*. Istanbul: Bilgi Yayınevi.

Özmucur, S. (1987). *Milli Gelirin Üç Aylık Dönemler İtibariyle Tahmini, Dolarla İfadesi ve Gelir Yolu ile Hesaplanması*. Istanbul.

Pamuk, Ş. (1986). "24 Ocak Sonrasında Sınıflar ve Gelir Dağılımı." *Onbirinci Tez*. No. 2, pp. 87-101.

Petek (various issues).

The Programme of the Motherland Party, 1983. Ankara.

Therborn, G. (1985). "The Prospects of Labour and the Transformation of Advanced Capitalism." *New Left Review*. No. 155, pp. 5-38.

Tünay, M. (1978). *The Political Role of Organized Labour in Turkey*. Unpublished Ph.D. dissertation. Department of Political Economy, University of Toronto, Canada.

Türel, O. (1987). "Türkiye'de Sanayinin Gelişimine Genel Bakış." *1987 Sanayi Kongresi Bildirileri*. Ankara: TMMOB.

Wolfe, A. (1981). "Sociology, Liberalism, and the Radical Right." *New Left Review*. No. 128, pp. 3-27.

Yeşilada, B. (1988a). "Problems of Political Development in the Third Turkish Republic." *Polity*. Vol. 21. No. 2 (Winter):345-372.

_____ (1988b). "Türkiye'de İslamcı Akımlar ve Suudi Bağlantısı." *Bilim ve Sanat*. (July):22-25.

_____ (1989). "Islam, Dollars, and Politics: The Political Economy of Saudi Capital in Turkey." Paper presented at the Twenty-third Annual Meeting of the Middle East Studies Association in Toronto, Canada. November 15-18.

2

Ideology, Social Bases, and Organizational Structure of the Post-1980 Political Parties

Ayşe Ayata

INTRODUCTION

In 1983, when military rulers permitted the formation of new political parties in Turkey, fifteen different parties applied for permission in a two months' period (Yeşilada, 1988). The fragmentation of the voters in the precoup period (Özbudun and Tachau, 1975) and the electoral system that resulted in a reflection of this fragmentation in the parliament (Turan, 1988) certainly served as incentives for this multiple party formation. Three political factors crucially affected the establishment of new parties in Turkey. The first was the dealignment of voters from their pre-coup political party loyalties as new societal cleavages evolved; the second was the emergence of new ideas to mobilize the voters; and the third was the change in the electoral system.

Theories of dealignment and electoral volatility constitute important aspects of election studies. The European and North American political systems have experienced a decline in class-based politics over the last few decades. In this dealignment of voters from class-based parties, the reshuffling of votes among the exisiting parties and the emergence of postindustrial values among the public have all led to the reevaluation of political behavior (Inglehart, 1977).

The process of dealignment has two outcomes. On the one hand, voter dealignment leads to a centrifugal instability. That is, there is an increase in the precariousness of links between class background and voting behavior. Political parties begin to lose their strongholds in certain classes, the emotional intensity decreases, and the voters become more volatile (Haerpfer, 1987). On the other hand, the process of dealignment leads to a discussion of the strength of party organizations and the intensity of party membership (Sundberg, 1986 and 1987; and Botella, 1987).

This dealignment process also affects the party system. First, the old parties that had a mass base with their ideological and doctrinaire appeal became catchall parties. This, in turn, reduced their ideological content and strengthened the role of the leader, while downgrading the role of the member and deemphasizing the class basis of the voter to secure access to a variety of interests (Kirchheimer, 1966). Second, this led to the emergence of a number of new parties, most of them small, in the US and Europe. This development represented more fragmented and specific interests (Harmel, 1985; Berrington, 1985; Harmel and Robertson, 1985; Rochon, 1985; and Lucardie, 1987). A closer analysis of this new dealignment along the lines of class demarcation indicates new cleavages in society that cut across middle-class votes along party lines. The new political parties seem to be more successful when they are based on new societal cleavages. Moreover, changes in the political system of a country, such as constitutional or electoral laws, led to a better milieu for the flourishing of such organizations. Despite these new trends, some recent studies indicate that class and religion are still the two most important factors in electoral behavior. Furthermore, volatility between the ideological left and right is very low, while within-area volatility is considerable (Mair, 1985). This can also be achieved by the adaptability of old parties to new cleavages (Daalder, 1985; and Mair, 1985).

All of the Turkish political parties of the 1980s were new. However, only one of the major parties, the Motherland party (MP), is based on new societal cleavages and mobilization of a relatively new ideological concept known as the new right. The remaining political parties represent adaptation of old changes to the new political order: the Social Democratic Populist party, the True Path party, the Welfare party, and the Nationalist Work party. This chapter focuses exclusively on the contender parties that hope to come to power, while mentioning only in passing the "promoter parties" (Hermall and Robertson, 1985) that are unlikely to win seats in the National Assembly.

In the Turkish party system the electoral volability between the left and right is very low. In the seven elections since 1960, with the exception of 1977, roughly one third of the electorate has voted for the political left and two thirds has voted for the political right. Therefore, the changing societal cleavages are more plausible in determining within-area fractures and volatility.

Despite the significance of changing cleavages, dealignments, the rise of new political parties, and electoral volatility, the major determinants of electoral behavior in Turkish politics seem to be class and religion (Heper and Evin, 1983 and 1988). These factors continue to retain their primacy as major sources and issues of conflict. Relatively less important, but still of considerable significance, are ethnicity and urban-rural differences.

In addition to the above-mentioned sources of electoral volatility, this paper will examine the organizational structure of three of the new political parties: the Motherland party, the Social Democratic Populist party and the True Path party. These parties represented the emerging cleavages in Turkish politics in the 1980s and were represented in the parliament at the time this chapter was written. Probably the only exception that stands for an important cleavage but was not represented in the National Assembly is the Welfare party. This party won seats in the National Assembly in the National Elections of October 1991.

THE MOTHERLAND PARTY (MP)

The 1982 constitution and new election law created a National Assembly with a strong MP majority. In the 1983 elections, the MP received 45 percent of the votes and 53 percent of the seats in the National Assembly. This trend was further accentuated in the 1987 elections, when the MP won 64.9 percent of the Assembly seats with only 36.3 percent of the votes. This disproportionately reflected the voter support base. However, criticism from the major opposition parties was mild, because the election law raised their hopes for future elections in which they might win a similar majority. The leaders of the main political parties also believed that the new law could eventually reduce the impact of smaller parties on voter fragmentation.

The emergence of the MP was undoubtedly the most important aspect of Turkish party politics in the 1980s. The prominence of the MP not only was due to its three consecutive election victories (the two general elections of 1983 and 1987 and one local election in 1984), but also to the new ideas it brought to Turkish politics. Views of scholars on the impact of the MP on Turkish politics fall into two opposite camps.

The first group (e.g., Tünay in this volume; Yeşilada, 1989; and Zaralı, 1986) view the MP as an extension of the 1980 coup government. According to these scholars, the party is corporatist in nature, an instrument in integrating the Turkish economy into world markets, essentially conservative and supported by the religious and nationalist groups, an executive committee of the Turkish bourgeoisie, and a reflection of the rise of the new right in Turkey.[1] According to an alternative view, however, the MP is seen as the "initiator" of liberal revolutions, antibureaucratic, pluralist, modern, and able to bring together a coalition including a wide range of ideological groups.[2] It is clear that these two perspectives are mutually exclusive and very much opposed to one another.

During the transition to civilian rule in 1983, the MP had a low profile and moderate start, and claimed no descent from any of the pre-1980 political parties. Instead, the party began to introduce an alternative viewpoint—a "synthesis" of the pre-1980 ideological strands of liberalism, social democracy, nationalism, and conservatism. Which of these views Özal himself preferred is not clear. Political analysts wondered whether he was pursuing a policy of non-alienation of potential votes or was trying to create a middle-of-the-road ideology for a catchall party. Another major disadvantage of the MP was that it lacked a party organization with a wide base. It neither had extended cadres nor an ample supply of influential candidates.

During the 1983 election campaign, the Motherland party focused primarily on economic issues. The issue of "law and order," later one of the basic themes of MP propaganda, became a minor point. The party emphasized that a return to civilian rule did not mean the reappearance of political turmoil and anarchy, and deliberately rejected any close association with the military regime. Özal gave the impression of being a competent administrator and a serious politician with a rational and calculating mind who had an excellent grasp on the problems of the Turkish economy. An effective television media campaign further reinforced this image.

Two days before the 1983 elections Evren gave a speech on national television announcing that the military leaders did not at all favor the MP. Despite this, however, the MP still won an expected victory. Moreover, the MP had the majority of its support from urban areas: 51.4 percent of total votes in Istanbul and 45.5 percent of total votes in Ankara. These were two major social democratic strongholds of the 1970s. In order to understand the reasons for this overwhelming support, we need to further clarify two points. First, although Turkish democracy has been interrupted three times in the last four decades, there has still been a tradition of elected governments. In fact, the longest-lasting nonelected government served during the 1980 coup-for almost three years-and even that government at one point implemented a constitutional referendum. The Turkish people strongly associate democracy with an elected government which they conceptualize as responsive to their demands (Güneş-Ayata, 1984). Second, following an extended period of austerity economic measures during the military regime, Özal's economic experience and his future-oriented policies gave the impression of being responsive to the demands of the people. Furthermore, one might add that in Turkey, right-wing governments were known not only for their growth-oriented and expansionist economic policies but also for their caring for the poor. No doubt Özal also benefited from this image. Hence, urban migrants (with their optimistic view of the future, aspirations for social mobility, and demands for tangible services) were among the major supporters of the MP. For example, in Altındağ, Ankara, the MP had 55 percent of the votes. Moreover, the MP had better success in provinces where the percentage of wage earners and employees was highest (McFadden, 1985). Also, the MP fared better in the most developed areas of Turkey than in the least developed areas, where the Nationalist Democracy party received the largest support. This indisputable support for the MP from the socioeconomically developed regions of Turkey can be explained by the fact that upward mobility enhanced the expectations of voters and their claim on the distribution of the benefits of economic growth. In the eyes of many voters, the MP policies were closely associated with policies of economic expansion and a more egalitarian distribution of benefits.

As Özal himself asserted, the MP received votes from supporters of the four previous political parties (Tekeli, 1984 and Ergüder, 1988). However, these authors also argue that the MP attracted primarily the votes of the two rightist parties of the 1970s, namely, the National Action party and the National Salvation party. This further complicated the picture. On the one hand, the MP gained support from the upwardly mobile, entrepreneurially minded, pragmatic, modernist groups that were predominantly urban and living in the developed areas of Turkey. This included considerable support from such occupational groups as the urban self-employed, businessmen, and upwardly mobile urban workers (see Tables 1 and 2)–especially those employed in the private sector. On the other hand, the MP also attracted a section of the electorate known for their anti-Western values, who were highly critical of the consequences of urbanization and modernization. A look at the geographical distribution of votes in the 1987 general election shows that the MP had a wide support base among the Sunni Turks of central Anatolia, who were the majority population in Turkey and are often characterized as traditional and conservative. Furthermore, the major Sunni sects, and especially the leading Nakşibendi orders, openly declared their backing for the MP.

Table 1
Party Choice of Fully Employed, 1988 (percent)

Political Party	Employees Public Sector	Private Sector	Profes-sional	Worker	Busi-ness	Small Shop	Farmer	Others
MP	20.4	26.2	15.1	13.2	29.5	26.6	18.6	20.5
SDPP	41.6	41.9	58.6	38.5	25.2	27.3	32.9	32.0
TPP	10.7	7.9	10.6	24.1	22.1	22.9	27.9	20.8
DLP	2.5	5.1	2.2	9.8	2.4	4.5	3.9	4.0
WP	6.0	2.2		2.1	10.4	4.0	1.6	4.9
NWP	0.3			0.4		2.5	0.6	
OTHERS	5.3							4.1
Nonvoting	9.5		7.8	3.8		2.8	2.1	5.8

Source: Tabulated from figures of Konda, 1988.

Table 2
Party Choice Prior to 1987 Elections (by occupation, percent)

Party	Civil Pensioners/ Servants	Workers Public	Workers Private	Business/ Merchant	Free Professional	Shop- keepers	Farmers	Agricultural Workers	House- wives
MP	38.4	33.2	51.7	46.1	37.5	42.9	46.8	52.2	43.5
SDPP	36.1	22.3	11.6	5.6	35.7	16.1	8.8	13.9	23.1
TPP	5.9	16.1	16.3	29.7	3.0	17.0	18.9	10.8	11.0
DLP	2.4	11.1	3.4	0.0	10.2	8.2	7.5	5.1	5.8

Source: *Milliyet*, November 15, 1987.

The 1983 elections brought to the parliament an inexperienced group of legistator. Only fifteen of the total membership had any previous political experience (Kalaycıoğlu, 1988 and Tachau, 1988). Immediately, however, the question of political identity and the future of the MP became an issue of interest in political circles and public opinion. This discussion centered on whether the party would survive if the pre-1980 political parties were to participate in the coming elections. In addition many people wondered whether the potentially antagonistic groups in the MP, that is, the "modernists" and the "reactionaries," could remain in the same party for long.

With regard to the first concern, the MP proved itself to have a longer life than the other two new parties by winning one local and two consecutive national elections, thus becoming a genuine "catchall" party. No single occupational, educational, or income group appeared to have decisively refrained from voting for the MP. The real test, however, came in the 1987 elections, when the descendants of the Justice party, the Republican People's party, the True Path party (TPP), and the Social Democratic Populist party (SDPP) entered the national elections. The MP had proportionately higher votes in the thirteen most developed provinces in the 1983 elections than it did in the 1987 elections. In the thirteen least developed provinces, the MP received 37.07 percent of the votes. This figure was about 8 percent below its national average. In 1987 MP votes seriously declined from 45 percent to 36.9 percent.[3] In this sense, no strong correlation appeared between MP votes and the socioeconomic development level of the provinces. The strong metropolitan accent that appeared in the 1983 elections tended to become less marked in subsequent elections.[4]

On the other hand, a public opinion survey conducted in 1988 showed that the MP appeal was stronger among younger voters, while the distribution of the votes among age groups was not very skewed (20-29, 20%; 30-40, 32.2%; 60+, 13.2%; Konda, 1988). As for education, support for the MP was particularly weak among university students and graduates, whereas the distribution was more even in the case of the primary-and-secondary educated and the noneducated. Finally, in terms of the occupational groups, the MP was a genuine catchall party even though an inclination for the party existed among merchants, small business owners, and shopkeepers.

Organizational structure was the MP's weakest aspect. Both the Justice party and the Republican People's party, which gave birth to two different parties in the 1980s, had strong party organizations. The origins of these institutions can be traced back to the 1950s or even to the early days of the republic. By the late 1970s, the structure of local party organizations was so crystallized and fragmented that some groups were only very loosely integrated (Güneş-Ayata, 1988). For instance, the old town notables tended to grow more and more uneasy as the RPP became a social democratic party, while the nouveau riche were denied leading positions in the Justice party. In contrast, the local branches of the MP were filled with such people. Significantly, these groups left their clientele networks in their previous parties or had no such following anyway. In this sense, the MP became the real caucus party. As in any caucus party, the local organizations became instruments for elections instead of being permanent organizations for mobilization. Against this background, it is not difficult to see that it was primarily the media that built up voter support for the MP; hence, the party relied on TV programs and Özal's omnipresence as the leader.

Another unique aspect of the MP organization was the nonexistence of primary elections. Despite pressures from other political parties, and the long tradition of primary elections in all of the political parties before 1980, the MP undervent two general and two local elections without extensive usage of primaries. This signifies the relative weakness of the peripheral party vis-à-vis the center. However, localism, defined by Frank Tachau and Frederick Frey as becoming a parliamentarian from one's birthplace, was not totally absent in the MP. This too was typical of the caucus parties, where local notables were appointed to positions with high potential for electability in order to attract votes. Nevertheless, these individuals had only delegated political power from the center. Since the nominations came from the center, the MP's elected party officials had to prove their allegiance and loyalty to the center, and ignored the need to build their own power bases with their voter clientele.

This weak structure of the MP peripheral party organizations was only one aspect of the organizational problem. In the significant absence of a hierarchically structured, powerful, intact, and close–knit local organization, ideologically motivated groups found it quite easy to infiltrate and dominate the local organizations. In fact, during the 1988 congress of the MP such a coalition of ideologically organized groups (known as the Holy Alliance) almost won the majority of administrative seats despite the strong opposition of the party leader. However, the relative effectiveness of the Holy Alliance among the electorate was not very clear. Ironically, a close examination of the publications of the religious and nationalist right within the Holy Alliance clearly demonstrated that these groups were antiliberal, anti-individualist and in many ways anti-Western (Meeker, 1988 and Yeşilada, 1988 and 1989). The paradox is that Westernism, individualism, and liberalism were the core ideals of the initial MP ideology. Therefore, it seemed as though the alliance of the liberals with the two right-wing groups within the Holy Alliance had the potential of falling apart and eventually resulting in the split of the MP along these two ideological lines. However, over the last half of the 1980s, the two forces managed to coexist, largely as a result of political maneuvering by Turgut Özal. This coexistence could be viewed as a pragmatic pact for vote hunting. However, I would propose another explanation from a cultural perspective.

The tendency to vote for right-wing political parties increased considerably in central Anatolia. This tendency reached its climax in Erzurum with 85.8 percent of the votes going to right-wing parties. In thirteen of the twenty-five central

Anatolian provinces (Ankara, Bitlis, Bilecik, Bolu, Çankırı, Eskişehir, Erzurum, Giresun, Gümüşhane, Kayseri, Malatya, and Yozgat), MP votes were over 40 percent and in six of them over 45 percent. These places were either largely homogeneous Sunni communities, or ethnically heterogeneous regions where the Sunni and Alevi groups lived close to each other, with the Sunnis almost always constituting the majority. In all, the MP scored 5 percent higher than its national average in these regions. The two factions of the MP seemed to appeal to two conflicting values of the conservative voters of central Anatolia. On the one hand, a great majority of the people desired economic prosperity, modernization, technological improvement, industrialization, and better life-styles (which in the modern world means extended consumerism). On the other hand, however, the same people were uneasy about the consequences of the modernization process, which meant individualism, competition, and erosion of traditional values and norms. What this contrast of values and attitudes highlighted was the deep-rooted conflict between economic and technological change on the one hand and cultural conservatism on the other. In fact, a study of MP propaganda in the 1987 general election pointed to the fact that the major party themes were directly oriented to this longing for modernization, coming usually under the banner of "moving to a new age," *çağ atlamak,* (Acar, Ayata, and Cesur, 1987). The MP propaganda focused on "modernization for the country" as a whole rather than addressing the problems of specific social groups or classes. At the same time, however, the party tried to appeal to the conservative Sunnis by making references to nationalist symbols and national pride. A progressive and modernist group in the party who called themselves the "liberals" drew an analogy to religious revivalism in the US. On the other hand, those attached to the Holy Alliance wanted to increase their share of power in the government in order to win concessions such as wearing head scarves in the universities and maintaining Koran courses without state control. This approach had wide appeal to the majority of the voters, who aspired to further modernization as long as their traditions were not totally dismantled and uprooted. This became more important as their main competitor, the True Path party (TPP), tended to adopt a more conservative, traditionalist stand. Hence, the ideology of the new right emerged as a synthesis of modernization and economic growth with safeguards against the fears of the conservative voters who felt threatened by the development program of the party.

THE TRUE PATH PARTY (TPP)

Contrary to the Motherland party, the True Path party claimed to have a long past, reaching back to 1946 and even back to Ottoman times. The party had a direct link to the pre-1980 Justice party which, in turn, was a direct descendant of the pre-1960 Democrat party. These ties were confirmed with the election of

Süleyman Demirel as the TPP's leader as soon as the voters lifted the ban on pre-1980 politicians in a general referendum in 1987. As a result of this linkage to the Justice party, the TPP also inherited the organizational network of the former through the country.

With regard to its organizational network, the TPP benefited immensely from Demirel's success in keeping intact his patronage networks through the years of military intervention. He is well-known for his strong personal ties to his followers. Throughout his political life, Demirel has also been known for his loyalty to his supporters. This, of course, is a very significant characteristic of a patronage type of organization. In fact, the True Path party represented traditionalism in Turkish politics. It adopted a traditionalist form of party organization backed by the traditional middle classes of artisans and shopkeepers.

The organizational network of the TPP extends to the entire periphery, covering every single village in Turkey. The TPP officials claim that 70 percent of their local representatives were from the Justice party (Acar, 1989). Patronage networks in the TPP were largely dependent on the personal resources, prestige, and networks of the patrons, the majority of whom were local notables, and on local businessmen who had sufficient personal resources and ability to maintain patron-client relations even without having to rely upon state resources. The cutthroat competition for party leadership that occurred two years before Demirel's reelection was also indicative of the strength of the party organization. During the general election primaries in 1987, center candidates decisively lost against the local candidates. Therefore, even though the military regime had introduced various bottlenecks to prevent resource distribution through patron-client networks, such networks did endure and survive to establish this new political party. In essence, the coup leaders failed to eliminate the traditional patron-client networks of the DP JP TPP.

Unlike the support for the MP and the SDPP, the support for the TPP was not evenly distributed among various social groups and categories. As the data in Table 1 indicate, the highest support came from the farmers (27.9%), followed by the workers (24.1%), and then the merchants (22.1%) and shopkeepers (22.9%). The TPP's lowest support came from civil servants, professionals, and managers. Clearly, these figures show that the members of the new middle class showed little sympathy for the TPP, whereas the old middle classes (peasants, artisans, shopkeepers) tended to support the party. It is important to note, however, that support for the party became even smaller as the education and age levels of the voters increased (Acar, 1988).[5]

At its electoral base, the TPP competes mainly with the MP. In fact, 53.1 percent of the TPP voters claimed they would definitely vote for the MP as their second choice (*Hürriyet*, November 15, 1987). In regional terms, the TPP obtained the best results in the western–central Anatolian provinces of Kütahya, Manisa, Muğla, and Isparta, which were typical DP JP strongholds during the pre-1980 period. In Süleyman Demirel's hometown Isparta, the TPP had its highest support during the 1987 national elections and obtained 60 percent of the votes. Finally, in five Eastern provinces (Kars, Erzurum, Rize, Elazığ, Bingöl, and Artvin) a clear shift from the MP to TPP was observed.

The TPP voters differ from the MP voters not only in terms of their socioeconomic backgrounds but also in ideological terms. First of all, the influence of the ideologies of the new right on the TPP was at best minimal. Both through his campaign style and in his more explicit messages, Demirel was careful to present himself as representative of conservative values and traits. Unlike Özal, who placed excessive emphasis on integration with the international sphere, Demirel showed vigilance in distancing himself even from Turkey's Western allies. His populist views and the sympathy he showed for the problems of the people became the overriding themes of his discourse. With colloquial language, he criticized the MP's liberal economic policies for leaving large numbers of lower-income groups vulnerable to the ills of market forces. With this view, Demirel thus became associated with the idea of a "benevolent state." This is quite ironic, because during the pre-1980 period, Demirel had the general support of Turkey's capitalist class and advocated the market-oriented economic growth model.

This duality or ideological schism was representative of two different dimensions of political conservatism in Turkey. In this regard Şerif Mardin drew attention to two trends of political philosophy in Turkish history. He described one trend as the "collectivist understanding of freedom" (Mardin, 1988) and the other as "the populist-egalitarian policies" of the right (Mardin, 1987). These two concepts could be highly useful in understanding both the role of the TPP in Turkish politics and the nature of the difference between this party and the kind of new right that ruled Turkey during the 1980s.

The philosophy of the traditional right in Turkey is based on the notions of economic justice and political egalitarianism. The concepts of human dignity and egalitarianism are simultaneously stressed. For example, much of the Democrat party's appeal to the masses was built on the idea that democracy meant equal contribution from everybody in ruling the country. Such a "liberal" understanding of democracy is a theme inherited by the TPP (Acar, 1988). In Demirel's emphasis on national will and the sovereignty of the people, he was hinting at a certain conception of order in society in which collective freedom is greater than individual freedom. Furthermore, this freedom is collectively used and embedded in the traditions of the country and the nature of the people. According to Levy (1988) this philosophy is particularly useful in appealing to and communicating with the masses. This is precisely what was at the heart of JP populism.

Second, the egalitarian tradition involved both a sense of social justice and a contractual understanding of the state as having an obligation to preserve the general well-being of its citizens. In this regard, the Democrat party tradition created a certain conception of an intermediary state that provided the basic needs of the people. Hence, one recurrent theme in the TPP propaganda after the 1987 elections was criticism of the MP government for non-distributive, non-egalitarian policies which placed the free market and the principle of efficiency above all other considerations. Parallel to this view, one could observe an antileftist and anticommunist orientation within the TPP which disclaimed any clear preference for any particular social group or class. The national will, according to Demirel, was something that should be collectively exercised.

Thus, although both the MP and the TPP emphasized nationalism, religion and some similar cultural symbols in their propaganda, they had important ideological differences. While the MP seemed more successful in mobilizing the innovative, Western-oriented urban population with an individualistic and competitive ethic, the TPP appealed to those who felt threatened by the MP policies.

THE DEMOCRATIC LEFT

Both political parties on the left, the Social Democratic Populist party (SDPP) and the Democratic Left party (DLP), associated themselves with social democratic values. Of these two parties, the SDPP specifically stated its ties to the former Republican People's party (RPP). After the military coup of 1980, the ideology of the left centered around democracy, the consolidation of democratic principles, and the development of a social democratic culture. Economically, the SDPP was particularly keen on the issue of rapid industrialization, which it saw as the only long-term solution to the economic problems of Turkey. The SDPP advocated a system of progressive taxation to achieve a more egalitarian distribution of wealth and favored a more controlled economy in which the state would assume a directing role. However, people from both right and left have criticized the SDPP for its etatist and centralist leanings. On the other hand, the DLP was supposed to be moving away from such "old-fashioned" principles and views (Alpay and Gürsel, 1986).

The differences that were observed between these two parties on the left were less ideological than a reflection of differences in their social class support. The major problems of social democracy in the 1980s were cultural and organizational. After the 1980 coup, one of the first political parties to be established was the Populist party. This new party was also trying to become the heir to the RPP inheritance, and unlike the Social Democratic party (SODEP), it took part in the 1983 elections. In the public view, however, the true heir was not the PP but SODEP (Yeşilada, 1988). In fact, the leadership cadres of the RPP, many of whom were not allowed to participate in active politics, supported SODEP although they knew that their previous leader, Ecevit, was openly rejecting this line of action. In general then, the local RPP organization was split between three new political parties: SODEP, PP, and

Ecevit's DLP, which came into existence after the 1983 elections. Despite, SODEP's call for cancellation of votes in the 1983 elections, the PP showed an unexpected success by getting 30.5 percent of the votes. This enabled the PP to be represented in the parliament with 117 seats, but its organizational base continued to remain thin. SODEP, on the other hand, was not allowed by the military government to enter the elections. The merger of the two parties in 1984 was specifically intended to eliminate the deficiencies on both sides.

The social democratic tradition in Turkey is markedly different from European social democracy. Turkish social democracy does not have strong links with organized groups, including trade unions. There are two basic reasons for this. First, there are legal limitations on establishing permanent and formal links with the trade unions as specified in the 1982 constitution and trade union laws. Second, the RPP adapted social democratic ideology in Turkey in the 1970s. Until that time, the party had a long tradition of strong local organizations, which could be considered "aberrant" in terms of basic social democratic ideals (Tuncay, 1981). Nevertheless, the tradition of strong constituency organizations was quite efficient in legitimizing and diffusing the new ideology among the RPP loyalists. In this regard, the representatives of the local organizations, who had influential ties to the National Executive Committee and the National Assembly, played crucial roles.

During the 1980s, however, the leadership cadres of the local organizations were prevented from taking official positions in political parties by a military ban. It was not until the 1987 general referendum that these local officials and key political figures of the pre-1980 period regained their right to reenter political life. In their absence, the new social democratic parties and, above all SODEP, were founded by a group of intellectuals and bureaucrats who were close to the educated new middle classes in the big cities (Levy, 1988 and Mango, 1988) but were quite remote from the grass-roots party activists of the RPP. Hence, from the very outset, a deep cleavage existed between the party elite and the peripheral party organizations. This problem was resolved in the 1987 and 1988 congresses, during which the founders of SODEP were largely replaced by the representatives of local party organizations. Finally, SODEP and the PP merged to form the Social Democratic Populist party (SDPP) on November 3, 1985.

In its organizational structure, the SDPP has strong clienele networks at local levels. These clientele networks represent ethnic and religious groups that feel threatened by the policies of the conservative right. Nevertheless, the SDPP failed to attract the overall support of the pre-1980 RPP loyalists.

During the 1970s, whether the RPP was in power or not, party activists always had access to state resources. Under the military regime, however, many local RPP officials were scrutinized, arrested, and humiliated. As a result, these party officials suffered a loss of prestige in the local communityies Furthermore, election results were not very promising for the SDPP, with a drop from an RPP victory in the 1977 elections with 42 percent of the votes to only 24.8 percent in the 1987 general election. Both factors seriously limited the ability of the local organizations to mobilize votes.

Nevertheless, SDPP support among the public showed a gradual increase during the latter half of the 1980s. According to the Konda Public Opinion Poll in 1988, the party's support increased to 38.5 percent from a low of 22.3 percent in 1987. The highest percentage (58.6%) was attained among professionals. Educated middle-class support for the party was further strengthened by the fact that 61 percent of the university educated tended to vote for the SDPP, while this ratio dropped to 28.4 percent among the least educated. Finally, the SDPP's appeal to young voters (19-29-year-olds) was also quite high with 38 percent. (Konda Public Opinion Poll, 1988).

Regionally, the SDPP performance was worst in the central Anatolian provinces. For example, in Gümüshane and Erzurum, support fell to 15 percent, which is less than half of its national average. More striking was the fact that the left votes, that is, including the DLP, decreased; in twenty-two central Anatolian provinces the votes for the left were below its 1983 level. Exceptions occurred in Burdur, Isparta, Sinop, and Sakarya where the Alevis or Kurdish-speaking people coexisted with Turkish-Sunni groups. In general we could say that wherever there was a dominance of Sunni Kurds, SDPP votes fell below its national average. It is interesting that the religious Welfare party gets most of its votes in such places. On the other hand, it seems that SDPP success was particularly marked in Erzincan and Tunceli, where Alevi Kurds constituted the majority population.

Since the mid-1960s, the Alevis have been loyal supporters of the RPP and then of the SDPP. The major reason for this is their strong secular views. Secularization represented a powerful check against domination by the Sunni majority and was one of the key principles of the RPP. As Islamic revival gained momentum in the 1970s and 1980s, more Alevis supported social democratic parties. In areas where there was a sizable concentration of Alevi population, the Alevis organized at the local party level to promote their interests and assert their collective identity. However, as they increased their power in the party organization, an increasing alienation of Sunni voters occurred. The outcome was net losses for the SDPP.

One other related factor deserves further attention. The Democratic Left party adopted a more moderate stand toward secularism. Ecevit repeatedly stressed that he wanted the leftist voters who were alienated from SDPP for cultural reasons. To some extent this was appealing to the leftist Sunni voters. On the other hand, Alevi concentrations in the DLP were much less likely to occur, since the party had at best a pseudo-organization and all of its candidates were nominated from the center-almost always by Ecevit himself.

As would be expected, in the Sunni majority areas of the central Anatolian plateau the SDPP came in second and sometimes third in the 1987 elections, scoring much lower than its national average (Konya 7.8%, Kayseri 7.8%, Çankırı 14.8%). In such provinces, clientele networks played a very important role at the local organization level (Güneş-Ayata, 1988). As the party continued to lose support in central Anatolia, the networks were further distanced from state resources. Parallel to this development, their relations with the center, dominated by the bureaucrats and intellectuals, was also loosening. This tendency toward isolation of the local party organization's from both the state and the central leadership cadres continued until the 1988 congress. The local party organizations responded to this process by supporting a faction, constituted predominantly of old RPP politicians who were able to keep their ties with clientele networks fairly intact. The 1988 congress brought this faction to power in the party. Meanwhile, although the party was more successful in three large urban centers (Istanbul, Ankara, and Izmir), the ethnic dimension of political participation was even more marked. The migrant ethnic groups from the eastern and southeastern provinces who were anxious to preserve their collective interests and identities began to form close-knit organizations. In some places they became so influential as to dominate the election primaries (e.g., Çankaya region in Ankara in the 1987 elections). Thus, ethnicity and nationalism became major problems in the parliamentary group of the party. In the general congress of 1988 there was a latent but serious conflict between groups representing old style clientele networks and those directly representing or collaborating with urban-based eastern ethnicity. In the absence of consociational democracy, which constitutes the backbone of social democratic parties in Europe, the struggle between the two factions contributed to internal cleavages and tensions in the SDPP.

In summing up the SDPP support base, one may conclude that this party had two types of electoral base. In the first type, one finds the predominance of the urban educated middle classes and the industrial workers. This was typical of all left-wing parties. The other type, however, included voters who were mobilized primarily through religious and ethnic affiliations. This latter form of support base was unique for the SDPP when compared with other European social democratic parties.

CONCLUSIONS

In terms of the electoral support base, traditional issues and sources of conflict such as class and religion dominated party struggles in Turkey during the 1980s. In very general terms we could say that the organized working class and the new middle classes (professionals, civil servants, and so on) tended to vote predominantly for the left while the traditional urban middle classes (small businessmen, shopkeepers, artisans) as well as the peasants were more inclined to vote for the right. A similar division seemed to have consolidated along religious-ethnic lines: The Alevis voted overwhelmingly for the leftist parties, and the less-educated provincial Sunni voters were likely to show a clear preference for the political right. The situation with the language-based eastern and urban ethnic groups was somewhat more complicated. Here one noticeable trend was the growing support for the religious Welfare party among the Sunni section of the Kurdish speaking people in eastern and southeastern Anatolia. Equally powerful was the tendency of the Alevi Kurds to vote, almost exclusively, for the political right. The first trend was more noticeable in fairly segmented communities while the second was one of cumulative coincidence (language and religion), a process noticeable in provinces where Alevi Kurds constituted the majority population, as in Tunceli or in large urban centers.

With regard to postcoup party life, the new political parties attempted to introduce new ideas. At the same time, however, they inherited many of the precoup societal cleavages that, in turn, hindered their effective functioning as new political organizations. In addition, there were two important factors at work. First, the new electoral system did not allow small parties to attain representation in the parliament. Among these parties, only the mobilizers with clear-cut ideologies and loyal mass followings were likely to perpetuate themselves in the long run. A case in point is the fundamentalist Welfare party.

The second factor was organization, as the parties tried to address the new concerns of the citizens: the physical and urban environment, religion revivalism, metropolitan problems, and human rights issues, to name a few. Such factors undoubtedly influenced the voting preferences of the electorate. However, by and large the new parties failed to effectively incorporate solutions to these new problems in their platforms. As a result, most of the newer parties, with their weak organizational networks, faced eventual disaster in the elections despite their attempts to use the media for propaganda purposes. As Rokkan (1970) emphasized, even communication through the media does not reach the mass public directly, and an organized network of effective leaders are needed to fill the gap. Such a defect was most evident in the case of smaller parties and, ironically, the Motherland party. In the case of the MP, this weakness explains how political factions (e.g., the Holy Alliance) could become so powerful at the organizational level. At the time of preparing this chapter, the MP faced the problem of sustaining the durability and stability of its constituency. The party largely lacked a permanent core of loyal voters. In comparison, the True Path party with its patronage networks, and the Social Democratic Populist party, with its clientele structures, seemed to have stronger voter support bases. Nevertheless, two additional problems are worth noting. First, Turkish political parties tend to be formed on individualistic and hierarchical lines rather than on group–based interests. And second, there are serious legal constraints on party-interest group linkages. Both factors greatly hinder the ability of political parties to establish and maintain ties to organized interest groups. Thus, in their efforts to attract volatile mass support, the new political parties adopt a "catchall" strategy, in which ideological differences and societal cleavage factors become low-priority issues for party officials. Thus, these parties' future success in attracting and maintaining stable mass support is rather questionable.

NOTES

1. See Yeşilada (1988), Zaralı (1986), and Tünay in this volume for discussions of issues raised by this perspective.
2. See chapters by Ergüder, Heper, Rustow, and Karpat in Heper and Evin (1988) for discussions on this perspective.
3. It should be noted that before the referendum no formal opposition was allowed; only informal networks asked for a no vote. The referendum was held in September to determine if the citizens wanted to lift the ban on participation in politics by pre-1980 political figures. The ban was imposed by the generals after the 1980 coup.
4. For instance, in 1989 local elections the MP came last in all five of the largest metropolitan centers.
5. The figures are from Konda polls carried out in 1987 and 1988.

REFERENCES

Acar, F. (1988). "The True Path Party." Paper presented at the Conference on Continuity and Change in Turkish Political Life. Bilkent University. Ankara. November 10-12.

Albaum, M., and J. Davies (1973). "The Spatial Structure of Socio-Economic Attributes of Turkish Provinces." *International Journal of Middle East Studies*. Vol 4. (July):288-310.

Alpay, S., and S. Gürsel(1986). *DSP-SHP Nerede Birleşiyor, Nerede Ayrılıyorlar*. Istanbul: Afa Yayınları.

Berrington, H. (1985). "New Parties in Britain: Why Some Live and Most Die?" *International Political Science Review*. Vol. 6. No. 4 (October):441-461.

Botella, J. (1987). "Does Party Membership Really Matter? In Search of an Electoral Model for Mass Parties." Paper presented at the ECPR Workshop on Party Strategies and Party-Voter Linkages. Amsterdam. April 10-15.

Daalder, H. (1985). "The Comparative Study of European Parties and Party Systems: An Overview." In H. Daalder and P. Mair., eds., *Western European Party Systems*. Beverly Hills, Calif.: Sage Publications.

Ergüder, Ü. (1988). "The Motherland Party." Paper presented at the Conference on Continuity and Change in the Turkish Political Life. Bilkent University, Ankara. November 10-12.

Ergüder, Ü., and R. Hofferbert (1988). "The 1983 General Elections in Turkey: Continuity or Change." In M. Heper and A. Evin, eds., *State, Democracy, and the Military: Turkey in the 1980s*. New York: Gruyter.

Güneş-Ayata, A. (1984). *Participation and Organization in Local Politics: A Comparative Study of Class and Clientage in Two Small Towns.* Unpublished Ph.D. dissertation .

_____ (1988). "Pluralism versus Authoritarianism: Political Ideas in two Islamic Publications." Paper presented at the Conference on Islam and Society in Turkey. School of Oriental and African Studies. University of London. May.

Haerpfer, C. (1987). "The End of Parliamentary Duopoly in Austria? The Impact of Electoral Behaviour upon Small Parties in Austria, Germany, Belgium, and Great Britain, 1974-1987." Paper presented at the ECPR Workshop on Small Parties in Western European Party Systems. Amsterdam. April 10-15.

Harmel, R. (1985). "On the Study of New Political Parties." *International Political Science Review.* Vol. 6. No. 4, pp. 403-418.

Harmel, R., and J. Robertson (1985). "Formation and Success of New Parties: A Cross-National Analysis." *International Political Science Review.* Vol. 6. No. 4, pp. 501-523.

Heper, M. (1988). "Conclusions." In M. Heper and A. Evin, eds., *State, Democracy, and the Military: Turkey in the 1980s.* New York: Gruyter.

Heper, M., and A. Evin. eds., (1988). *State, Democracy, and the Military: Turkey in the 1980s.* New York: Gruyter.

Hürriyet. Turkish daily. (November 15, 1987).

Inglehart, R. (1977). *The Silent Revolution.* Princeton: Princeton University Press.

Kalaycıoğlu, E. (1988). "The 1983 Parliament in Turkey: Changes and Continuities." In M. Heper and A. Evin ,eds. , *State, Democracy, and the Military: Turkey in the 1980s.* New York: Gruyter.

Kirchheimer, O. (1966). "The Transformation of Western European Party Systems." In J. Lapalombara and M. Weiner, eds., *Political Parties and Political Development.* Princeton: Princeton University Press.

Konda Public Opion Polls (1987 and 1988).

Levy, A. (1988). "Change and Continuity and the Justice Party." Paper presented at the Conference on Continuity and Change in Turkish Political Party Life. Bilkent University. Ankara. November 10-12.

Lucardie, P. (1987). "The Role of the Small Parties in the Netherlands: Prophets, Correctors, and Cliques." Paper presented at the ECPR Workshop on the Role of Small Parties in the West European Party Systems. Amsterdam. April 10-15.

Mair, P. (1985). "Adaptation and Control: Toward an Understanding of Party and Party System Change." In H. Daalder and P. Mair, eds., *Western European Party Systems.* Beverly Hills, Calif.: Sage Publications.

Mango, A. (1988). "The Social Democratic Populist party." Paper presented a tthe Conference on Continuity and Change in the Turkish Political Party Life. Bilkent University. Ankara. November 10-12.

Mardin, Ş. (1987). "Türk-Toplumunu İnceleme Aracı Olarak Sivil Toplum." *Defter.* Aralık-Ocak. No. 2.

_____ (1988). "Freedom in an Ottoman Perspective." In M. Heper and A. Evin, eds., *State, Democracy, and the Military: Turkey in the 1980s.* New York: Gruyter.

McFadden, J. (1985). "Civil-Military Relations in the Third Turkish Republic." *Middle East Journal.* Vol. 39. No. 1, pp. 69-85.

Meeker, M. (1988). "The Muslim Intellectuals of the Turkish Republic." Paper presented at the Conference on Islam in Turkey. School of Oriental and Asian Studies. University of London. May.

Rochon, T. (1985). "Mobilizers and Challengers: Towards a Theory of New Party Success." *International Political Science Review.* Vol. 6. No. 4, pp. 419-439.

Rokkan, S. (1970). "Nation-Building, Cleavage Formation, and the Structuring of Mass Politics." In S. Rokkan, ed., *Citizens, Elections, Parties.* Oslo: Universitest for Laget.

Rustow, D. (1988). "Transition to Democracy: Turkey's Experience in Historical and Comparative Perspective." In M. Heper and A. Evin, eds., *State, Democracy, and the Military: Turkey in the 1980's.* New York: Gruyter.

Sundberg, J. (1986). "The Failure of Maintaining Party Membership in Denmark: A Scandinavian Comparison." Paper presented at the ECPR Workshop on Internal Party Arenas. Göteborg. April.

_____ (1987). "The Role of Party Organizations in the Electoral Process." Paper presented at the ECPR Workshop on Party Strategies and Party Voter Linkages. Amsterdam. April 10-15.

Tachau, F. (1988). "The Republican People's Party." Paper presented at the Conference on Continuity and Change in Turkish Political Party Life. Bilkent University. Ankara. November 10-12.

Tekeli, Ş. (1984). "Cumhuriyet Döneminde Seçimler." *Cumhuriyet Dönemi Türkiye Ansiklopedisi.* Vol. 5, pp. 1797-1824.

Tuncay, M (1981). *Türkiye Cumhuriyetinde Tek Parti Yönetiminin Kurulması, 1923-1931.* Ankara: Yurt Yayınları.

Turan, I. (1988). "Political Parties and the Party System in Post-1983 Turkey." In M. Heper and A. Evin, eds., *State, Democracy, and the Military: Turkey in the 1980s.* New York: Gruyter.

Yeşilada, B. A. (1988). "Problems of Political Development in the Third Turkish Republic." *Polity.* Vol. 21. No. 2 (Winter):345-372.

_____ (1989). "Islam, Dollars, and Politics: The Political Economy of Saudi Capital in Turkey." Paper presented at the Twenty-third Annual Meeting of the Middle East Studies Association in Toronto, Canada. November 15-18.

Zaralı, R. (1986). "ANAP Üzerine Tezler ve Düşünceler." *11. Tez.* No. 2.

3

The Rise of Islamic Fundamentalism and Its Institutional Framework

Sencer Ayata

INTRODUCTION

During the 1920s and 1930s, Turkish officials adopted a policy of laicism to make religion a personal matter of individual conscience. This narrowing of religious influence in social life marked a major break from almost a millennium of accumulated Islamic traditions that constituted the basis of education, law, jurisprudence, ethics, and social norms. With the growth of an educated urban elite and its adoption of Western values and life-styles, laicism expanded. This vast secularization program almost eliminated religion from public life and institutions. Those who tended to think and act otherwise, sometimes even including ordinary devout Muslims, were blamed for "obscurantism." In practical terms, religion meant the denial of modern science, technology, progress, the independence of the country, and the unity of the nation. Religion, however, survived in family and small community life. In essence, religion became a diffuse ideology for individuals in small communities dissatisfied with the elite's values and institutions. A cultural divide between a ruling Westernized elite and the deeply religious masses in the countryside and in the small towns was thus established as one of the most outstanding societal cleavages of Turkish society and polity.

At the same time that laicism continued to expand rapidly in Turkey, the country also experienced a revival of religious fundamentalism in public life especially, during the last two decades. In this chapter, I do not examine the more comprehensive process of increasing religiosity, that is, changes in the family, community, and social interactions of everyday life. Rather, my focus is on the two closely related processes of rising fundamentalism and penetration of public institutions by organized Islamic groups. Accordingly, changes in four major institutions (economy, education, political parties, and the state) are examined in relation to the worldviews, ideologies and political strategies of two basic fundamentalist movements (the neo-traditional and radical). Although differences between such groups exist, both generally emphasize "religious vision propelling groups into political action" (Stowasser, 1987:10).

MASS MEDIA AND ISLAMIC PERSPECTIVES

The area where the rise of religiosity as well as Islamic fundamentalism is most visible is the world of communications: books, periodicals, newspapers, magazines, videocassettes, and so on. The daily circulation of Islamist newspapers reaches 5,000, while the nearly sixty monthly periodicals sell over 700,000 copies. Manuals on Islamic practices, translations of the works of modern Islamist ideologies, and classical religious texts are printed in the hundreds of thousands. These publications vary greatly in their basic views of Islam and society but can be examined under the following headings: the traditional Sufi orders–primarily the Nakşibendi, but also the Kadiri, Rufai, and others; religious movements of republican origin–Nurcu, Süleymancı, Işıkcı; and the independent or nontraditional Islamists (radicals), consisting of numerous groups and factions, each following its almost distinct track. Due to limited space, this chapter limits the analysis to the views of the Nakşibendi, the Nurcu, and the radicals.

The Nakşibendi Order

The basic traditions and tenets of the Nakşibendi order, some of which are also part of the general Sufi doctrine, emerged as important organizational assets in the context of a rapidly changing Turkish society. This particular form of Sufi teaching emphasizes the purification of the soul, pious asceticism, strengthened faith, superior morality, personal integrity, and self-control in resisting materialistic desires and hedonistic pleasures. Typically, the Sufi orders aim to create exceedingly devout people superior in their commitment to ordinary believers. Such an intensified inner life of belief and conscience is extremely important for a religious movement operating in a rapidly changing society where the traditional culture is eroding under the impact of rising consumerism, hedonism, and status competition.[1] Moreover, the primary allegiance and loyalty of the members is expected to be to the order itself and especially to its leader, the sheikh. In this context, total submission requires, at least in ideal terms, the annihilation of the individual's ego in his relationship with the sheikh. The emphasis on hierarchical relations of super- and sub-ordination emerges as yet another significant asset for social and political mobilization. Finally, a uniquely Nakşibendi notion of a communion of hearts, which links the members of the order living in different parts of the world, as well as the past generations, through the mediation of the sheikh, helps to foster a wide network of influence and solidarity that goes beyond the confines of narrow local groups. In summary, the Nakşibendi appear as highly loyal and strong believers, deeply committed to the organization and its leader, disciplined in their action, and extremely solidaristic in developing connections that may often cut across regional and national differences.

The Nakşibendi, however, do not take an extremist position in their asceticism. On the contrary, compromise with the material world is considered necessary for establishing the mastery and domination of Islam over society. For example, the neo-traditionalist approach of the Nakşibendi to science, technology, and economy argues that technological innovation and economic power, normally rejected when considered separately, are essential for Islam as long as they are used within the confines of Islamic purposes. Hence, if it is spent to uphold the power and glory of Islam, accumulation of wealth is encouraged. However, wealth directed at avaricious consumption and economic domination of others is condemned.

The hallmark of Nakşibendism is its catechism, which places an extremely powerful emphasis on ritual and religious observance. The attempt to control every single aspect of daily social life by infinitely extending the sphere of canonical jurisprudence is the Nakşibendi challenge against opposing non-Islamic ethical and value systems. Indeed, the Nakşibendis are utterly intolerant and exclusivist toward other value systems and life-styles. In order to render Islam supreme in social life, the leading Nakşibendi authorities rely on a highly developed strategy. Here, they assume that once this most fundamental sphere is successfully controlled, others will necessarily follow. They target the residential communities and bazaar environment of the self-employed where, through catechism, they can effectively exercise a strong sense of community and increased social control. The extremely detailed rules of conduct confine the individual so that virtually no scope is left for autonomous action. Thus, the external social control that is exercised by the community complements the internalized self-control which the individual gains through spiritual education. The Nakşibendis have at their disposal a vast stock of rules inherited from the past, while they create new ones in response to new situations. Thus, proper behavior according to divine ordinances and standards is constantly counterposed to secular norms and values.

In this process of the sacralization of social life, the roles of the sheikh or *tarikat* leaders is crucial, in that they pass judgment on proper conduct in new or conflicting situations. Importantly, they also maintain and regulate the pressure of the community on deviant individuals. The sheikh has legitimate authority because of not only spiritual guidance, but also personal charisma and divine illumination. Here, we see how the spiritual and social domains are closely intertwined.

Politically, the Nakşibendi journals emphasize supranationalist values, the strengthening of Islamic consciousness and solidarity on a worldwide basis, and respect for past Islamic traditions. In the 1970s, the religious National Salvation party (NSP) was known for its glorification of Ottoman history, but the Nakşibendi of the 1980s proved less enthusiastic in following this track. In recent publications, a national frame of reference is not particularly prominent. On the contrary, Islam is the relevant political unit, with news about Islamic countries and people taking priority. A league of Islamic nations, a unified Islamic economy, and the oneness of the Islamic community (*Ummet*) emerge as themes overriding nationalist ones. The historical outlook strictly focuses on orthodox Islam. In this respect, races and nations are not ranked on the basis of their contribution to the Islamic cause and civilization.

In their political strategy the Nakşibendi are peaceful and gradualist. Open confrontation with the state and other secular republican institutions is deliberately avoided.[2] In their strategy for success the Nakşibendis encourage the growth of a rich propertied Islamist bourgeoisie, the consolidation of an Islamist sector in the economy, and the use of political party connections to increase the influence of the Nakşibendi networks within state institutions and to promote the expansion of communities that adopt the Islamic way of life. The mainstream Nakşibendi orders tend to take an open stand against radical militarism, but splinter groups that use the basic Sufi and Nakşibendi discourse as a basis for radical militant action also exist.

The Nurcu Order

The Nurcu are even further divided in their views and strategies for action. Said Nursi, the founder of the movement, was deeply influenced by Sufism and Nakşibendi Islam as a *medrese* student in various parts of southeastern Anatolia. However, he never became a truly *tarikat* man. He rejected the latter on grounds that the apparent decline of Islam under the threat of Western culture, civilization, and institutions imposed other priorities and urgencies. Specifically, these were twofold: a reinvigoration of the Islamic faith and the spread of the knowledge of modern sciences among the Islamic population. Closer scrutiny of his work reveals these objectives as two facets of the same unfolding principle. Nursi's *Risalei Nur* collection presents a cosmological framework that explicates the relationship between God, nature and men. According to Şerif Mardin (1982), Said Nursi focused primarily on the more metaphorical and allegorical verses in the Koran. This emerges as an important contrast with the Nakşibendi tradition of placing the primary emphasis on rules and standards of conduct. To follow Mardin's explanation, Said Nursi describes the bountiful creativity of God, the richness of the biological universe, and the regularity of nature where God is "present" (Mardin, ibid.).

Taking these fundamentals as their point of departure from the Sufi orders, the Nurcu journals, in hundreds and thousands of brief articles, try to show how an inquiry on divinity and rigorous scientific investigation can become one and the same thing. Man, in accordance with his very purpose of (inquiry) is in constant search of God. When carefully examined, even the smallest particle in the universe is a wonder in itself as a sign and proof of the masterly work of God. The discovery of such wonders in the universe by means of scientific investigation is elevated to the status of worship of God. The regularity, the perfection, the faultlessness and immaculateness of the order of nature, repeated over and over again in infinite multitudes, signal the Divine Wisdom which men can grasp through scientific observation.[3]

The fairly high level of sophistication of the popularized science articles indicates that the reader must have some formal educational background in the natural sciences. In fact, the Nurcu order receives substantial backing from technically oriented people and teaching institutions which specialize in the natural sciences. In this order, science and technology are not only praised for their instrumental functions, as in the case of the Nakşibendi, but are divinely sanctioned. Scientific investigation and worship of God are closely integrated as the Nurcu's particular appeal gains a fundamentally religio-philosophical character.

The nationalist emphasis, which is more marked in the Nurcu journals, takes the form of Ottomanism: a glorification of the social, political, and economic organization of the Ottoman Empire as an ideal society. Many issues of the Nurcu journals contain at least one or two articles that exalt various aspects of Ottoman civilization and institutions. Nurcu authors readily accept the supremacy of the Ottoman system in cultural, scientific, and military terms. They perceive the ruling establishment of the empire as having strictly observed Islamic faith and principles. Another aspect of the preoccupation with Turkishness in Nurcu teaching is the belief that Turks have been the leading contributors to the Islamic cause in the Muslim world.

Since their foundation some of the Nurcu groups supported the Democrat party of Adnan Menderes in the 1950s and the Justice party (1962-1980) and the True Path party (since 1983) of Süleyman Demirel. Other Nurcus, critical of this long lasting and overtly committed relationship with Demirel, supported the religious National Order party and its successor, the National Salvation party of Necmettin Erbakan. During the 1980s the leading Nurcu group that follow Fethullah Gülen, the so-called Fethullahcı order, backed the center rightist Motherland party (MP) of Turgut Özal. This political party remained in power until October 1991.

In terms of their political strategies, the Nurcu are not fundamentally different from the Nakşibendi. They too employ peaceful means and adapt gradualist methods to promote Islam in society and politics. The Nurcu are also nonconfrontationalist; that is, they try to work from within the existing secular institutions of the state in order to counter and reduce the power of the state. For example, the Fethullahcı are known for their efforts to provide food and accommodation for poor students in dormitories established by the order. From these establishments, the students are directed toward various schools and professions as part of the overall indoctrination process. From time to time, their attempts to infiltrate the army do appear on the national press. Infiltration of strategic state institutions like the Ministry of Education, the police, the State Planning Organization, and the like is also a strategy used by other religious groups that originated during the republican period of Turkey.

The Radical Islamic Groups

The traditional orders and religious movements of republican origin together constitute the neo-traditionalist Islamic block in Turkey. As elaborated by Shepard (1987:318-19), neo-traditionalism established itself when traditionalism faced the challenge of Westernization. While the neo-traditionalists value the depth and complexity of past Islamic tradition, they accept the need for modern science, technology, and some aspects of modern civilization.

Radicals, on the other hand, consist of numerous splinter groups with different views and approaches. Common to all, however, is a break from past Islamic perspectives and paradigms and especially from those of traditional and neo-traditional orders. Many radicals are deeply influenced by the very modern ideologies and worldviews from which they strive to disassociate themselves. In other words, radicalism is primarily ideological in nature. Being remote from the Islamic masses, the radicals live in a hostile world of competing ideologies and ideological groups. A typical radical politicizes every aspect of social life and places religion on a distinctly political plane. Also, as Meeker (1988) indicates, the radicals tend to ideologize and intellectualize their past experience with a nostalgia not so much oriented to the past as to the future. Islam in this sense is transformed into an ideology essential for defining personal and social identity.

Islamic radicalism is an urban phenomenon. The radicals are intellectuals living in big cities, professionals employed in large-scale organizations, or, in the majority of cases, students in higher education. The radical approach to Islam is less historical; other than the Golden Age of the Prophet and his companions, no other period of Islamic history is glorified. The Golden Age in turn is seen more as a "state of nature" to deduce the basic Islamic ideals and to use them as a measure of deviations and aberrations from the ideal Islamic society.

We can distinguish two major radical tendencies among these groups. In the 1980s a small group of intellectuals has interpreted social and political problems from an Islamic viewpoint and started a new trend that has gradually established itself among the educated young Islamists. These Muslim intellectuals address themselves to the general public not only by writing in Islamist journals and newspapers but also by joining debates with secular intellectuals in the national press and panels. Interestingly enough, these Muslim intellectuals study Western ideas, philosophies, and ideologies, and a few have a good grasp of modern social science literature.

An international orientation also accounts for these groups' influence in society. Radical Islamic groups, unlike the Nurcu and Nakşibendi, adopt a tolerant and, in some cases, even sympathetic view of the Iranian revolution. They are, however, critical of nationalist tendencies. The radicals view nationalism and national boundaries as artificial creations of the Western powers to divide and weaken solidarity among the Islamic people.[4]

Nevertheless, radical Islam is predominantly militant. As one goes from the more advanced educational institutions of the cities to peripheral ones and to lycées and religious schools in the Anatolian provinces, this tendency becomes even more marked. This type of militant Islam makes considerable use of traditional religious views and practices. The majority of militants, however, are influenced by Islamist ideologists whose works are widely translated into Turkish. Qutb and Mawdudi are influential militant Islamists while Ali Sheriati is an important figure for the Muslim intellectuals. In their strategies, the intellectuals and militants both adopt confrontationist, antistate, antisystem methods. Even so, the intellectuals are somewhat more peaceful, as they emphasize changing people's minds through education. Militant Islam, on the other hand, is more action-oriented, and some sections, though admittedly few, openly argue for the use of physical force to fight against the non-Islamic groups. Although the center of gravity in fundamentalist Islam in Turkey is clearly the neo-traditionalist bloc, militant Islam could become influential by evolving into a modern urban protest movement or by adopting revolutionary tactics. As argued in other contexts, increasing inequality, reduced possibilities for upward social mobility, and mounting social discontent are likely to make socioeconomic matters more significant and the slide toward leftist themes and ideologies more pronounced among radical groups (Davis, 1987:51-57).

RELIGION AND THE ECONOMY

Until the 1950s and 1960s, the traditional petty bourgeoisie, consisting of artisans and shopkeepers, remained as the main bearers of Islamic pietism and culture in urban Turkey. From then on, the traditional middle class split spatially, as the artisans gradually moved to areas with concentrations of small industry located in the outskirts of towns, where the traditional culture and life-styles of the bazaar existed. Indeed, at present, especially in the provincial towns and cities, the shopkeepers' bazaar and the small industrial areas of artisans and small craftsmen include the two major strongholds of religious pietism. This traditional middle class of propertied people preserves the *gemeinschaft* of a society which can effectively exercise powerful social control over individuals to maintain the values, life-styles, and worldview of the religious majority.

Since the 1960s Islamic fundamentalism has gained support from two new social groups. The first is a *moyenne bourgeoisie* of industrialists in labor-intensive sectors and of merchants in retail and wholesale trade. The leadership cadres of the NSP in the 1970s and those of the Welfare party (WP) in the 1980s contained people largely from this group, who helped finance religious and fundamentalist activities through generous donations to religious foundations and associations. The *moyenne bourgeoisie* is a product of the market and operates in this framework. Thus, its local character is less marked when compared with the traditional bazaar people. This partly explains why the *moyenne bourgeoisie's* participation in politics has been more fundamentalist in nature and distinct from the more religious pietism of the traditional petty bourgeoisie.

The second important development is the emergence of a new large bourgeoisie committed in various degrees to the Islamic movement. This new social class grew as a result of the conscious efforts of Islamists in the Motherland party governments who provided the Islamist bourgeoisie access to credit from official sources. They were also given preferential treatment in receiving government contracts. Hence, especially in the 1980s, many such firms benefited significantly from state-directed patronage and these companies, in turn, financially backed Islamist movements. With the emergence of this bourgeoisie, it became possible for international Islamic capital to find qualified Turkish collaborators for joint investments.[5] Furthermore, given the rapid expansion of Islamic banks and financial institutions in Turkey, this new economic sector continues to have good prospects for further growth and expansion.

The Islamic bourgeoisie comprise no more than a tiny fraction of the total Turkish bourgeoisie. However, its significance is more political, due to its finance of Islamist activities. A widely shared Islamic principle is that all property, and nature in general, including man's own body and organs, are ultimately owned by God. The supreme owner indicates in detail how all property is to be used. Furthermore, this should not be according to the "whims and whips" of individual human beings. Rather, use of property ought to comply with divine ordinances. As the expression goes, the learned men of Islam join the Islamic struggle (*Cihad*) with their science (*ilm*), others with their bodies, and men of property with their wealth.

In the neo-traditionalist publications, the identification of Islam with poverty is condemned, for this is conceived to be tantamount to saying that religious people are the weak, the impotent, the desperate, and the miserable. To the extent that it carries the footprints of men of substance, Islam will be associated with effectiveness, influence, and power. Hence, accumulation of wealth by the religiously devout is explicitly encouraged, provided that this form of economic activity is subordinated to the general religious political cause, that is, the transformation of economic power into the worldly power of God. This may take the form of financing Islamist publications, student dormitories, and social security organizations. One deliberate aim behind this is to produce tangible results that indicate Islam can institute more efficient and more humane organizational alternatives than the secular institutions of the state. As opposed to radicalism, conservative neo-traditionalist strategy includes an emphasis on private property, capital accumulation, and reformist zeal in matters of social security (Lawrence, 1987).

In sum, one could argue that Islam in the economy clearly indicates that civil society itself is the major source of the dynamism of the fundamentalist movement in Turkey. In this process the groups that seem to hold the upper hand are not the splinter radical groups but the neo-traditionalist Islamists, who adopt a strategy of consolidation of religion at the base of the society, and pursue nonconfrontationist policies in their relations with the state and other public institutions.

EDUCATION

Historically, the relationship between religion and education in Turkey has evolved in four major stages. Until the middle of the nineteenth century, education in the Ottoman Empire was overwhelmingly a religious affair, undertaken in different institutional contexts corresponding to different areas and levels of instruction. The religious monopoly no education was not challenged until the introduction of new schools and higher education institutions that taught modern sciences. From the mid-nineteenth century onward, the sphere of secular education gradually expanded at the expense of religious institutions. These new institutions concentrated mainly on such fields as the military, medicine, and engineering, and they were staffed with new people who had secular educational backgrounds. Meanwhile, the traditional educational system decayed along with the old religious elite, who remained largely outside the main orbit of reform and change. During this period of the Ottoman Empire, pluralism in education was characterized by the presence of "modern" and secular schools operating side by side with the traditional religious institutions. Also, some hybrid forms of schools combined elements of both the secular and religious educational systems.

During the republican period, the single-party rule (1923-1946) imposed a totally new educational system. The "Unity of Education" Act placed all educational activity under strict government control and introduced a state monopoly on education. This decision undermined the pluralist structure of education that had prevailed in the second phase described above. Religion, on the other hand, was left almost totally outside the scope of formal eduction. As Akşit explains:

It (the Act) was not only a rejection to the traditionalism of Medreses but it also put an end to the pluralism of the educational system: thus asserting a centralist, modernist, national educational system under the guidance of rationalism and scientism to establish a new nation with a new identity and a new unified morality. (1988:18)

Under such circumstances, the transmission of religious knowledge from one generation to the next was possible only through informal channels: family, the small community, and clandestine *tarikat* activity.

The last phase started during the multi-party period in 1946 and consolidated in the early 1990s. It marks a return to the pluralist framework of the second stage found during the pre-republican period. However, this new educational pluralism is radically different from the previous one. The hallmark of this change is the reintroduction of religious teaching in the secondary schools and in the theology schools of higher education. The secondary schools which offer religious instruction are known as the *İmam Hatip Okulları*. The number of these schools and their students have multiplied over the last three decades. By 1987, the students in the *İmam Hatip* schools made up 10 percent of total secondary school students. In all, a total of 240,000 students were studying in 717 such schools (Akşit, 1988:2). The schools include modern sciences in their curriculum, and their graduates are quite successful in the university entrance exams. Once in universities, these students begin new careers in secular educational fields. Another institution worthy of mention in this context is the so-called "Koran Course," which has been run officially by the Directorate of Religious Affairs since 1981. In these schools, children recite the Koran and learn basic Islamic teaching and practices. Finally, in 1981 the military government passed an act that made the teaching of a course on religious education compulsory for all students in primary and secondary public schools. One major implication of this act is that Sunni teaching in religious classes is used with both Sunni and non-Sunni students.

The discussion on increasing pluralism, however, should not be limited to the formal sector of education. Dormitories organized by religious groups also teach and transmit religious knowledge, values, and practices. Recently, various religious groups started centers which specialize in the training of students for the university entrance exams. In these places, fees are lower than those found in private dormitories sponsored by private companies like Koç and Sabancı. Equally significant in this context is the revival of traditional *medrese* schools in eastern and southeastern Turkey: These are typically run by a single *hoca* and his few assistants who teach the traditional curriculum of the *medreses* to a small group of students. Islamist groups also finance private secondary schools, which are in turn licensed by the Ministry of Education. So far, there has been at least one unsuccessful attempt to found a private Islamic university (*Bezm-i Alem*). In conclusion, one could say that while religion has not yet seriously challenged the supremacy of secular education, it has been highly successful in penetrating and expanding its influence in formal and informal education.

POLITICAL PARTIES

Since the transition to a multi-party system in 1946, almost all of the main political parties have attempted to appeal to people's religious sentiments by adopting religious symbols, extending religious services provided by the government, and relaxing legal and police controls over clandestine religious activities. Political parties to the right of center have always gone further in this direction than the more secular Republican People's party (RPP) and its successor since 1983, the Social Democratic Populist party (SDPP). In this chapter, however, the discussion of the relationship between religion and political parties has a much narrower focus: examining the strategies of cooperatation and compromise adopted by political parties in power toward organized religious groups.

Perhaps such relations were never extinct at the local provincial level, but their first appearance in national politics can be traced back to the formation of a strong alliance between the Nurcu group and the Democrat party during the 1950s. Since then the Islamist groups have adopted two basic strategies in their relations with political parties. First, they support a political party that struggles to bring about a society and polity in which all institutions are organized primarily according to Islamic principles and practices. And second, they support the leading cente-right parties.

The NSP/WP line in Turkish politics is indicative of the first approach. At the local and electoral base, the NSP derived its recruited power from traditional religious groups, while it recruited national leadership cadres from among young university-educated technocrats who, if not of urban origin, had wide-ranging contacts within urban centers. Hence, a strong regional accent was noticeable in the party's electoral support. Turkey's least developed regions (the East and Southeast), where the traditional leadership of landowners, local notables and sheikhs reigned supreme, had emerged as major NSP strongholds. Second, the party's performance was considerably better in small towns and some Anatolian provinces than in other rural and metropolitan areas. Gradually, the NSP/WP increased their metropolitan votes. During the 1987 elections, the WP votes in Istanbul were higher than the party's national average.

As a result of this dualism in its leadership and electoral base, the NSP had bitter and ongoing internal strife, and always received heavy criticism from the Islamist groups. These critiques emphasized the highly manipulative, exclusive, and conciliatory tactics of party leaders as well as the party's close integration with an overtly non-Islamic regime. Within the party, centripetal forces always retained power and employed careful tactics to hold different groups together. Curiously, one way of doing this was by creating tangible benefits for the cooperative members. This, in turn, required NSP's participation in coalition governments and further co-optation with secular institutions. Despite efforts in this direction, the policies and tactics of the NSP leadership alienated some Nurcu and Nakşibendi groups .

NSP propaganda focused on issues such as technological change, industrialization, and national development. It also criticized social inequality, government waste, and exploitation. With a unique emphasis on moral crisis, the party attempted to draw attention to the undesirable social and cultural effects of modernization and secularization. In this environment, the NSP declared its role in politics as one of filling the moral and cultural vacuum resulting from Turkey's Westernization policies.[6]

At the local level, the NSP adopted a more pronounced fundamentalist tone. The leader of the party, Necmettin Erbakan, maintained that only Islam, and not secularism, was in harmony with human nature and that parliamentary democracy was a dangerous Christian and Jewish trick to deceive the faithful. He also argued that Islamic institutions should serve as models for reorganizing Turkish society from top to bottom and that Islamic law and jurisprudence ought to reign supreme in all realms of life. This so-called "nationalist view," the official party ideology, was nothing other than a fundamentalist ideology that seriously challenged the secular state. In fact, this tendency to move from political conservatism to religious fundamentalism became more obvious in the Welfare party during the 1980s.

As to the second strategy of supporting the leading center-right wing parties, these organized Islamic groups are divided. During the 1980s the Süleymancı and some sections of the Nurcu voted for the True Path party. The Fethullahcı and the Kadiri supported the MP, and the Rıfai voted for the Nationalist Work party. The support of the most influential group, the Nakşibendi, was divided between the MP and the WP. And finally, the radical splinter groups either stood firmly against forming such alliances or supported the WP. Recent public opinion polls indicate that support for the WP is at least 10 percent of the voters. Judging by the distribution of support, one may assume that about the same amount of support goes to the remaining religious parties. This places the religiously mobilized voters at some 20 percent of the electorate.

The so-called "Holy Alliance" (*kutsal ittifak*) in the MP was often described as a confederation of divergent Islamist groups. What makes this relationship different from previous alliances observed during the DP and JP periods is that members of the Holy Alliance were directly represented at the local, national, and parliamentary groups of the MP as well as at the cabinet level. In other words, this was not a typical relationship between a political party and pressure groups. This extensive network of religious groups in the MP partly explains why the influence of Islamist groups in Turkey has become so overwhelming at the state level and in public life in general.

RELIGION AND THE STATE

The changing relationship between the state and religion is likely to constitute one of the most important debates in Turkey in the 1990s. Here, I limit the discussion of state institutions to the army, the bureaucracy, and the legal establishment. These institutions, together with secular educational institutions, are often seen as the main pillars of the secularist republican state.

During the single-party period, the state strictly controlled religion. Furthermore, the influence of religion in state affairs was eliminated, and religious activities in public life were tightly controlled. During this time, *tarikat* activity, which had been experiencing a steady decline since the last decades of the Ottoman Empire, moved underground. And finally, the newly formed Directorate of Religious Affairs remained only as a minor state department preaching a privatized civic religion that relegated Islam to the conscience of the individual.

The Democrat party rule significantly revised this pattern. During this period religion became a useful instrument in appealing to the masses in elections. As the leaders of the DP deployed more religious slogans and symbols in their propaganda, religion represented opposition to the laicist elitism of the early republic.[7] Once in power, the DP adopted a conciliatory attitude toward religion and relaxed government control over religious activities. Thus, DP rule also marked the beginning of various forms of co-optation between organized Sunni religious groups and political parties of the center right. However, for the DP, and even for its successor, the Justice party, it would be incorrect to say that this co-optation reached the point of allowing fundamentalist networks to infiltrate state institutions. Blatant attempts to infiltrate state institutions occurred only when the NSP participated in coalition governments in 1973-1979 and during the MP rule in the 1980s.

Following the 1980 coup, military leaders attempted to find a medium between religion and the secular state by adopting ideas from both the single–party and DP/JP periods. From the single–party period, the tradition of strong state control over religion, or direct state intervention into religious affairs, was adopted. At the same time, following the DP/JP model, religion was accepted as a significant social and political datum in people's lives.

Beyond this though, other considerations also affected the military leaders' policy preferences.

First, the growing significance of the Islamic Middle East as a trade partner and closer diplomatic alliances with Islamic countries, both occurring at a time when Turkey's relations with Western Europe were deteriorating, pressured the Turkish leaders to look favorably to the Islamic countries of the region. Second, officials recognized the potential of religion as a legitimizing force for their policies. Lastly, they saw religion as an important instrument in the struggle against anarchy and terror.

Despite these tendencies, military officials still viewed Islam and Islamic organizations with suspicion, while causing a serious and potentially dangerous dilemma in state-religion relations. On the one hand, the state tried to increase the religiosity of the people through the policies discussed above. On the other hand, the state continued to oppose religious movements by (1) arresting fundamentalist leaders, (2) banning fundamentalist organizations, (3) attempting to impose state control over Koran courses, though this was quickly abandoned by Turgut Özal's MP government, and (4) dictating the content of all sermons delivered by mosque personnel. These seemingly paradoxical policies provoked criticism from both secular intellectual and fundamentalist leaders. The secular intellectuals saw these policies as the main reason for the revival of fundamentalist Islam in Turkey. The fundamentalists, however, condemned the attempts of the military government to define what the "true religion is."

The hallmark of the changes that occurred after 1983 was the unprecedented level of penetration of state institutions by neo-traditionalist Islamic groups. Many official departments became vehicles for the promotion of fundamentalist ideas and interests. In some ministries the personnel departments fell into the hands of the fundamentalist networks, which used the opportunity to draw upon the graduates of *İmam Hatip* schools and students who had religious ties to "dormitories." These individuals, in turn, used their newly acquired power and prestige to promote the Islamic cause in their respective state institutions. Even the military was not immune to this development. For example, in 1990, 813 officers and students were dismissed for having ties to fundamentalist organizations. The trend over the last few years suggests that such developments are likely to increase in the near future.

Considering the developments of the 1980s, it would be incorrect to see state action as homogeneous and one-sided in its support of secularist reforms and institutions. The state and the secular are no longer monolithic. They have been penetrated by Islamists. Who will prevail at the end is difficult to guess. It is, however, correct to say that the state institutions will become the battleground for laic and fundamentalist forces.

CONCLUSION

The findings of this study show that some Islamic groups operate within the boundaries of the Turkish political system. In this capacity they clearly represent antiestablishment forces. Other Islamic groups are more secretive and use clandestine tactics to challenge the state. As a result of these developments, Islam is becoming highly politicized in all aspects and sectors of social life. In an attempt to expand its sphere of influence and to keep up with the rapid pace of social change, Islamic organizations have increasingly diversified their ideological orientations and political strategies. It is highly likely that we will witness a further proliferation of Islamic organizations. Therefore, it is essential to understand the complexity of believers' motives and responses to the Islamic appeal, the different forms which this appeal takes, and the magnitude of revivalist tendencies.[8]

The above analysis demonstrates a close affinity between religious fundamentalism and right-wing political parties. At the other side of the political spectrum, the social democratic parties represent the hard-line secularist opposition to Islamic revival in Turkey. However, this distinction is seriously confused when one considers the political allegiance of the Alevis (Shia) in the country. Contrary to the position of the Sunnis, the Alevis have a strong tendency to support the social democratic parties. This dichotomy resulted in serious clashes between the two religious sects. During the 1970s Turkey witnessed several open clashes between the Sunnis and the Alevis in which several hundred people died. Although there was little evidence of this conflict in the 1980s, the further spread of Sunni fundamentalism could generate a strong, but latent, reaction from the Alevi population.

Given the intensity of the situation, is a major clash between secularist and religious groups likely in the near future? From the Islamic point of view, one particular development may help to mitigate the harshness of the situation and postpone the inevitable conflict. During the past decade, various social problems (such as rapid urbanization, inadequate housing and health care, unemployment, and worsening income distribution) have become even more acute. Some religious groups may respond to these problems more actively than the incumbent political parties. In such a scenario, religion would not only legitimize the rightist parties but also represent a voice of widespread social discontent.[9] Speaking for the underprivileged can powerfully challenge the mainstream conservative neo-traditionalist groups of Turkish Islam.

Other than those already polarized at the laical and the fundamentalist fronts, crucial forces that are likely to determine the course of future events are the government, big business, and the military. In a country where the government acts as the main distributor of resources, those who hold power can be highly effective in increasing or curbing the influence of political groups or movements. Hence, a government in the hands of politicians strongly dedicated to republican laical principles can at least reduce state-directed patronage favoring organized religion. This, however, should not be exaggerated: Pushing all fundamentalist groups into opposition may help these otherwise divided groups to unite against the state.

As for the other two institutions, the laical section of big business is likely to emerge as the most significant deterrent to fundamentalism. This predominantly Istanbul-based bourgeoisie is pro-Western in its views, business ties, and life-style. The military, on the other hand, while still opposing fundamentalism, is preoccupied with sociopolitical disorder in southeastern Turkey. Furthermore, there is a new tendency among the general staff to view religiosity favorably in spite of still vehemently opposing fundamentalism. The danger in this case is where one draws the line between religiosity and fundamentalism in Islam.

In the 1990s Turkey is likely to experience the most serious "legitimacy crisis" ever witnessed since the early days of the republic. First, separatist groups in the Southeast are challenging the unity of the nation and the principle of the unitary state. How ethnicity, regionalism, and demographic divisions in an Islamic country are influenced by religiosity and fundamentalism is an extremely important question which has not been seriously studied.[10] Second, some intellectual groups on the far left and far right criticize the "strong state" principle of the republic as being nothing more than dictatorship. Finally, Islamic fundamentalists' attack on laicism and Western civilization challenges the very fabric of the republican state.

NOTES

1. In one of the very rare empirical studies on *tarikats*, Vergin provides evidence to substantiate this argument. In a small town, Ereğli, that experienced rapid industrialization, the author underlines the following as being highly characteristic of *tarikat* people: "controlling temper and playing down aggression, the ability to strike a balance between worldly and other worldly considerations as to withdraw from excesses of leisure and entertainment: discipline in work and a sufficient self-control to distance oneself effectively from the flux of deep involvement in everyday life" (Vergin, 1985:16-18).

2. Algar goes even one step further to argue that the Nakşibendis have implicitly and unconsciously accepted the secularist republic. The author also notes that they have important reservations about the basic principles and functions of the existing regime (Algar, 1984:188-189).

3. A highly sophisticated and comprehensive account of the work of Said Nursi can be found in Mardin (1982 and 1989).

4. For more detailed accounts of radical Islam see Toprak (1985), Ayata (1988), and Meeker (1988). For a study of radical fundamentalist women see Acar (1988).

5. In his study on the connections between foreign capital and Islamic fundamentalists in Turkey, Yeşilada (1988) argues that complex economic and

political ties exist between the two groups. The economic investments of Saudi finance institutions in Turkey do not aim simply at achieving profits. Rather, these investments provide an economic support base for the fundamentalists in Turkey in their struggle against the secular state.

6. For further readings on the NSP and ideology see Landau (1976), Alkan (1984), and Özbudun (1987).

7. According to Sunar and Toprak, the cleavage between the cultures of the center and the periphery that had existed since the Ottoman Empire widened during the early republican period. In their explanation they argue that "the tension between the Ottoman center and the periphery had been partly reduced by the linkage function served by Islam. When this major connection with the periphery was weakened by the state, the tension was exacerbated and the distance between the central elite and the ascriptive, religious groups of the periphery greatly increased. The state elite now faced, without much intermediation, a religiously anchored primordially embedded segmental society which it was supposed to reshape and reform" (Sunar and Toprak, 1983: 426-427).

8. Pointing to the distinct clusters within the usually "undifferentiated Muslim setting," Heper argues that Islam is multifunctional and is used by different groups for entirely different purposes (Heper, 1981:346).

9. Sarıbay stresses that relative deprivation and loss of prestige by social classes are the major factors behind the rise of religious fundamentalism in Turkey (Sarıbay, 1985:45).

10. For a detailed discussion see Hudson (1984:39).

REFERENCES

Acar, F. (1988). "Women in the Ideology of Islamic Revivalism: Three Islamic Women's Journals." Paper presented at the Conference on Islam and Society in Turkey. School of Oriental and African Studies. University of London. London. May.

Aksu, B. (1988). "Islamic Education in Late Ottoman Medreses and Republican Turkish Imam Hatip Schools." Paper presented at the Conference on Islam and Society in Turkey. School of Oriental and African Studies. University of London. London. May.

Akşit, B. (1988). "Islamic Education in Late Ottoman Medreses and Republican Turkish Imam-Hatip Schools." Paper presented at the confernce on Islam and Society in Turkey. School of Oriental and African Studies. University of London. London. May.

Algar, H. (1984) "Der Naksibendi Order in der republikanischen Türkei." In Jochen Blaschke and Marlin van Bruinessen, eds., *Islam und Politik in der Türkei*. Express Edition. Berlin:

Alkan, I. (1984). "The National Salvation Party in Turkey." In Metin Heper and Raphael Israeli, eds., *Islam and Politics in the Modern Middle East*. London: Croom Helm.

Ayata, Ayşe G. (1988). "Pluralism versus Authoritarianism: Political Ideas in Two Islamic Publications." Paper presented at the Conference on Islam and Society in Turkey. School of Oriental and African Studies. University of London. London. May.

Davis, E. (1987). "The Concept of Revival and the Study of Islam and Politics." In B. F. Stowasser, ed., *The Islamic Impulse*. Washington: Croom Helm.

Heper, M. (1981). "Islam, Polity and Society in Turkey: A Middle Eastern Perspective." *The Middle East Journal*. Vol. 35.

Hudson, M. C. (1984). "The Islamic Factor in Syrian and Iraq'i Politics." In J. P. Piscatori, ed., *Islam in the Political Process*. Cambridge: Cambridge University Press.

Landau, J. (1976). "The National Salvation Party in Turkey." *Asian and African Studies*. Vol.11. No. 1.

Lawrence, B. B. (1987). "Muslim Fundamentalist Movements: Reflections Toward a New Approach." In B. F. Stowasser, ed., *The Islamic Impulse*. Washington: Croom Helm.

Mardin, Ş. (1982). "Bediuzzaman Said Nursi (1873-1960): the Shaping of Vocation." In J. Davis., ed., *Religious Organization and Religious Experience*. London: Academic Press.

_____ (1989). *Religion and Social Change in Modern Turkey: The Case of Bediuzzaman Said Nursi*. New York: State University of New York Press.

Meeker, E. M. (1988). "The New Muslim Intellectuals of the Turkish Republic." Paper presented at the Conference on Islam and Society in Turkey. School of Oriental and African Studies. University of London. London. May.

Özbudun, E. (1987). "Islam and Politics in Modern Turkey: The Case of the National Salvation Party." In B. F. Stowasser, ed., *The Islamic Impulse*. Washington: Croom Helm.

Sarıbay, A. Y. (1985). "Turkiye'de Siyasal Modernleşme ve İslam." *Toplum ve Bilim*. No. 29/30.

Shepard, W. E. (1987). "Islam and Ideology: Towards a Typology." *International Journal of Middle East Studies*. Vol. 19.

Stowasser, B. F. (1987). *The Islamic Impulse*. Washington: Croom Helm.

Sunar, I., and B. Toprak (1983). "Islam in Politics: The Case of Turkey." *Government and Opposition*. Vol. 18. No .4.

Toprak, B. (1985). "İki Müslüman Aydın: Ali Bulaç ve İsmet Özel." *Toplum ve Bilim* No. 29/30.

Vergin, N. (1985). "Toplumsal Değişme ve Dinsellikte Artış" *Toplum ve Bilim*. No. 29/30.

Yeşilada, B. (1988). "Islamic Fundamentalism in Turkey and the Saudi Connection." *UFSI Field Staff Reports*. Africa/Middle East. No. 18.

4

The Development of Turkish Manufacturing Industry during 1976–1987: An Overview

Oktar Türel

INTRODUCTION

This chapter, which aims to review the main features of the development and transformation of Turkish manufacturing industry during the period 1976-1987, is composed of six sections. Following this brief introduction, the growth of manufacturing output, employment, and productivity will be discussed in general terms in the second section. Structural change within manufacturing industry will be briefly examined in the third section. The fourth section will be devoted to an analysis of productivity changes in industry, both in the aggregate and by sector. The main trends in industrial capital accumulation are presented in the fifth section. The sixth and last section is earmarked for a summary and the basic conclusions of the chapter.

For a study of Turkey's economic development in the 1980s, the choosing of the year 1976 as the starting point may look rather inappropriate at the first glance. The choice is justified, however, when one takes into account the fact that this year was perhaps the last "normal" year conforming to past trends in the economy, bringing the expansionary phase of the early 1970s to a close. The downturn starting from 1977 did not manifest itself only with a slowing-down of GNP growth, but also with a dramatic setback in manufacturing activity, to be recovered in 1981-1982. There are indicators that the upturn in 1981-1987 may now be paving the way to a recession from the second half of 1988 onward; hence the period 1976-1987 will most likely coincide with the full cycle. Thus, it will be of much interest for students of the Turkish economy to understand the nature of changes in the structure of production and levels of productivity over the entire span of the cycle. Although the available data lack either precision or coverage for the last two years of the period under study, the picture that emerges from them is sufficiently clear to make the underlying trends explicit.

Additional complications arise, however, in obtaining constant-price output and output per man series, due to the rapid inflation experienced in the period and the major relative price changes concomitant with it. Therefore, the reader is urged to be circumspect in the interpretation of the productivity changes presented in the next three sections and related tables, which should be regarded as representative trends and not as precise estimates. Further improvement on the data base seems to be an urgent need.

With minor exceptions, we take the 1982 prices as a basis for reference partly because the year 1982 was the median, which helps minimize telescopic faults backward and forward. Other important reasons for this decision include the fact that the relative price structure in the Turkish manufacturing sector attained a fairly stable pattern in that year, following price adjustments in the public enterprises, the dismantling of most of the price controls, currency depreciation in real terms, and steps taken toward trade liberalization in 1980-1982.

A few comments are also in order for the classification of manufacturing activities which are given in the appendix to this chapter. The classification conforms, by and large, to the sector classification of the State Planning Organization (SPO) adopted in Annual Programmes. It enables us to present series on output, foreign trade, and investment in a consistent manner, and also satisfies the compatibility of SPO and State Institute of Statistics data.[1]

Obviously, the performance of Turkish manufacturing industry in the period concerned cannot be judged solely in the national context; it must be compared and contrasted especially with that of the semi-industrialized less developed countries (LDCs). Apart from occasional remarks, however, we shall not attempt to make such a comparison mainly for two reasons: The first is the limitations of time and space. Second, additional research effort needs to be directed toward improving the statistical data base, if one wishes to derive hard-and-fast conclusions from international comparisons of this kind.[2]

THE GROWTH OF MANUFACTURING OUTPUT AND PRODUCTIVITY: GENERAL OBSERVATIONS

The growth of manufacturing value added (MVA), employment, and MVA per man in absolute terms and as a rate of change summarized in Tables 1 and 2. With the help of these tables, the following observations can be made.

For the period 1976-1987, MVA and MVA per man increased by 5.1 percent and 2.7 percent per annum (p.a.) on average, respectively. This shows a significant slowing down in comparison to the rates of growth of output and productivity attained over the previous cycle 196619-76 (9.5% and 5.4%, respectively). The Turkish performance also looks modest compared with the achievement of lower-middle-income LDCs over the period 1973-1981 (8.1% p.a. growth of MVA, on the average). However, Turkey's manufacturing output has been growing faster than that of the developed market economies (DMEs) which increased their MVA by 1.7 percent p.a. on the average for the period 1973-1981. In the last fifteen years for which comparable data are available, the growth rate of MVA per man in Turkey seems to be smaller that that of the lower-income LDCs and approximately equal to or slightly greater than that of the DMEs.[3]

The speeding up of MVA growth in the 1980s should be interpreted with caution. If the year 1980 is taken as an arbitrary starting point, the growth of MVA and productivity are impressive indeed (8.4 and 4.5% p.a., respectively, for the subperiod 1980-1987). However, as noted above, the growth of manufacturing output from 1980 to 1987 should not be taken in isolation from the cycle, since it was basically dependent on two conditions which are unlikely to be enjoyed in near future: the available stock of idle capacity inherited from the 1970s, and a balance of payments support which was not usually extended to other large semi-industrialized LDCs at a commensurate level of generosity. Although it would be an exaggeration to say that the Turkish economy lived through a foreign exchange bonanza in 1980-1987, to argue that it was foreign exchange-strangled is also wrong.

If capital-labor substitution is ruled out, it can be conjectured from the figures in Tables 1 and 2 that *almost all* of the increase in productivity per man during 1980-1987 is attributeable to improvements in capacity utilization. If, alternatively, one starts from a Cobb-Douglas production function with a capital coefficient around 0.7, almost two thirds of the improvement in MVA per man is due to increased use of industrial capacity, the rest being accounted for by technological change and/or capital deepening. Noting the fact that the capacity utilization rates in the second half of the 1980s are fairly high by past standards, one cannot be very optimistic for the growth of MVA and productivity in the 1990s in view of the sluggishness of capital formation observed in the 1980s (see the section on fixed capital formation below).

STRUCTURAL CHANGE IN MANUFACTURING INDUSTRY

Changes in the Composition of Gross Output

One might prefer to work with the change in the composition of MVA as an indicator of structural change in manufacturing. However, there are serious difficulties in obtaining or producing that type of information in current, let alone in constant, prices.[4] Therefore, we had to figure out structural change in manufacturing industry by the changes in composition of gross output published by the SPO in its Annual Programmes.

Table 1
Value Added, Employment, and Output per Man in Manufacturing Industry, 1976-1987

Year	Manufacturing Value Added (MVA) (TL billion, at 1982 prices)	Employment in Manufacturing (thousands)	MVA per Man (TL million, at 1982 prices)
1976	1593.6	1555.3	1.025
1977	1710.6	1591.6	1.075
1978	1771.8	1609.6	1.101
1979	1678.6	1571.5	1.068
1980	1571.3	1547.7	1.015
1981	1720.2	1593.5	1.080
1982	1812.8	1628.4	1.113
1983	1970.7	1684.9	1.170
1984	2171.2	1748.2	1.242
1985	2290.9	1802.0	1.271
1986	2509.9	1.904.2	1.318
1987[1]	2758.6	1999.8	1.379

1. Annual Program estimates.
Source: Manufacturing VA is calculated from SIS national accounts data and employment figures are compiled from SPO Annual Programmes.

Table 2
Development of Manufacturing Industry, 1976-1987

Year	Index values (1976=100)			Rates of increas, percent p.a.		
	MVA	Employment	MVA per man	MVA	Employment	MVA per man
1976	100.0	100.0	100.0			
1977	107.3	102.3	104.9	7.3	2.3	4.9
1978	111.2	103.5	107.4	3.6	1.1	2.4
1979	105.3	101.0	104.3	-5.3	-2.4	-3.0
1980	98.6	99.5	99.1	-6.4	-1.5	-5.0
1981	107.9	102.5	105.4	9.5	3.0	6.3
1982	113.8	104.7	108.6	5.4	2.2	3.1
1983	123.7	108.3	114.2	8.7	3.5	5.1
1984	136.2	112.4	121.1	10.2	3.8	6.2
1985	143.8	115.9	124.1	5.5	3.1	2.4
1986	157.5	122.4	128.6	9.6	5.7	3.7
1987[1]	173.1	128.6	134.5	9.9	5.0	4.6
1976-1987[2]				5.1	2.3	2.7
1976-1980[2]				-0.3	-0.1	-0.2
1980-1987[2]				8.4	3.7	4.5

1. Annual Program estimates.
2. Average.
Source: Computed from data in Table 1.

Due to sizable changes in relative prices, especially in 1976-1982, the SPO data based on current prices would give a distorted picture of structural change. Furthermore, sectoral price indexes to be used for deflating the current values of output are either short (like those of the series produced by State Institute of Statistics (SIS) after 1981), or unsuitable for deflation due to incompatibilities in sector classification, like those of the Treasury. In order to obtain a more meaningful composition, we tried to take at least the most drastic dislocation in relative price structure into account, that is, the change in relative prices of oil products vis-à-vis all non-oil manufactured products. Obviously, this kind of correction bypasses the relative price changes inside the non-oil manufactures category, but even so the correction seems to be better than none at all. The deflator for the oil products sector is obtained from a weighted average of ex-depot prices of seven major oil products. To deflate gross output at current prices in all other manufactured products, we singled out the non-oil component from the wholesale price index of the Undersecretariat of Treasury and Foreign Trade (1968=100).

Some of their peculiarities notwithstanding,[5] the sector shares presented in Table 3 enable the reader to make the following observations:

1. The decrease in the share of consumer goods industries by 8.5 percentage points is almost totally offset by the increasing share of intermediates.
2. The share of investment goods and consumer durables has not shown a marked increase over time. The recovery observed in this category after 1980 is basically the outcome of buoyant domestic demand for consumer durables, including automobiles and communication equipment.
3. At a more disaggregated level, the shares of chemicals, nonmetallic products, and electrical machinery and electronics in total gross output have been increasing in the last eleven years, whereas there is a definite decrease in the share of food and beverages. The Turkish export drive seems to have led to a rebound in the shares of textiles, clothing, and leather products after 1981-1982, which, on domestic demand considerations alone, were expected to fall. The shares of other sectors, including nonelectrical machinery, do not show definite directions of change.

Perhaps the most disturbing aspect of Table 3 is that the relative share of engineering industries in total gross output has not significantly increased over the last eleven years, in contrast with the experiences of large, semi-industrialized, middle-income LDCs. According to UNIDO's estimates, the share of engineering industries (ISIC 38) in total MVA were 17 percent in Turkey, 17 percent in Korea, 24 percent in Mexico, 26 percent in India and 29 percent in Brazil for the year 1975. In 1980, the corresponding figures for the five countries mentioned were 20, 22, 27, 28, and 30 percent respectively (see UNIDO, 1986a: Statistical Annex). Industrial experience suggests that the share of engineering output in MVA is positively correlated both with the share of MVA in national income and with the level of per capita income, as confirmed both by cross section and time series data. For the DMEs, the share of engineering industries in MVA now is already around 50 percent, a target which middle-income LDCs can hardly expect to reach by the end of the century. In relation to her GNP per capita and share of MVA in GNP, Turkey seems to possess a weaker base for engineering industries; and there seems to be no determined policy stand to change this state of affairs. Although in almost all of the Development Plans (including the fifth one, shaped by some of the members of present economic administration), the declared objective of the government has been the promotion of engineering industries, the political authorities do not seem to be committed to these statements of intent.[6]

Table 3
Sector Shares in Manufacturing Gross Output,
1976-1987 (percent)

Sectors				Years			
	1976	1978	1980	1982	1984	1986	1987[1]
CONSUMER	45.4	40.0	47.7	42.8	40.0	38.0	36.9
Food	(30.0)	(26.4)	(33.6)	(30.1)	(27.3)	(24.5)	(23.4)
Beverages	(1.4)	(1.4)	(1.8)	(1.3)	(1.1)	(1.2)	(1.2)
Tobacco	(2.3)	(3.1)	(3.9)	(2.8)	(2.6)	(2.4)	(2.2)
Textiles /Cloth.	(11.7)	(9.1)	(8.3)	(8.5)	(9.0)	(9.9)	(10.1)
INTERMEDIATES	40.3	46.8	41.2	45.4	45.8	47.4	48.4
Wood Products	(5.4)	(5.4)	(3.4)	(4.8)	(5.0)	(5.6)	(5.4)
Paper Products	(1.2)	(1.0)	(0.9)	(0.8)	(1.1)	(1.2)	(1.1)
Printing /Publish.	(1.0)	(1.3)	(1.4)	(1.0)	(0.8)	(0.7)	(0.7)
Leather Products	(2.9)	(2.4)	(1.9)	(1.8)	(3.5)	(3.9)	(4.5)
Rubber and Plastics	(1.5)	(2.9)	(1.9)	(2.2)	(1.7)	(2.1)	(2.2)
Chemicals	(5.8)	(7.0)	(7.4)	(8.1)	(7.8)	(8.9)	(9.4)
Petroleum Prod.	(13.6)	(17.1)	(15.3)	(16.0)	(14.1)	(12.0)	(12.1)
Glass	(0.5)	(0.5)	(0.4)	(0.9)	(1.1)	(0.8)	(0.9)
Pottery, China & Earthenware	(0.2)	(0.4)	(0.4)	(0.3)	(0.3)	(0.7)	(0.7)
Cement and Other Non-Metallic Pr.	(2.1)	(2.3)	(2.4)	(3.1)	(2.8)	(3.7)	(3.6)
Iron and Steel	(4.4)	(4.2)	(4.1)	(4.8)	(6.1)	(6.2)	(6.3)
Non-ferrous Metals	(1.7)	(2.3)	(1.6)	(1.5)	(1.4)	(1.7)	(1.6)
INVESTMENT AND CONSUMER GOODS	14.3	13.2	11.1	11.8	14.2	14.6	14.7
Metal Products	(2.6)	(3.1)	(2.8)	(3.5)	(3.7)	(4.0)	(3.9)
Non-Electrical Machinery	(3.9)	(3.2)	(3.1)	(2.2)	(2.9)	(2.9)	(3.1)
Electrical Mach.	(2.6)	(2.5)	(1.8)	(2.3)	(3.5)	(3.7)	(3.9)
Transport Equip.	(5.2)	(4.2)	(3.4)	(3.7)	(4.1)	(3.9)	(3.8)
Scientific Equip.	(0.1)	(0.1)	(0.1)	(0.1)	(0.1)	(0.1)	(0.1)

1. Provisional. Figures may not precisely sum up to the totals because of rounding.
Source: Computed from SPO Annual Programs data.

International Trade Orientation

An important indicator of the direction of structural change in industry is, undoubtedly, the place to which Turkey is heading in the international division of labor. If a country exports (imports) a commodity in large quantity relative to its volume of economic activity in that community, such a situation is regarded as revealing her comparative advantage (disadvantage) in this product. One of the most commonly used indicators of revealed comparative advantage is the ratio of net exports (i.e., exports-imports) to sectoral gross output, which is also used in this study.[7]

The net export/gross output ratios in various sectors from 1976 to 1987 presented in Table 4 show the following developments for Turkey in the 1980s:

1. The economy has been increasingly specializing in textiles, clothing, leather, glass and to a lesser extent, food industries.[8]
2. It has been partly reducing the import surplus in iron and steel industries in comparison to the 1970s and emerging as an exporter of unsophisticated products of this sector.
3. It has been keeping its net importer position in most of the process industries like paper, chemicals and nonferrous metals.
4. With the exception of metal products, it has been developing into a net importer of engineering products at an accelerating pace.
5. It has been rapidly losing its net exporter status in tobacco due to the rising imports of final products as against sluggish exports of processed leaf.
6. It has been marginally involved in trade in beverages, wood products, printing and publishing, rubber and plastics, oil products, and nonmetallic products other than glass.

In comparison to the late 1970s, the Turkish trade orientation has not changed much in qualitative terms, but specialization in some subsectors of manufacturing industry seems to have intensified in the 1980s. This has been leading Turkey to specialize in nondurable consumer goods and a few relatively unsophisticated intermediates which have a bias for using natural resources as inputs. This specialization pattern does not necessarily imply that commodity orientation in foreign trade is also rising. Actually, the reverse has been taking place in the case of exports, with the Gini-Hirschmann concentration coefficient falling from 48.2 in 1976 to 38.0 in 1987. Import concentration, on the other hand, showed a modest decline (with concentration coefficients of 41.2 and 38.2 for the benchmark years).[9] The trend toward diversification is also confirmed by other studies (see Togan et al., 1987:35-39).

Table 4
Trade Orientation of Manufacturing Industries, 1976-1987
(net export/output ratio, percent)

Sectors	1976	1978	1980	1982	1984	1986	1987[1]
CONSUMER							
GOODS	5.7	5.4	7.2	14.1	19.2	16.8	19.3
Food	3.2	4.0	5.0	7.5	8.7	8.6	8.3
Beverages	1.0	0.8	0.8	1.1	1.5	---	1.1
Tobacco	30.2	14.1	17.7	34.2	19.8	10.6	11.8
Textile/cloth.	7.9	7.5	12.1	327	53.2	40.6	48.6
INTERMEDIATES	-16.4	-13.5	-16.7	-5.4	-7.1	-6.9	-8.2
Wood prod.	0.1	---	0.4	3.3	3.1	2.7	-0.2
Paper prod.	-9.7	-12.7	-22.4	-21.0	-11.1	-11.8	-15.2
Print/publish.	-2.0	-1.0	-0.4	-1.2	2.0	-2.8	-2.0
Leather prod.	7.0	4.0	7.0	18.1	27.3	15.2	29.3
Rubber/plastic	-12.6	-3.4	1.4	2.5	8.3	-0.3	0.2
Chemicals	-56.7	-36.4	-43.8	-31.5	-51.7	-33.9	-33.2
Petroluem prod.	-7.1	-19.2	-17.3	1.8	2.5	0.1	0.1
Glass	12.3	13.1	14.4	22.9	20.2	24.7	24.3
Potter, china,							
and earthenware	-2.9	0.3	3.1	11.3	-3.7	6.0	4.1
Cement & other							
nonmetal. prod.	1.7	4.3	2.9	13.3	1.5	-2.0	-5.3
Iron and steel	-36.4	-23.9	-23.6	-17.9	-11.2	-8.6	-19.4
Nonferrous							
metals	-14.1	-2.8	-8.6	-14.6	-23.2	-17.4	-35.2
INVESTMENT &							
CONSUMER GOODS	-58.0	-30.7	-37.3	-52.9	-51.7	-56.8	-41.9
Metal prod.	-18.0	-15.5	-23.3	-11.1	-8.4	-4.5	-1.5
Nonelectrical							
machinery	-114.6	-58.8	-60.5	-141.8	-125.0	-148.6	-104.8
Electrical mach.							
and electronics	-36.8	-22.8	-48.0	-37.1	-47.0	-49.2	-36.4
Transport equip.	-43.3	-23.9	-18.1	-43.1	-33.5	-40.2	-27.6
Professional and							
scientific equip.	-517.2	-95.6	-227.6	-355.4	-418.7	-320.2	-388.3
TOTAL	-12.1	-7.7	-7.5	-1.8	-2.9	-5.2	-2.9

1. Provisional.
Source: Computed from SPO Annual Programs.

Another implication of Table 4 is that although the import dependence of manufacturing industry in relative terms does not seem to have been rising much in recent years, it hass not been falling either in comparison to the year 1982, when the trade deficit in absolute as well as in relative terms was at a minimum for the 1980s. The sustainability of import surpluses of that magnitude in the next decade is questionable, in view of Turkey's debt servicing profile.

Factor Use

In order to have a better understanding of the direction of structural change, we can also investigate the pattern of factor use in manufacturing sectors. As a proxy to represent factor intensity, recourse is usually had to factor payments and/or factor shares, assuming the absence of factor price distortions caused by monopoly power. If one notes that, conceptually, the wage payment is composed of two elements, that is, the compensation for unskilled labor effort and the cost of purchasing services embodied in the skilled worker, we could take the industry-wide differentiation of wages as a measure of skill intensity. In the same vein, the non-wage component of MVA per worker could serve as an indicator of physical capital intensity; and eventually MVA per employee may be treated as a measure of intensity in human and physical capital taken together.

We take the average wage ranking for the years 1982-1984 in the private manufacturing sector as an indicator of skill intensity, noting that the bargaining power of the labor unions was at a low ebb at that time. When the pattern of trade orientation and skill intensity levels are compared, an inverse and significant rank correlation is observed between the two, the Spearman rank correlation coefficient being -0.463. In other words, the hypothesis that the Turkish economy is specializing in industrial activities of low skill is supported by this evidence.

Moreover, there is a weaker but again negative association between trade orientation and MVA per employee, the Spearman rank correlation coefficient being -0.205. This suggests that the specialization pattern does not tend toward sectors with higher total factor intensity. The most favored indicator of the intensity of technology in a given sector is the share of R&D expenditure in sector value added. We have ranked manufacturing sectors according to the R&D share in value added observed in the US economy (taken as a proxy) and sought a relationship between technology intensity and trade orientation. The result is a negative and highly significant rank correlation between the two, with a correlation coefficient of -0.654. With due caution for the fact that product composition in Turkish manufacturing sectors may be different than that in the US economy and that our proxy for technology use could be rather crude, we can confirm the hypothesis that the Turkish economy in the 1980s has been specializing in sectors with lower technological sophistication.[10]

In summary, if the structure of foreign trade toward the end of the 1980s is taken as indicative of the specialization pattern in the 1990s, the apparent tendency is that Turkey is specializing in sectors with lower skill, capital, and technology intensity. This tendency is sufficient cause for concern. In the past two decades, the major industrial exporters among LDCs have shown a similar pattern. But changes in comparative advantage have led quite a number of semi-industrialized LDCs (including Argentina, Brazil, India, Korea, and Mexico, not to mention the city-states) to move to a more capital-oriented export structure, reflecting progress to a later stage in comparative advantage and marking a new and higher stage in the course of economic development as well. This seems to be virtually absent in the Turkish case. As far as total (i.e., physical and human) capital endowment in international trade in the late 1970s is concerned, Turkey was placed among the countries which exported significantly below their expected levels and imported significantly above their expected levels (see UNIDO, 1986b:34-52).

PRODUCTIVITY CHANGES IN MANUFACTURING

At present, annual MVA at sector detail is available only for large establishments (i.e., those having ten or more employees). Furthermore, the data for 1986-1987 have not been published yet. In spite of these deficiencies, the productivity trends obtained from the available statistical material are sufficiently informative.

According to the 1980 census figures, 62 percent of total manufacturing employment and 88 percent of MVA is accounted for by large establishments, and these shares show a secular upward trend. The productivity gains obtained by shifts in employment from the pool of small-scale, low-productivity jobs to the large scale, high productivity establishments will be largely exhausted by the turn of the century, and productivity performance will increasingly depend on the performance of large-scale industry. Hence no serious error is committed by taking only the performance of large-scale establishments into consideration in the analysis of productivity changes at the sectoral level.

The deflation problem again poses a difficulty in obtaining constant-price, sectoral MVA series. The considerable changes in relative price structure, especially in 1978-1982, have led to important transfers of MVA among sectors; hence using a single deflator, for example, the implicit industrial value added deflator, obscures the productivity change in real terms. The way out of the difficulty is, obviously, double deflation (i.e., deflating outputs and inputs separately), but unreliable and/or incomplete price indexes hamper such a practice.

The current-price MVA of sector (i) is correctly double deflated when it is divided by where P_i and n stand for the price level of sector (i) and number of sectors providing inputs, respectively. If the expression in brackets is sufficiently close to unity (as it turned out to be in our experiments with the 1979 I-O table), then $d_i \approx P_i$:

$$d_i = P_i - \sum_{j=1}^{n} P_j a_{ji} \; / \; 1 - \sum_{j=1}^{n} a_{ji} \; = \; P_i \left[\; 1 - \sum_{j=1}^{n} (P_j/P_i) \, a_{ji} \; / \; 1 - \sum_{j=1}^{n} a_{ji} \; \right]$$

Therefore, we have deflated the current value added in oil products and non-oil products with the respective price indexes mentioned above in the section on structural change as a first-order approximation to a constant-price series. This treatment is similar to the one applied in the context of sector shares above, and its results are summarized in Table 5.

The "adjusted" series point the a disturbing fact that labor productivity was lower in 1985 than in 1976, both at the aggregate and at most of the sector levels.[11] The inclusion of productivity gains in 1986-1987 would hardly alter this picture. Even if we isolate the years of recovery, 1981-1985, from the entire cycle, the increase in labor productivity is only 3.2 percent p.a. on average. If we take into account the increase in capacity utilization, which is in the range of 5-6 percent p.a. according to the estimates of the Istanbul Chamber of Industry, nothing is left which can be attributed to capital deepening and/or technological change. If the increase in capacity utilization peters out (which seems to be the case after 1984), this will imply a setback and even a decline in the overall industrial productivity of large establishments in the near future.

These findings are also confirmed by other research. With the help of data given in Odabaşı et al. (1987:397-403), who have used almost the same sources of information as ours, one can calculate a 24.5 percent fall in productivity per worker for the period 1976-1984 in contrast to our estimate of 20.7 percent (see Table 5). The difference between the two is due to the definition of output and the deflation methods employed. Figures in Odabaşı et al. imply a 23.6 percent increase in the growth of total gross output and a 20.0 percent increase in *total* factor productivity.[12] This leaves a negligible fraction to be accounted for by technological change.

Table 5
MVA per Employee in Large-Scale Establishments,
1976-1985 (TL million at 1982 prices, adjusted)

Sectors	1976	1978	1980	1982	1984	1985
				Years		
CONSUMER GOODS						
Food	1.69	1.74	1.30	1.56	1.34	1.50
Beverages	3.86	4.21	3.75	4.49	3.94	5.29
Tobacco	3.76	1.60	1.15	4.01	3.10	3.95
Textiles and Clothing	1.90	1.67	1.18	1.28	1.32	1.34
INTERMEDIATES						
Wood Products	1.83	1.91	1.04	0.98	1.01	1.26
Paper and Paper Products	2.15	2.50	1.49	1.77	1.69	2.18
Printing and Publishing	1.99	1.87	1.21	2.14	2.33	2.03
Leather Products	1.15	1.09	0.85	1.03	0.97	1.87
Rubber and Plastics	1.68	2.52	2.00	1.97	1.97	2.04
Chemicals	4.29	3.57	3.30	3.41	2.91	3.00
Petroleum Products	28.36	18.87	22.86	45.46	36.89	40.15
Glass	2.06	2.10	1.59	2.55	2.16	2.36
Pottery, China and Earthenware	2.54	1.94	1.43	1.31	1.42	1.77
Cement and Other Non-Metallic Pr.	1.84	2.11	1.69	2.13	1.51	1.86
Iron and Steel	2.34	2.82	1.90	1.75	2.39	2.47
Non-ferrous Metals	2.38	3.94	1.83	1 .44	1.70	1.61
INVESTMENT GOODS & CONSUMER DURABLES						
Metal Products	1.81	1.99	1.43	1.46	1.36	1.63
Non-Electrical Machinery	1.76	1.75	1.42	1.72	1.67	1.69
Electrical Machinery and Electronics	2.46	2.69	1.99	2.13	2.43	2.64
Transport Equipment	3.67	2.62	1.48	2.14	1.92	1.81
Professional and Scientific Equipment	1.40	1.00	0.79	1.07	0.91	0.81
TOTAL	2.65	2.54	1.93	2.45	2.10	2.26

Source: Computed from SIS survey/census data.

Some conjectures for explaining this mediocre productivity performance can be put forward as follows:

1. The tendency for the Turkish economy to specialize in low-skill, low-productivity fields could well be a process repeated within subsectors of manufacturing activity.

2. The data in Table 6 seem to suggest that productivity per man rises together with the size of establishment, although the relative productivity positions of establishments employing more than 500 persons is rather uncertain. Table 7, on the other hand, shows that the average size of establishments has been declining. This could well be a factor explaining the decrease in average productivity.

3. The erosion of real wages throughout the period 1976-1985 has considerably reduced the share of wages in prime cost. This might lead industrial establishments to be less keen on productivity improvements, while industrial markups are maintained and even raised by monopolistic practices.[13]

4. The apparent fall in productivity might be influenced partly by errors in deflation and partly by the pricing of imported inputs. The overvaluation of the Turkish currency in the period 1976-1979 might have led to underestimation of total input costs and therefore to overestimation of MVA. This is particularly so, if rents originating from overvaluation of currency accrue to manufacturers due to quota allocations, and so on. However, the improvements in MVA accounting cannot be expected to yield changes in estimates of productivity per man sizable enough to reverse the declining trend.[14]

The poor record of productivity change in the late 1970s and even in the 1980s explains why the competitiveness of Turkish exports in recent years is predicated upon real devaluations, high rates of export premiums and suppression of wages. If the competitive struggle in international markets is to be won by lowering prices, the Turkish style of doing it is unlikely to be the best practice sustainable in the long run.

Table 6
MVA per Man and Size of Establishments (1980-1985)

Size of Establishment in Number of Persons Employed	MVA per Man Index (Large Establishments=100)			
	1980	1982	1984	1985
1 to 9 persons	20.9	n.a.	n.a.	n.a.
10 or more	100.0	100.0	100.0	100.0
10 to 49	51.1	45.1	52.3	46.0
50 to 99	85.3	61.5	70.5	66.6
100 to 199	102.2	80.4	94.1	85.9
200 to 499	130.4	161.9	108.9	117.9
500 to 999	105.3	101.4	109.6	121.9
1000 or more	108.4	109.9	121.7	123.6

na.: not available
Source: Computed from SIS survey/census data.

Table 7
Average Size of Large Establishments (1976-1985)

Years	Number of Establishments Covered	Number of Wage and Salary Earners (thousands)	Average Size
1976	6054	696.0	115
1977	6522	762.8	117
1978	7134	767.1	108
1979	7441	777.9	105
1980	8710	787.0	90
1981	9194	798.4	87
1982	9457	828.4	88
1983	9266	862.3	93
1984	8779	891.0	102
1985	10646	927.6	87

Source: Computed from SIS survey/census data.

One would also like to inquire whether there is an association between the change in productivity per man and trade orientation. If manufacturing sectors are ranked according to their rate of change in labor productivity and a correlation is sought between this ranking and the trade orientation, the result turns out to be insignificant, with a Spearman rank correlation coefficient of +0.143. Therefore, it cannot be confidently argued that the export drive in the 1980s has made a considerable impact on productivity change. Alternatively, if the direction of causality is reversed, Turkey does not seem to have captured export markets in the fields with higher productivity gains (or the fields where productivity losses are lower). More product-oriented research needs to be done on this issue.

TRENDS IN FIXED CAPITAL FORMATION

Although the estimates for capacity utilization rates in Tables 8 and 9 are rather imprecise, there is general agreement over the fact that these rates have been increasing throughout the 1980s and reaching maximum feasible levels around 1986-1987. Therefore, the future path of output growth and trade orientation will be dependent upon the volume and sectoral composition of manufacturing investments.

In the early 1980s, major investment projects initiated by the public sector in the 1970s required fairly large funds to be completed. When the public investment program was substantially reduced in 1981-1982 in line with advice from the World Bank, the ax generally fell upon projects in engineering industries which had barely started. Investments in industrial intermediates (like oil products, petrochemicals, paper, iron and steel, and rubber), on the other hand, were allowed to be completed almost by default, since these projects had already reached an advanced stage.

Constraints of that kind have shaped the public investment program in the first half of the 1980s (see Table 10); but when this backlog of projects was finally eliminated, the share of public sector manufacturing investment in total fixed investments was drastically sequeezed to its lowest level since the 1950s. This share, which was around 12 percent by the end of the 1970s, was drastically reduced to 7.3 percent in 1985, 5.7 percent in 1986, and 3.3 percent in 1987.[15] As a crude estimate, the (realized) manufacturing investment in the public sector in 1987 is around 2-3 percent of total productive capital in this sector, which could barely keep up with wear and tear, let alone extension, modernization, and renewal.

Table 8
Weighted Capacity Utilization Rates of Establishments Registered to Istanbul Chamber of Industry (1977-1986, percent)[1]

Sectors	1977	1978	1980	1982	1984	1986	1987[2]
CONSUMER GOODS	63	66	57	72	74	76	80
Food	53	76	55	74	72	74	74
Beverages				77	77	75	67
Textiles and Clothing	69	62	58	71	76	80	83
INTERMEDIATES	57	55	49	68	72	73	76
Wood Products	60	72	26	58	55	63	70
Paper and Paper Prod.	65	57	50	73	79	83	86
Printing and Pub.				71	73	74	81
Leather Products[3]				53	62	59	64
Rubber and Plastics				70	80	69	78
Chemicals	54	50	50	70	72	70	75
Petroleum Products				68	73	74	73
Glass				69	78	81	86
Pottery, China, and Earthenware	77	65	63	61	68	76	78
Cement and Other nonmetallic Prod.				72	82	81	82
Iron and Steel	50	55	42	69	72	78	76
Nonferrous Metals				54	59	56	55
INVESTMENT GOODS AND CONSUMER DURABLES	49	51	51	60	69	73	71
Metal Products				63	66	72	75
Non-Electric. Mach.	51	51	52	54	71	69	78
Electrical Mach.				65	74	71	72
Transport Equipment	43	54	49	58	61	64	62
Professional and Scientific Equip.	n.a.	n.a.	n.a.	42	69	78	71
TOTAL	n.a.	n.a.	n.a.	67	72	73	75

n.a.: not available.
1. These figures are rounded.
2. Provisional.
3. Treated under wearing apparel in 1977-1980.
Source: ICI Research Department Reports on Capacity Utilization.

Table 9

A Comparison of Weighted Capacity Utilization Rates Found in ICI and SIS Records, 1983

Sectors	ICI	SIS[1]
CONSUMER GOODS	76	64
Food	74	65
Beverages	83	57
Tobacco	50	81
Textiles and Clothing	76	63
INTERMEDIATES	69	65
Wood Products	59	53
Paper and Paper Products	79	70
Printing and Publishing	70	76
Leather Products	56	59
Rubber and Plastics	72	62
Chemicals	75	n.a.
Petroleum Products	73	69
Glass	75	74
Pottery, China, and Earthenware	52	65
Cement and Other Nonmetallic Prod.	72	64
Iron and Steel	69	n.a.
No-ferrous Metals	58	58
INVESTMENT GOODS AND CONSUMER DURABLES	62	64
Metal Products	63	63
Nonelectrical Machinery	56	64
Electrical Machinery and Electronics	65	69
Transport Equipment	64	63
Professional and Scientific Equipment	69	76
TOTAL	70	65

n.a.: not available on a comparable basis.
1. According to the definition coded as U3W in SIS capacity utilization survey.
Source: SIS and ICI capacity utilization surveys.

Since the share of the public sector in total manufacturing investment has also been radically decreased (falling from around 40 percent in the late 1970s to 31 percent in 1984, and 22 percent in 1987), the volume and sectoral composition of manufacturing investment is now largely determined by private investors' behavior. As Table 11 shows clearly, even as late as 1986-1987, private investors in the manufacturing sector have not yet overcome the low spirits of the early 1980s. In real terms, almost all sectors have shared in this reluctance to invest, with a few exceptions like leather products, nonmetallic products and transport equipment. Among the sectors with considerable investment allocations in the past, those with more or less unchanged shares in total investment are textiles and clothing, paper, metal products, and electrical machinery. The sectors which seem to be less attractive to investors are food, wood products, rubber and plastics, chemicals, iron and steel, nonferrous metals, machinery, and professional equipment.

This sector orientation is by and large in harmony with Turkey's trade orientation during the 1980s examined earlier. Some cases to the contrary are not hard to explain. For example, investment allocations in electrical machinery, electronics, and transport equipment are propelled by the buoyant domestic demand for second generation consumer durables and communication equipment, together with replacement demands. The iron and steel exports are much influenced by regional economic and political conditions. All these may not be long-lasting phenomena.

Since the Turkish economic administration in the 1980s has placed much of its hopes on the contribution of foreign capital to restructure the economy, it is worth investigating whether the foreign investors' behavior can conform to that of domestic capital. The figures in Table 12 are rather erratic and not much amenable to straightforward judgments. But if these figures are converted into US dollar terms, they lead to the conclusion that foreign capital seems to be not far removed from the sector choices of the 1960s and 1970s. Of about 630 million dollars invested in manufacturing sectors in 1980-1987, 19 percent went to chemicals, 16 percent to transport equipment, 13 percent to electrical machinery and electronics, and 17 percent to food and beverages.[16] These sectors were also the favorites of foreign capital prior to 1980. In cumulative terms, the respective figures were 21 percent for chemistry, 31 percent for transport equipment, 14 percent for electrical machinery and electronics, and 7 percent for food and beverages at the end of 1977, as a rather crude approximation.

Table 10
Sectoral Breakdown of Public Sector Manufacturing
Investment,[1] 1976-1987 (TL billion, at 1983 prices)

Sectors	1976	1978	1980	1982	1984	1986[2]	1987[3]
CONSUMER GOODS	59.5	53.0	50.8	43.1	33.0	18.2	8.3
Food	(37.3)	(34.0)	(27.6)	(26.4)	(22.8)	(9.9)	(6.0)
Beverages	(1.5)	(1.2)	(1.0)	(0.8)	(0.6)	(0.7)	(0.5)
Tobacco	(10.8)	(12.9)	(14.7)	(10.8)	(2.4)	(1.4)	(1.2)
Textiles and Clothing	(10.0)	(4.9)	(7.6)	(5.1)	(7.2)	(6.2)	(0.6)
INTERMED.	219.4	220.3	257.6	198.3	123.6	100.5	69.4
Wood Products	(0.8)	(1.4)	(1.6)	(0.9)	(0.1)	(...)	(0.1)
Paper Products	(2.0)	(2.3)	(2.0)	(1.4)	(0.7)	(0.5)	(0.5)
Printing & Pub.	(26.2)	(36.9)	(28.9)	(17.2)	(6.5)	(1.1)	(0.6)
Leather Products	(0.4)	(0.3)	(0.2)	(0.3)	(0.5)	(1.0)	(1.0)
Rubber/Plastics	(44.9)	(72.6)	(109.4)	(78.4)	(62.3)	(55.0)	(35.2)
Chemicals	(76.0)	(41.0)	(46.9)	(36.6)	(15.1)	(15.5)	(5.7)
Petroluem Prod.	(0.6)	(1.6)	(1.3)	(6.0)	(3.4)	(9.3)	(14.0)
Glass/nonmetal	(10.8)	(10.7)	(15.1)	(17.4)	(7.1)	(4.9)	(6.3)
Iron and Steel	(47.1)	(49.9)	(48.9)	(36.6)	(26.2)	(12.1)	(5.4)
Nonferrous Met.	(10.6)	(3.6)	(3.2)	(3.7)	(1.6)	(1.0)	(0.6)
INVEST. GOODS & CONSUMER DURABLES	23.2	26.9	24.8	21.1	17.3	12.0	7.3
Metal Products	(2.1)	(1.4)	(1.8)	(3.4)	(6.3)	(2.0)	(0.2)
Nonelectrical Machinery	(10.0)	(15.6)	(10.9)	(9.4)	(3.9)	(4.1)	(4.2)
Electrical Mach., and Electronics	(0.5)	(2.6)	(3.7)	(2.9)	(1.6)	(1.4)	(0.4)
Transport Equip.	(8.1)	(5.3)	(8.1)	(5.3)	(5.3)	(4.4)	(2.5)
Professional & Scientific Eq.	(2.6)	(1.9)	(0.3)	(0.2)	(0.1)	(0.2)	(...)
TOTAL	302.1	300.3	333.3	262.4	173.9	130.8	85.0

1. Three-year moving averages except for the year 1987. Figures are rounded, and may not sum up to the totals.
2. Provisional
Source: SPO.

Table 11
Sectoral Breakdown of Private Manufacturing
Investment,[1] 1976-1987 (TL billion, at 1983 prices)

Sectors	1976	1978	1980	1982	1984	1986[2]	1987[2]
CONSUMER GOODS	166.1	118.0	68.1	79.2	94.6	107.7	97.8
Food	(47.2)	(40.0)	(24.5)	(22.4)	(16.6)	(21.9)	(24.7)
Beverages	(5.7)	(6.7)	(2.0)	(8.2)	(7.5)	(3.4)	(1.4)
Tobacco	(0.2)	(0.6)	(7.4)	(7.3)	(0.4)	(0.3)	(0.0)
Textiles and Clothing	(113.1)	(70.7)	(34.2)	(41.3)	(70.0)	(82.1)	(71.7)
INTERMED.	282.5	268.2	213.4	187.4	175.8	178.4	167.3
Wood Products	(17.7)	(22.8)	(6.1)	(1.7)	(1.2)	(1.9)	(1.8)
Paper Products	(13.1)	(9.4)	(13.3)	(10.1)	(10.5)	(9.4)	(8.1)
Printing & Pub.	(5.4)	(3.0)	(1.9)	(1.3)	(2.1)	(6.5)	(12.1)
Leather Products	(5.6)	(3.0)	(0.8)	(0.9)	(0.8)	(6.4)	(10.0)
Rubber/Plastics	(38.7)	(30.2)	(6.1)	(19.5)	(41.6)	(18.7)	(8.5)
Chemicals	(49.8)	(50.4)	(66.2)	(61.4)	(56.3)	(38.6)	(25.7)
Petroleum Prod.	(2.7)	(2.3)	(18.7)	(21.6)	(4.0)	(4.4)	(1.5)
Glass/nonmetal	(53.5)	(50.1)	(38.7)	(37.3)	(30.9)	(56.0)	(68.6)
Iron and Steel	(81.6)	(85.7)	(51.3)	(25.9)	(25.1)	(34.5)	(29.4)
Nonferrous Met.	(14.5)	(11.5)	(10.3)	(7.7)	(3.2)	(2.0)	(1.7)
INVEST. GOODS & CONSUMER DURABLES	139.6	133.1	61.6	55.7	72.1	96.8	109.3
Metal Products	(22.1)	(24.8)	(9.4)	(9.0)	(11.1)	(15.8)	(15.9)
Nonelectrical Machinery	(39.8)	(38.8)	(18.5)	(15.6)	(16.4)	(19.0)	(18.5)
Electrical Mach. & Electronics	(27.8)	(26.5)	(8.4)	(13.4)	(19.7)	(24.5)	(21.5)
Transport Eq.	(36.0)	(34.2)	(24.7)	(16.5)	(23.6)	(35.7)	(50.9)
Professional & Scientific Eq.	(14.0)	(8.8)	(0.5)	(1.2)	(1.4)	(1.8)	(2.4)
TOTAL	588.3	519.4	343.0	322.2	342.5	382.9	374.4

1. Three-year moving averages except for the year 1987. Figures are rounded.
2. Provisional.
Source: SPO.

These observations suggest that foreign capital is basically interested in strengthening monopolistic positions (some of them gained earlier) in the import substituting industries and are not much interested in activities where the Turkish export drive of the 1980s has been taking place. Obviously, this is only a general tendency which may be contradicted by individual examples. But if the expected contribution of direct foreign investment lies, first and foremost, in bringing new technology in form of new processes and products, it has to be said that export sectors did not benefit much from these transfers of technology; if they did at all, it took place largely through spillovers. The reluctance of foreign capital to enter into activities like the production of machinery and professional and technical equipment in the 1980s is clearly visible from Table 12.

SUMMARY AND CONCLUSIONS

In this paper, we have first tried to review the growth over the period 1976-1987 of manufacturing output and productivity, both of which have grown more slowly than in the previous cycle. Taken in isolation, growth of output and productivity in the subperiod 1980-1987 was fairly satisfactory even by international standards. But the performance in this subperiod rested mainly upon the utilization of idle capacities taken over from the pre-1980 years and a bountiful balance of payments support which was being maintained even when the total private capital inflows to LDCs was rapidly dwindling. These are not likely to be repeated in the near future.

It was shown that a very large fraction of the increment in productivity in manufacturing is accounted for by improved capacity utilization, leaving at best a modest part to be attributed to technological change and/or capital deepening. What is more alarming, however, is the fact that the overall productivity per man in large establishments has declined by almost one fifth from 1976 to 1985. This was also confirmed by other research. The reasons for the apparent fall in productivity of large establishments are discussed above and need not be repeated here.

This fall in productivity has not been observed, however, at the aggregate level, due to the ongoing process of structural transformation, which increases the share of large-scale, high-productivity establishments at the expense of small-scale, low-productivity ones. But the latter category will be expected to approach insignificance in the 1990s as far as its share in output is concerned. Thus, overall increase in productivity will increasingly depend on the performance of each sector on the one hand, and on the resource shifts from low-productivity sectors to high-productivity sectors on the other. But as noted above, neither the Turkish trade orientation nor the trend in capital accumulation has been conducive to obtaining productivity gains from these sources.

Table 12
Sectoral Breakdown of Private Foreign Capital Inflow
(registered entries at current prices, TL million)

Sectors	End-1977 (Cum.)[1]	1980-1981	1982-1983	1984-1985	1986	1987
CONSUMER GOODS	169	4912	5393	22072	4778	11256
Food and Beverages	148	2480	3536	18535	4007	8521
Textiles and Clothing	21	2431	1857	3537	771	2735
INTERMEDIATES	810	4821	10812	24088	11471	52230
Wood Products	---	268	554	336	0	-263
Paper	49	505	895	301	-126	3047
Rubber and Plastics	226	436	613	2851	1	307
Chemicals	465	2245	4732	8905	12496	27389
Glass	46	184	1364	190	1467	-225
Earthenware, Cement, & Other Nonmetallic Prod.	24	151	1459	368	-238	1535
Iron and Steel	---	754	1045	10303	-2210	19584
Nonferrous Metals	---	278	150	834	81	856
INVESTMENT GOODS AND CONSUMER DURABLES	1210	3642	8344	29645	22134	27536
Metal Products	99	4	1174	1045	-89	637
Nonelectrical Machinery	119	469	840	6515	2235	-389
Electrical Machinery and Electronics	316	1348	2043	7365	10766	20033
Transport Equipment[1]	676	1821	4287	14720	9222	6889
Professional and Scientific Equipment	---	-	-	-	-	366
OTHERS (Nonclassified)	2	200	1487	200	-878	1921
TOTAL	2191	13575	26027	76005	37505	92943

1. Accumulated inflows through December 1977.
2. Includes industries producing spare parts and accessories.
Source: SPO Annual Programmes and SPO, Department of Foreign Capital records.

The orientation of Turkish industry in the 1980s has been toward sectors with low skill and low technology intensity. In qualitative terms, the trade orientation did not change much from the 1970s to the present, but international specialization has proceeded further toward nondurable goods and a few intermediate goods sectors. Although this pattern resembles that of major industrial exporters among the LDCs in the past two decades, it seems that Turkey has been spending, if not to say wasting, too much time at this juncture. Histories of development in late industrializers need not follow a linear path.

At present, the chance of obtaining further productivity gains through increased capacity use seems rather weak. Thus, Turkish manufacturing performance in the near future will depend on the volume and the composition of private fixed investment undertaken in recent years, since no meaningful role has been envisaged in the 1980s for public sector investment. Unfortunately, in the period under study, private enterpreneurs have been rather reluctant to invest in manufacturing industries as well as in other fields of production. At a disaggregated level, they have also not shown much interest in engineering and process industries, which receive much emphasis in the development efforts of middle-income, semi-industrialized LDCs today as a source of technological spillovers.

The present Turkish economic administration seems to prefer leaving industrial development to its "natural" course in the belief that eventually the profit motive will reassert itself and stimulate manufacturing activity. The absence of any conscious industrial policy in the 1980s has amply demostrated that this "natural" course has transferred profits away from industrial pursuits to rentiers and traders (domestic or international) and hampered industrial capital formation. This intra-class redistribution of surplus is clearly demostrated in Boratav (1987a, 1988).

The trouble with these tendencies is that the future growth of the Turkish economy might be rapidly choked off either by capacity constraints in, or rising import dependence of, the manufacturing sector. The sooner such a prospect is perceived and the need for a conscious policy for industrial development is conceded by the present economic administration, the better.

NOTES

Department of Economics at the Middle East Technical University (METU), Ankara, Turkey. The financial support expended by METU to the research for this paper under Project AFP 87.04.03.02 is gratefully acknowledged. Thanks are also due to Dr. F. Şenses for his valuable advice and to Ms I. Akşın, Messrs. H. Arslan, E. Aslanoğlu, and I. Yıldız for their research assistance. The remaining errors in the paper are the writer's own responsibility. Since the 1989 Annual Program was not in print at the time of writing, the author was unable to use the actual data for 1987 in place of the estimated figures. However, this is not expected to alter the conclusions significantly.

1. In order to preserve the continuity of the time series we have (1) excluded ginning from the manufacturing sector and (2) classified all leather products and wooden furniture under intermediates.

2. For an imaginative attempt in this field, see Boratav (1987b).

3. The grouping of countries is that of UNIDO (1985:Chapter 2).

4. The sources and methods of compilation of quinquennial data in UNIDO (1986a) are not clear to the present writer. Obviously, one can work with SIS survey data on large establishments for this purpose, making approximations about the small-scale enterprises, but we preferred not to do so.

5. For example, the shares of food and oil products in 1978 look rather strange, and the drastic reduction in the share of food after 1982 can hardly be attributed to the lack of demand. These anomalies, which are probably products of improper deflation, could be removed by improvements in the data and method.

6. "Some people argue that we have to establish heavy industry. This view is wrong. [Suppose] you produce everything, what is the use of it if you cannot sell? I am of the opinion that industrial development must be left to its natural course" (The former Prime Minister Mr. Özal speaking in an interview with Mr. N. Doğru, *Milliyet*, October 6, 1987).

7. An alternative indicator of the revealed comparative advantage is the ratio of net exports to the volume of international trade (i.e., exports + imports). We opted for the first indicator in order to use the same SPO data base and avoid problems of definitional inconsistency. In any case, the results would not be much different, had the alternative approach been chosen (see UNIDO, 1986b:186-188).

8. This picture is unlikely to change much even when account is taken of fictitious exports.

9. The Gini-Hirschmann coefficient would take a value between 100.0 and 21.8 in our case of twenty-one subsectors.

10. In the three correlation calculations mentioned above, we excluded professional equipment (ISIC 385), which is a very heterogeneous batch, together with printing and publishing, which does not seem to have a meaningful place in international trade.

11. A caveat is also necessary for the oddities of deflation and perhaps of reporting errors. See, for example, productivity levels in tobacco (1978-1981) and oil products industries (1978, 1980) represented in Table 5.

12. To compute the total factor productivity, Odacıbaşı et al. (1987) use a constant returns to scale function and obtain productivity by dividing MVA by a weighted sum of capital and labor, with the weights being the factor payments in the base year. We opted for the established practice of working with labor productivities alone, partly due to our misgivings about the reliability of the estimates of the capital stock.

13. In the second half of the 1970s, when the relative price of oil was low in Turkey, it was argued that this was a disincentive for industry to take energy-saving measures. A similar argument can be invoked for labor use in the 1980s.

14. The sharp decreases recorded in 1980 are partly due to the ban on layoffs by the government established after the military coup. We would like to thank Professor Merih Celasun, who brought this point into our attention.

15. The public sector investment program has become so thin in the 1980s that even an uninitiated observer could identify major new entries (a speciality tire factory, investments in machinery, transport equipment, and avionics related to defense, etc.) and completions (Aliağa Petrochemical Complex, Middle Anatolian Refinery, Akdeniz Paper Mill, extensions to Iskenderun Steel Mill, etc.).

16. Foreign investment in iron and steel was largely in 1984-1985. Later figures are, generally speaking, investment in portfolio.

APPENDIX: SECTOR   DEFINITIONS

Sectors	ISIC Code Nrs.
CONSUMER GOODS	
Food	311, 312
Beverages	313
Tobacco	314
Textiles and Clothing	321, 322
INTERMEDIATES	
Wood Products	33
Paper	341
Printing and Publishing	342
Leather Products	323, 324
Rubber and Plastics	355, 356
Chemicals	351, 352
Petroleum Products	353, 354
Glass	362
Pottery, China, and Earthenware	361
Cement and Other Nonmetallic Products	369
Iron and Steel	371
Nonferrous Metals	372
INVESTMENT GOODS AND	
CONSUMER DURABLES	
Metal Products	381
Nonelectrical Machinery	382
Electrical Machinery and Electronics	383
Transport Equipment	384
Professional and Scientific Equipment	385

REFERENCES

Boratav, K. (1987a). *Stabilization and Adjustment Policies and Programmes-Country Study 5/Turkey*. Helsinki: World Institute for Development Economics Research.

_____ (1987b). "International Comparisons of Wages and Labor Productivity from the Viewpoint of the Future Prospects of Turkish Manufacturing Industry within the EC." In *Proceedings of the 1987 Conference on Industry*. Ankara: The Union Of Chambers of Engineers, pp. 211-219 (in Turkish).

_____ (1988). "Inter-class and Intra-class Relations of Distribution under Structural Adjustment: Turkey during the 1980s." Paper presented at the Conference on Turkey's Development in the 1980s, organized by Harvard University, mimeo.

Milliyet. October 6, 1987.

Odacıbaşı, M., G. Çoygun, and N. Atalay-Ilgaz (1987). "Productivity in Manufacturing Industry." In *Proceedings of the 1987 Conference on Industry*. Ankara: The Union of Chambers of Engineers, pp. 395-411.

SIS (State Institute of Statistics, 1976-1985). *Annual Surveys/Censuses on Manufacturing Industry*. Ankara: SIS Publications.

SPO (State Planning Organization, 1978-88). *Annual Programmes*. Ankara: SPO Publications.

Togan, S., H. Olgun and H. Akder (1987). *Report on Developments in External Economic Relations of Turkey*. Research Center of the Foreign Trade Association of Turkey, Pub. No. 1987/1.

UNIDO (1985). *Industry in the 1980s: Structural Change and Interdependence*. New York: United Nations.

_____ (1986a). *Industry and Development: Global Report 1986*. Vienna: United Nations.

_____ (1986b). *International Comparative Advantage in Manufacturing: Changing Profiles of Resources and Trade*. Vienna: United Nations.

5

Turkey's Labor Market Policies in the 1980s against the Background of Its Stabilization Program

Fikret Şenses

INTRODUCTION

The Turkish Stabilization Program, introduced in January 1980 and still in force after nearly ten years of uninterrupted implementation, has generated a great deal of interest and controversy both at home and abroad. The Program, composed initially of short-term measures to cope with growing inflationary pressures and balance of payments difficulties of the late 1970s, has been gradually extended in subsequent years to address other objectives like the liberalization of the foreign trade regime, shifting the system of incentives toward export orientation, and privatization of economic life.

The objectives and main impact of the Program have been subjected to extensive scrutiny (Kopits, 1987; Öniş, 1986; Şenses, 1983; and Wolff, 1987). One sphere which has remained largely neglected, however, is the interaction of the Stabilization Program with broader political issues surrounding Turkish society in the 1980s. This neglect has also been apparent in the meager attention devoted so far to the labor market aspects of the Program, which, with their strong political as well as economic connotations, are of crucial importance in understanding the nature and extent of this interaction.

The Turkish labor market, like many of its counterparts in other developing countries, consists of a large agricultural sector together with the informal and modern sectors in urban areas. Rapid population growth averaging 2.4 percent per annum during 1965-1985, accompanied by heavy rural-urban migration, has introduced strong supply-side pressures on the labor market, especially in urban areas (Kuran, 1980 and Şenses, 1979). The slow pace of employment creation in the modern sectors, most notably in manufacturing, has meant both open unemployment and rapid growth in generally low-productivity jobs in the informal sector.

Labor market policies from the early 1960s until 1980 were, despite some attempts in the other direction, generally characterized by liberalism, which led to rapid growth in trade union membership, and, until 1977, also in real wages (Işıklı, 1986:141-167). There was, however, a sharp reversal of these trends in the 1980s. During this time, heavy interventionism in the labor market occurred, especially during the course of the military government from September 1980 to November 1983.

The main objective of this chapter is to draw attention to the possible links between economic policies implemented under the Stabilization Program and the labor market, and present a somewhat detailed account of the highly interventionist policy environment for labor during the 1980s. As economic stabilization coincided with military intervention in political life, especially in the crucial initial years, I focus on relevant political as well as economic issues to provide a broader picture of this policy environment. The following section of this chapter discusses the factors behind the reversal of the policy environment for labor in the 1980s and serves as background for the subsequent discussions. The next section presents a detailed account of the new labor legislation that began in the 1980s and mentions its impact on real wages and employment. The last section considers the outlook for the policy environment for labor in the years ahead.

THE BACKGROUND OF INTERVENTIONIST POLICIES IN THE LABOR MARKET

The factors responsible for the emergence of a highly interventionist policy framework for the labor market in the 1980s can be grouped under three broad and interrelated headings: (1) growing economic crisis in the late 1970s and the 1980 Stabilization Program, (2) growing trade union activism, and (3) the military takeover.

Growing Economic Crisis in the Late 1970s and the 1980 Stabilization Program

Turkey's traditional trade and industrialization strategy based on import substitution through protectionist policies attracted growing criticism after the early 1970s from a variety of sources. While accepting its record in generating rapid growth and industrialization, much of the debate centered around the sustainability of growth under the traditional strategy. Skepticism grew in the 1970s as import substitution extended into the relatively more capital-and import-intensive manufacturing branches. With the system of incentives heavily biased against exports, this situation, as elsewhere, resulted in growing balance of payments difficulties which were further aggravated by successive oil shocks. This, along with heavy import dependence, created widespread shortages of both intermediate and finished products, had an adverse effect on new investment and domestic production, and further provoked inflationary pressures.

The Stabilization Program, enacted in January 1980 under the auspices of the IMF, signaled right at the outset that there would be a gradual shift to export-oriented policies. Although there was initially no explicit statement about labor market and employment issues, certain aspects of the Program had strong connotations for these issues in two ways. First, the creation of an exportable surplus beyond domestic requirements, as well as controlling inflation, required domestic demand restraint, especially restraints on wages. Wage restraint was also important for attaining international competitiveness under an export-oriented strategy, as wages were regarded as a significant cost element in the manufacturing sector. Reactivating the excess capacity in this sector for export markets, as well as success in wage restraint, required smooth and peaceful industrial relations which in turn would increase Turkey's relative attractiveness in the eyes of potential foreign investors. Second, exchange and interest rate reforms implemented under the Program were aimed at removing the underpricing of capital goods in general, and thereby the capital-using bias of earlier policies. This, together with wage restraint, was expected to correct factor price distortions and boost employment generation under the spur of export growth.

This shift toward export-oriented policies was to reorient the pattern of production and investment in accordance with Turkey's comparative advantage in world markets. As this would involve relatively labor-intensive activities in a labor-abundant economy like Turkey, such a reorientation was also expected to have favorable employment effects.

Growing Trade Union Militancy and the Quasi-Political Argument

The relatively more liberal environment for organized labor during the 1960-1980 period led to rapid growth in trade union membership and militancy.[1] This generated a significant shift in power and influence toward the labor movement and led to its emergence, for the first time in Turkish history, as a major force in society. Such a tendency did not go unnoticed by employers, who did their best to restrain this challenge,[2] especially during periods of military intervention into the political process. Employers' concern with and opposition to this challenge grew in severity as the emerging economic crisis began to threaten the profitability of their enterprises, most notably through production bottlenecks and high wage settlements. This opposition was further aggravated by growing trade union militancy in the wake of accelerating inflation after the mid-1970s,[3] became stronger and more concerted over time, and led the employers' associations to adopt a common antiunion stand. The common elements of this position included demands for wage restraint, limitations on the scope and amount of severance pay as well as other non-wage payments, restrictions on the number of trade unions and their financial resources, imposition of compulsory auditing of trade union activities and financial accounts, removal of links between trade unions and political parties, and the incorporation of government representatives into the process of collective bargaining in the hope of obtaining lower wage settlements. As inflation hit the three-digit mark for the first time in recent Turkish history, strike activity by the trade unions hit a new peak, affecting mostly enterprises in the private sector. In September 1980, on the eve of the military takeover, for example, there were 227 strikes involving 46,216 workers, 74.8 percent of whom were in the private sector (SIS, 1985:202). Against this background of worsening industrial relations and increasing political turmoil, growing signs indicated that the employers' demands were heard more sympathetically in decision-making circles.

The Military Takeover and the Political Argument

Even before the military takeover in September 1980, there were certain moves in the direction of a restrictive labor environment.[4] The dividing line in policies toward the labor market was, however, the military takeover, which clearly put a major portion of the blame for the political instability of the preceding period squarely on the labor movement in general and on the relatively more militant sections in particular. During its first few days in office, the military government introduced banning of all trade union activity, instructions to end all ongoing strikes, and the imprisonment of a large number of trade union leaders among its immediate measures. The government's program, announced in September 1980, indicated a firm intention to introduce new labor legislation which, as it turned out, had to wait until May 1983. The 1982 constitution and a number of measures taken before that, however, gave a strong hint of the likely elements of the new legislation.

RESTRICTIVE LABOR MARKET POLICIES, EMPLOYMENT, AND WAGES

Against the background of the factors discussed in the previous section, the military government's measures were intended to reverse earlier policies and thereby shift the balance of power away from trade unions. Although policy intervention in the labor market involved heavy bureaucratization of the system through a wide variety of measures, the 1982 constitution and Law 2821 (Law on Trade Unions) and Law 2822 (Law on Collective Bargaining, Strikes, and Lockouts) provided the basic guidelines. These laws followed the intent of the constitution itself. The discussion of labor market policies in this section will therefore be confined largely to changes implemented within the framework of these three pieces of legislation and will focus on four interrelated spheres of intervention.

The Process of Collective Bargaining

The right to take part in collective bargaining agreements has been granted only to those trade unions with authorization by the Ministry of Labor. This authorization, on the other hand, was made on the condition that the relevant trade union represent the majority of workers in the establishment as well as at least 10 percent of all workers working in that branch of activity. Furthermore, the process of concluding a collective bargaining agreement itself depended on a complex series of formalities. The failure to comply with any one of the rigid stages in this process meant the loss of authorization by the union concerned, and required the total recommencement of the process. Estimates state that a collective bargaining agreement would take a minimum of 2.5 months from the day the union applied to the Ministry of Labor for authorization until its conclusion (Ketenci, 1987:187-188).

Administrative Controls of Trade Union Activity

Strict requirements were imposed to guide the eligibility of founding and executive members of trade unions. Eligiblity for becoming a founding member, for instance, required at least one year of active service as a worker in that branch of activity. The period for active service necessary for executive posts was much longer, a minimum of ten years (Güzel, 1987:84). Another restrictive clause demanded that new members of a trade union inform their employers of their membership. As Şükran Ketenci (1987:183) explains, the membership of a trade union in an international organization was conditional on the approval of the government which, much more significantly, was empowered with the right to ban a trade union or suspend its activities if any of the union executives were convicted on the basis of certain clauses of the Turkish penal code. As argued by many critics, administrative control of trade union activity on such a wide scale provided the government with considerable leeway to exert its powers rather arbitrarily. Equally severe intervention into the financial autonomy of trade unions occurred with the avowed aim of controlling the sources and level of their financial resources. The right to deduct membership fees at source, for example, was confined only to those trade unions which had managed to conclude a collective bargaining agreement. Likewise, nonmembers paying only a fraction of the membership fee could take advantage of the benefits obtained under a collective bargaining agreement, with obvious negative implications for trade union membership. Other attempts to restrict the financial resources of trade unions included the imposition of an upper limit for trade union membership fees, the prohibition of collecting funds other than membership fees from members, and the procural of government approval before receiving contributions from non-Turkish sources.

Restrictions on Political Activity and the Right to Strike

Trade union activities were restricted to those related specifically to conflicts arising from the process of collective bargaining. Particularly strict stipulations were imposed on trade unions having political objectives, conducting political activities, or even supporting official political parties. However, by far the most severe restrictions were imposed on the right to strike. The increase in the number of activities in which strikes were prohibited was accompanied by strict prohibition of politically activated strikes, as well as general strikes and strikes in solidarity with other trade unions. Even when strikes were permissible, there was heavy regulation, giving governments considerable control vis-à-vis the timing, duration, and effectiveness of the strike. It has been estimated that even if the collective bargaining process was deadlocked right from the start, it would take as much as 3.5 to 5 months for a trade union to bring the strike into effect (Sönmez, 1984:134). Furthermore, even when the trade union managed to call a strike, the government, for national security and general health reasons, reserved the right to suspend the strike. Likewise, striking workers were not permitted in any way to interfere with the entry of raw materials to and the exit of manufactures from the workplace. Unions were also prohibited from paying any wages or social benefits to the striking workers.

The degree of administrative control over the right to strike was also evident from the detailed regulations guiding even the number of pickets and their distance from the workplace (Işıklı, 1986:196). Even after the end of the ban on strikes, which had remained in force from September 1980 to September 1983, the above rules and regulations were highly effective in restricting trade unions from calling strikes. In the first year after the lifting of the ban, for example, there were only four strikes throughout the country, involving only 561 workers (Central Bank, 1988:108). A period of increased strike activity followed, with the number of strikes rising to 21 in 1985, 307 in 1987, and 156 in 1988, and involving 2,410, 29,734, and 30,057 workers, respectively. However, in terms of man-days lost, this activity was still nowhere near the levels reached in the several years preceding the military intervention in 1980.

Policies for Employment and Wages

Employment

Employment has been one of the most neglected areas in the history of Turkish policy-making, lagging far behind objectives like rapid growth and industrialization. Three factors emerge as possible explanations for this neglect.

First, the basic problem of the labor market lay on the supply side as the rapid pace of population growth in the past created a large number of new entrants into the labor market with little hope of being productively employed. In this argument, unemployment is a structural problem with no short-term solutions. The reluctance of the government to implement a systematic population policy has obvious implications for the future level of the labor supply and further aggravates the problem.

Another factor is that under Turkey's traditional industrialization strategy, rapid growth was expected to create enough employment over time to alleviate the disequilibrium in the labor market. This expectation, however, was not based on a systematic evaluation of the direct and indirect employment effects either of industrialization nor of the interaction between the labor market and policies in key spheres like education and technological change.

The availability of stopgap solutions, like large-scale labor emigration to Western Europe in the 1960s and early 1970s, together with the tacit social security system provided by strong family ties, have also played a major role in this neglect. No significant changes in policies toward employment occurred during the post-1980 period, which, while emphasizing the severity of the problem, has continued to demonstrate the difficulties of finding a solution in the shortterm. The establishment of the High Coordination Council for Employment Promotion for this purpose has not made any significant impact to date. Similarly, the Fifth Five-Year Plan, published in 1985, and Annual Programmes published thereafter have not offered a fresh approach, emphasizing instead the potentially favorable employment effects of export-oriented policies. Two noteworthy developments in the 1980s in the field of employement were (1) the ban on worker dismissals, imposed by the military government shortly after it came to office, which, with certain modifications, remained in force until 1984, and (2) the policy of restricting public sector employment through natural attrition and slowdown in the pace of new employment creation, especially in the Public Economic Enterprises (PEEs). Although detailed, reliable information on the first of these is missing, indications are that the ban was not implemented strictly and that its lifting resulted in a large number of dismissals. As regards the contraction of public sector employment, the only available information comes from the General Reports on PEEs published by the Prime Ministry High Board of Auditors (PMHBA), which indicate that total employment in the PEEs increased (in thousands) from 581.2 in 1979 to only 742.1 in 1984 and 776.0 in 1986.[5]

Data on aggregate employment trends for the economy as a whole, on the other hand, indicate an increase at an average annual rate of 2.6 percent during 1980-1985, with nonagricultural employment rising a little faster at 3.2 percent during the same period.[6] Consequently, surplus labor as a proportion of the total labor supply increased from 14.0 percent in 1979 to 18.2 percent in 1982, stabilized somewhat at around 16 percent during 1983-1986, and while showing a slight tendency to decline toward the end of the period, remained very high at around 15.2 percent in 1987.[7] This was accompanied by a rise in open unemployment (in thousands) from 189.5 in 1979 to 468.7 in 1982, 863.6 in 1984, 1,081.3 in 1986, and 1,162.5 in 1988.[8]

Wages

By far the most significant impact of the restrictive labor environment that emerged in the 1980s was on real wages. With trade union activity highly restricted throughout the 1980-1984 period, wage settlements were reached through the Supreme Arbitration Board. The latter based wage settlements on the government's target rate of inflation, with no attempt to readjust when the actual rate turned out, as was often the case, to be much higher than the target rate. Even when there was a return to free collective bargaining after 1984, a highly bureaucratized process of collective bargaining and strike procedure strongly discouraged workers' demands for higher wages. Not surprisingly, these developments were instrumental in generating a sharp fall in the welfare of a large section of the working population. This was evident from the changes in social welfare legislation as well as more directly from trends in real wages. These changes were as follows.

1. With the introduction of the Stabilization Program there was a major price decontrol instrumental in removing government subsidies on a large number of goods and services prominent in the consumption baskets of wage earners.

2. There were restrictions on the scope and size of payments that could be made under the severance payments scheme, a reduction in pensions as a share of basic wages, a reduction on the number of days designated as public holidays and the loss of payments at overtime rates on those days, a reduction in the maximum number of bonus payments that could be made each year, and an increase in the contributions by workers for social security and health services during this period.

3. The government significantly neglected a number of activities with strong welfare implications like education, health, and housing, while there was a noticeable increase in private sector activity, especially in education.

4. The poor quality of data notwithstanding, the available evidence from a variety of sources points to a sharp fall in real wages. First, our calculations, based on total payrolls in manufacturing value added as well as payrolls per employee, indicate a sharp decline during 1980-1985.[9] Data on real daily net wages for insured workers available only for the 1980-1985 period confirm a fall (in Turkish liras) from 40.93 in 1979 to 34.27 in 1985 (Central Bank, 1980 and 1985). Our calculations, on the other hand, based on more recent data on daily wages published by the State Planning Organization, indicate that real wages fell slightly from 2.34 in 1982 to 2.19 and 2.26 in 1983 and 1984 respectively, before recovering in 1985 to their 1982 level and falling again thereafter, to 2.11 in 1986, 2.20 in 1987, and, much more sharply, to 1.62 in 1988 (SPO, 1988:322).[10] Other data on wage costs, incorporating basic wages as well as non-wage payments, compiled by PMHBA for the public sector and by the Confederation of Turkish Employers' Unions for the private sector, point in the same direction.[11]

PROSPECTS AND CONCLUSION

The above discussion of the post-1980 changes in labor market policies and the factors responsible for these changes has indicated that there was a major reversal from the generally liberal environment of the preceding two decades. In this reversal it seems that employers' organizations have been largely effective in getting their demands accepted, as evidenced by the similarity between their pre-1980 proposals and the actual measures introduced by the 1982 constitution and subsequent labor legislation. Two basic conclusions can be drawn from our discussion.

First, the policy framework for the labor market exhibited a great deal of parallelism with broader political issues and the extent of state intervention into the workings of the political system. The post-1980 and pre-1980 periods were alike in this respect. While the relative openness and noninterventionism in political life in the 1960-1970 and 1974-1977 periods reflected significant gains made by organized labor with respect to their right to strike and free collective bargaining, and significant increases in real wages, interventions into the political process like those in 1971-1973 were felt in the labor market primarily through restrictive legislation.[12]

It was therefore no coincidence that the most decisive steps for restrictive labor market policies after 1979 were taken during the military rule period of 1980-1983. Likewise, the relative normalization of political life following the general election in 1983, from which certain political parties were banned, was the beginning of a new phase in labor market policies. This phase faciliated a more open discussion of restrictive labor legislation and enabled trade unions to air their grievances more freely. With DISK, representing the more militant sections of the trade union movement, removed from the scene, TÜRK-IŞ had to lead the campaign. This in itself was significant, if one recalls the fact that the conservative leadership of TÜRK-IŞ, representing the biggest chunk of the labor movement, was in close cooperation with the military government, with its general secretary actually serving as the minister of social security during 1980-1983. The post-1983 opposition to restrictive labor legislation centered mostly on interventions into the free collective bargaining process, and on the restrictions imposed on the right to strike andon the union members' freedom to choose their own leaders. The International Labor Organization (ILO), a strong ally of the trade union movement in this campaign, pressed hard for the removal of certain clauses in the new labor legislation which they considered to be in breach of the basic ILO statutes, particularly those determining the preconditions that a union must fulfill before it can participate in the collective bargaining process. It should be emphasized that the changes enacted in 1988 were in large part a response to ILO demands. Although these changes did not go very far in altering the restrictive institutional framework envisaged by the original legislation, they nevertheless represented an important development with regard to direction.[13]

The second conclusion is that the interaction between restrictive labor market policies and the Stabilization Program appeared more intense than envisaged. Although the links between the two were manifold, here we have confined our discussion to policies affecting only organized labor in urban areas. Even on the basis of this partial treatment, however, one can argue that labor market policies were an integral part of the Stabilization Program and were mutually reinforcing with other aspects of the program in at least three ways. First, the severe fall in real wages in 1980-1984, thanks to restrictive labor market policies, may have contributed significantly to the domestic demand restraint envisaged by the government as part of its anti-inflationary program and to the emergence of a sizable exportable surplus in the initial, but crucial, years of the export boom. It seems that an additional contribution of declining wages to the export boom occurred through the reduction of costs to exporting industrialists. Second, the fall in real wages, accompanied by an effective ban on strikes and restrictions on trade union activity, corresponded closely with the pre-1980 demands of employers and may have been instrumental in creating a more favorable environment for foreign investors. Finally, although its potentially favorable effects on employment do not appear to have materialized, the fall in real wages throughout the period under consideration, together with the removal of effective subsidies for capital utilization through foreign trade liberalization and interest rate reform, may have helped remove factor price distortions.[14]

The prospects for labor market policies in the 1990s seems, as in the past, to rest on two main factors. First, international organizations, headed by the ILO, may continue to exert pressures for the continued liberalization of the labor environment. An additional force in the same direction may be the EC, especially in the light of Turkey's application for full membership in April 1987. Second, domestic politial developments are likely to be the most significant determinants of labor policies. If the democratization continues uninterrupted, one would expect to see trade unions exerting increased pressure to recover their lost ground vis-à-vis their freedom of action as well as real wages. Two weeks after the local elections in March 1989, there was a largely spontaneous upsurge of protest by organized labor that may indicate what is likely to come in the future. The fact that the government has so far seemed responsive to demands for higher wages has shown that, despite the restrictive labor legislation, there is room for an effective expression of grievances and for obtaining sizable wage increases. One should not overlook the fact, however, that these increases go only part of the way toward recovering the substantial loss in wages during the past decade. It seems apparent that the leniency toward wage claims of the former Motherland party governments and the present True Path party-Social Democratic Populist party coalition may have been guided by economic considerations like boosting domestic demand. Nevertheless, progress in liberalizing labor policies in the years ahead will depend on how high this ranks on the list of objectives of trade unions and on the degree of openness of the political system in allowing freedom of expression.

NOTES

1. The number of workers covered by collective bargaining agreements (in thousands) increased from 9.5 in 1963 to 551.0 in 1970, 590.1 in 1977, and 371.3 in 1979 (SIS, 1971:169-171 and SIS, 1985:201).

2. This was also evident from the establishment in the second half of the 1970s of a number of employers' associations, which rapidly grew in influence.

3. The number of man-days lost through strikes increased (in thousands) from 12.3 in 1963 to 479.9 in 1973, 2,217.3 in 1978, and 5408.6 in 1980 (SIS, 1971:169-171 and SIS, 1985:202).

4. One notable move in this direction was the establishment of the Coordination Council for Collective Bargaining Agreements in order to restrain excessive wage claims.

5. *Total employment* refers to total personnel by end of each year (PMHBA, 1980:69 and PMHBA, 1988:36). A similar picture emerges from the Annual Survey of Manufacturing Industries, which indicates that the number of persons engaged in public sector manufacturing enterprises decreased (in thousands) from 294.0 in 1979 to 271.8 in 1981, and 266.1 in 1982 before picking up slightly to 278.9 in 1983 and 276.0 in 1985 SIS, 1988 and SIS, 1985).

6. Figures refer to average annual rates of growth for the employees component of the economically active population during the intercensal period (SIS, 1988:79).

7. Information tabulated from Ministry of Finance, *Annual Economic Report*, various issues.

8. Data obtained from the Central Bank, *Annual Report*, various issues.

9. Total wages and salaries as a portion of total manufacturing value added fell from 28.8 percent in 1980 to 20.4 percent in 1985 (SIS, 1988:134-135 and 140-141). Manufacturing payrolls per paid employee in real terms during the same period, on the other hand, fell from 104.5 to 91.8 TL. Wholesale price indexes used in our calculations are based on 1963 prices and are from *Central Bank Annual Report,* 1980 and 1986.

10. Nominal wages are deflated by the urban consumer price index (1978-1979 = 100), given in the same source.

11. Total wage costs including the basic wages together with bonus payments, social security, and other payments, with the exception of 1987, declined steadily in both the public and private sectors, falling in real terms from 6.09 to 3.48 and from 6.34 to 4.50, respectively during 1982-1988.

12. Some observers link the fall in real wages during 1978-1979 to the prevalance of martial law in a large number of provinces throughout the country in this period.

13. A relaxation of the conditions required for individuals to be founding or executive members of trade unions, an increase in the number of pickets allowed during a strike, and an extension of the time period between official auditings of unions were among the principal changes introduced in the new legislation.

14. One reason for the slow employment growth during this period may be found in the factor content of the manufactured exports accounting for the bulk of export growth during this period. Our estimates elsewhere have shown that whereas 28 percent of total manufactured exports in 1984 were in capital-intensive categories, 76.1 percent of these were directed to the Middle East, a major trading partner, especially until the mid-1980s. For details see Şenses (1989:25) for details.

REFERENCES

Central Bank of Turkey (various years). *Yıllık Rapor.* [Annual Report]. Ankara: Central Bank Publication.

Güzel, S. (1987). "1980 Sonrasında İşçi Haklarında Gerilemeler." *11. Tez.* No. 5 (February).

Işıklı, A. (1986). "1960-1986 Döneminde İşçi Hakları." In Türkiye Yol-İş Sendikası, ed., *Türkiye'de İşçi Haklari.* Ankara: Yorum Matbaası.

Ketenci, Ş. (1987). "İşçiler ve Çalışma Yaşamı: 1980'lerde Sınırlar ve Sorunlar." In B. Kuruç et al., eds., *Bırakınız Yapsınlar Bırakınız Geçsinler-Türkiye Ekonomisi 1980-1985.* Istanbul: Bilgi Yayınevi.

Kopits, G. (1987). *Structural Reform, Stabilization and Growth in Turkey* Occasional Paper No. 52. Washington: International Monetary Fund.

Kuran, T. (1980). "Internal Migration: The Unorganized Urban Sector and Income Distribution in Turkey, 1963-1973." In E. Özbudun and A. Ulusan, eds., *The Political Economy of Income Distribution in Turkey.* New York: Holmes and Meier.

Ministry of Finance. *Annual Report*. (various issues). Ankara: Ministry of Finance.

Öniş, Z. (1986). "Stabilization and Growth in a Semi-Industrial Economy: An Evaluation of the Recent Turkish Experiment, 1977-1984." *METU Studies in Development*. Vol. 13., Nos. 1 and 2:7-28.

PMHBA (Prime Ministry High Board of Auditors) (1980). *Annual Report on Public Economic Enterprises*. Ankara: The Prime Ministry.

_____ (1988). *Annual Report on Public Economic Enterprises*. Ankara: The Prime Ministry.

Şenses, F. (1979).*The Effect of Economic Policies on the Pattern of Trade and Development in Turkey, 1950-1970*. Unpublished Ph.D. thesis. London School of Economics and Political Science. London.

_____ (1983). "An Assessment of Turkey's Liberalization Attempts since 1980 against the Background of Her Stabilization Program." *METU Studies in Development*. Vol. 8, Nos. 1 and 2: 271-321.

_____ (1989). "The Nature and Main Characteristics of Recent Turkish Growth in Export of Manufactures." *The Developing Economies*. Vol 27. No.1, (March):19-33.

SIS (State Institute of Statistics) (1971). *Statistical Yearbook 1971*. Ankara: SIS Publications.

_____ (1985). *Statistical Yearbook 1985*. Ankara: SIS Publications.

_____ (1988). *Statistical Pocket Book of Turkey*. Ankara: SIS Publications.

Sönmez, M. (1984). *Özal Ekonomisi ve İşçi Hakları*. Istanbul: Belge Yayınları.

SPO (State Planning Organization) (1988). "1989 Yılı Programı." *Resmi Gazete* No. 19974, October 30.

Wolff, P. (1987). *Stabilization Policy and Structural Adjustment in Turkey, 1980-1985*. Berlin: German Development Institute.

6

The World Bank
and the Transformation
of Turkish Agriculture
Zülküf Aydın

INTRODUCTION

Discussions of Turkish agriculture often isolate certain issues from their larger context and their international determinants. The works of several scholars (Arsevik, 1975; Berk, 1980; Boratav, 1980; Bulmuş, 1981; Erdost, 1984; Kip, 1988; Ergüder, 1980; and Ulusan, 1980) are just a few examples of such omissions. Issues like internal terms of trade between industry and agriculture, agricultural price policy, and provision of chemicals and other inputs are quite often treated in relationship to the activities of certain political parties or governments, and conclusions arrived at therefore remain conjectural, providing no hint of long-term tendencies. This paper examines the role of the World Bank in the transformation of rural structures in Turkey.

The World Bank is a very powerful agency of international capital, and as such, it aims to ensure a particular type of transformation for Third World countries. It has been able to dictate certain types of developmental policies to these countries' governments. Through withholding or granting loans, it can direct governments to adopt policies in the interest of international capital. The World Bank's involvement in Third World agriculture at the national level is mediated through existing governments and state institutions like the *Ziraat Bankası* (Agricultural Bank) and cooperatives. In other words, these institutions act as invisible hands of the World Bank in transforming underdeveloped countries' structures in accordance with the interests of international capital.

Often the agricultural development projects supported by the World Bank appear to have humanitarian aims such as eliminating poverty and increasing the standard of living. However, these aims are incompatible with the conditions set and policies imposed by the Bank and the IMF prior to any major lending. I shall argue that the measures suggested for a particular rural development project aim to intensify the commercialization of agriculture rather than to eliminate poverty, and that this is more in line with the austerity and/or structural adjustment policies imposed on the country as a whole.

This chapter does not isolate a particular rural development project and its rhetorical aims from the general, more effective policies imposed on the receiving countries, but analyzes them within the framework of such policies. It shows that projects like the Çorum and Çankırı Integrated Rural Development and Erzurum IRD are part and parcel of the international agencies' attempts to further integrate Turkey into the world capitalist system. Furthermore, the commercialization of agriculture in Turkey has been nesessary for industrializing the country. Thus, the World Bank has played a significant role in the commercialization of Turkish agriculture since the 1960s. The incorporation of a large number of agricultural producers into the capitalist system has occurred in stages. To open up subsistence areas to market forces, the World Bank has made investments in the infrastructure and offered cheap credits, favorable prices, and input subsidies. Then, once the market orientation of the producers is irreversibly entrenched, it withdraws subsidies, favorable prices, and cheap credits from the producers. While earlier populist agricultural policies contributed to the viability of small producers, the later policies, which came as part of a structural adjustment policy package, have accelerated class differentiation in the countryside. This chapter argues that the measures taken, which have led to the long-term differentiation of the countryside, have been enacted with the goal of improving the lot of the poorer section of the countryside through production schemes.

THE WORLD BANK

By using its financial power, the World Bank imposes socioeconomic policies that are congruent with the interests of international capitalism on Third World governments; these policies intensify the dependence of the Third World. Although the preferred policies for complete incorporation of the Third World are privatization, raising interest rates, controlling bank credits, removing subsidies, limiting public spending, and keeping wages down, in the early years the World Bank made concessions from these strict policies with the hope of increasing the market orientation of the Third World. Among these concessions was the financing of rural development schemes which would include subsidies and price supports as well as public expenditure in large-scale infrastructural development. However, in each case the World Bank considered the commercializing effects of such schemes. Before financing any project, its experts carefully examined the suitability of the project and, in most cases, imposed their own priorities. Even so, the Bank's policy recommendations to the Third World have not remained the same since its establishment; on the contrary, they reflect the changes in the international division of labor and the socioeconomic and political relationship between advanced capitalist countries and the Third World. Until the late 1960s, the World Bank provided the foreign exchange costs of dams, railways, roads, ports, power stations and telecommunications, which in turn provided the necessary infrastructure for the movement of foreign capital and goods.

From the 1970s onward, the World Bank's lending policies have shifted significantly. Under the new approach, the Bank has emphasized the need for reaching the rural and urban poor (target groups) in the Third World (see McNamara's Nairobi speech in 1973). To counter mounting criticisms of the World Bank's support for Green Revolution policies and to ease the social tension and militancy caused by extreme class differentiation and inequalities in rural areas, the World Bank designed policies to alleviate the situation without compromising the principle of integrating rural areas into the orbit of the market economy (McNamara, 1968). Therefore, Third World poverty had to be tackled by reaching "target groups." Chenery et al. (1974) expressed theoretical formulations of this view in a semiofficial document produced for the Bank. The most crucial formulation was the "redistribution with growth" strategy, which was supposed to alleviate poverty and increase productivity through integrated rural development projects. This strategy now appears to have failed all over the world (de Janvry, 1981; Feder, 1977 and 1981; and Hayter and Watson, 1983), resulting in only some insignificant production increases achieved through the producers' intensified dependence on the market for inputs and outputs. However, due to unequal terms of trade between agricultural and other sectors, increased productivity has failed improve standards of living for the producers.

In the 1980s the leading policy of the World Bank shifted again. Because Third World agriculture had become closely integrated into the market economy, there remained little need to devise special distribution measures. At the same time, many underdeveloped countries experienced a problem of debt burden and had difficulties in meeting their debt servicing. Thus, the global policy of World Bank lending is now designed to cause structural changes which will transform Third World countries into states capable of repaying debts including interest. However, the rhetoric of increasing the standard of living has remained largely unchanged in specific rural development projects (a case in point is the Erzurum Integrated Rural Development Project). Therefore, one should consider specific projects within the overall policies of the Bank to determine the contradictions between the rhetorical aims and more comprehensive policies.

THE WORLD BANK, TURKEY, AND AGRICULTURE
IN THE 1980s

This shift in the World Bank's lending policies is definitely reflected in its relationship with Turkey. In the 1950s Turkey was encouraged to invest mostly in infrastructural and agricultural development. However, in the 1980s lending to Turkey became conditional on the implementation of liberalization and outward-oriented policies. The place of Turkey in the international division of labor ever since the 1950s has been that of a producer of traditional export crops and an importer of technology. As can be seen in Table 1, of all the sectors the highest loans went to agriculture between 1975 and 1988. While the Turkish state has borrowed 1,228 million US dollars for agriculture and rural development, industry has received less than half of this amount, a mere 539.7 million US dollars. Considering that some of the money lent to industry was used to develop agro-industrial plants such as fertilizer factories, the difference between the money lent to industry and thast lent to agriculture becomes even bigger. With the recommendations and impositions of the World Bank and IMF between 1960 and the late 1970s, Turkey emphasized agricultural development for export purposes, and import substitution industrialization for meeting the internal demands for some manufactured products.

The demands of import substitution industrialization on agriculture were twofold. First, it was expected that agriculture would continue its role as the major foreign currency-earning sector, and second, that rural areas would serve as a very large internal market for the import-substituting industrial products. The achievement of these two depended, however, on whether the agricultural sector would continue to increase its marketable surpluses. Therefore, governmenetal policies focused on achieving this end through what may be termed *vertical concentration*. The state has attempted to control, coordinate, and supervise the production of agricultural commodities of the small and medium-sized producers who constitute the overwhelming majority of rural producers in Turkish agriculture.

This shift from a mainly export-oriented agricultural development in the 1950s to import-substituting industrialization in the 1960s fitted nicely with the general aims of international agencies like the World Bank and the IMF. Import substituting industrialization meant dependence on the importation of technology and intermediate goods (Alpar, 1980; Keyder, 1987; and Uras, 1979) and necessitated agricultural commoditization for the reasons previously mentioned. Turkey's inability to finance rural development programs increases agricultural production allowed the World Bank to penetrate Turkish agriculture.

Table 1
World Bank Lending to Turkey, 1975-1988 (Million US Dollars)

State	1975-78	1979	1980	1981	1982	1983	1984	1985	1986	1987	1988	Total
Agriculture	269.5	85.0	51.0	40.0	40.0		187.5	300.0	255.0			1228.0
Development and Finance				40.0					300.0	32.9	400.0	772.9
Industry	95.0		83.0	110.0	44.1		7.6		100.0		100.0	539.7
Tourism	26.0											26.0
Transportation		75.0			71.1		186.4	134.5		197.0		664.0
Energy			120.0	87.0					252.0	457.0	30.1	946.1
Water Supply and Sewerage			6.0									6.0
Non-Project		150.0	200.0	375.0	304.5	300.8	376.0					1706.3
Education							36.8	55.1		58.5	115.8	266.2
Total	390.0	310.0	460.0	652.0	459.7	300.8	794.3	489.6	907.0	745.4	645.9	6155.2
State as a Guarantor												
Agriculture						150.4						150.4
Development and Finance	353.0		140.0		100.0						200.0	719.0
Industry	158.0			70.0								158.0
Tourism												0.0
Transportation												0.0
Energy		2.5				55.2		142.0				199.7
Water/Sewage					88.1					184.0	218.0	490.1
Power	56.0					163.0						219.0
Total	623.0	2.5	140.0	70.0	188.1	368.6	0.0	142.0	0.0	184.0	418.0	1866.2

Source: The World Bank. *Annual Report* for the relevant years.

With no further possibility of enlarging cultivable areas from the 1960s onward, large-scale infrastructural developments and the use of improved technology and chemical products in agriculture were necessary for increased production. To improve the infrastructure, investments had to increase in communications, energy storage, local processing facilities, and health and rural education. On the other hand, investments were essential for the direct planning and financing of production involving the introduction and provision of agricultural machinery, improved seeds, insecticides, pesticides, the provision of credits and inputs, and the implementation of a price support policy. All of these were possible with the availability of state and parastatal resources. These funds were in large part obtained from international agencies, most notably from the World Bank. The need for foreign currency since the 1950s had quite often led to various governments applying to the World Bank for help. This in turn enabled the World Bank to determine the direction of the transformation of Turkish agriculture in accordance with its global aims.

As the indebtedness of the country to international financiers has increased, her bargaining power vis-à-vis these organizations in terms of resisting the stringent conditions attached to the loans has gradually eroded. From 1980 onward, Turkey has implemented the most liberalized international policies of her history (Sertel, 1988 and Kazgan, 1988). As a result, multinational concerns have strengthened their control of industry while the commercialization and market orientation of agriculture have increased (Harris, 1988).

Import-substituting industrialization policies implemented in parallel with agricultural development policies until the late 1970s have augmented the flexibility of the World Bank and IMF. At the same time, the need for import-substituting industry for foreign currency has increased Turkey's dependence on the West and enabled these agencies gradually to determine the country's long-term developmental patterns.

Structural Adjustment

Turkey heavily borrowed to meet the demands of import substitution industrialization for foreign currency and rising oil bills in the wake of 1973. Such heavy borrowing made the country lose its credibility in the eyes of lenders. Therefore, multinational and bilateral creditors pushed Turkey to adopt a structural policy which was intended to have lasting positive effects on her balance of payments. Supported by the IMF, World Bank and OECD, and implemented between 1980 and 1985, the medium-term structural adjustment policy was in accordance with "the main strategic lines of the IMF's and World Bank's adjustment concepts: outward orientation, liberalization, deregulation and priority given to the private sector" (Wolff, 1987:2). In return for the loans received (totaling 1,556.3 million US dollars between 1980 and 1984), Turkey agreed to implement a large number of policies which affected almost every sphere of economic life (for the nature of these policies, see Wolff, 1987). Briefly, the large number of measures related to the liberalization of imports, promotion of exports, reformation of the public sector and the capital market, and the transformation of the agricultural and energy sectors were all geared to improving Turkey's long-term debt-paying ability.

However, the price of improving this ability seems to have been the furtherance of inequalities in income distribution in the country. Continual price increases, suppression of wages, low floor prices for agricultural products, and the increasing tax burden on the masses all led to a significant decrease in the standard of living of the people, but at the same time resulted in a transfer of resources to capital. The share of agriculture in the national income decreased from 23.9 percent to 14 percent between 1980 and 1988, while the share of wages and salaries dropped from 26.7 percent to 15.8 percent in the same period. According to one calculation, the transfer of resources from agriculture and wages to capital was worth about 51.1 billion U.S. dollars between 1980 and 1988 (Yıldırım, 1988). The general contention is that structural adjustment policies have exacerbated the already uneven income distribution in Turkey (Kazgan, 1988:375).

Structural Adjustment and Agriculture

Of all the sectors of the economy, agriculture drew the most attention from the structural adjustment policies. The IMF and World Bank had been complaining for a long time that state subsidies burdened the economy. Without touching the structural specifics of the Turkish countryside, the implemented adjustment policies were intended to increase production and exports (Yağcı et al., 1985:61). For reduction of subsidies and state controls, reliance on market forces and the improvement of agricultural technology were considered necessary. Measures were taken to let prices adjust to world prices, eliminate fertilizer subsidies, increase water charges, remove restrictions on exports, make agricultural sale cooperatives financially self-sufficient with credit obtained on commercial terms, establish crop insurance schemes, and improve medium-term planning and research capabilities (Yağcı et al., 1985:61).

Most of the price policy measures were implemented, but the institutional reforms were not taken very seriously (Wolff, 1987:40). The World Bank gave 300 million US dollars in 1985 to continue the policies that were already in operation. The Bank emphasized reforms to reduce producer subsidization while maintaining adequate incentives to increase the effectiveness of public investments (particularly irrigation), enhance technical services, and strengthen sector planning and programming (World Bank, 1985).

The policies concerning Turkish agriculture, advised by the Bank and implemented by the Turkish government, suggest no change in attitude of the

World Bank toward the agricultural sector in the Third World. It continued to incline toward incorporating small producers into the market economy and extracting surpluses from them through impersonal market relations. The structural adjustment policies reflect the contention that agricultural producers have now become dependent upon the market and that it is time they pay back the concessions made to them through the populist policies which furnished them with the knowledge of improved technology. A technically informed, market-oriented small producer, who utilizes recent technology but shoulders all the increasing costs of modern inputs without challenging price increases, is the desired type of producer.

However, Turkish small producers have proved not to be docile to the desired degree. Organized protests against the state's policies of minimizing the subsidies, while at the same time keeping agricultural prices at a depressed level, have recently occurred in some parts of Turkey (*Financial Times*, September 11, 1989). For example, about 10,000 farmers in Manisa demonstrated in protest against the state policies of increasing the prices of agricultural inputs but not the floor prices of agricultural crops at the same level.

World Bank Activity Areas in Turkish Agriculture

In the last three decades or so, the World Bank has penetrated every imaginable area of agricultural production in Turkey. I use the term *penetration* because, although in day-to-day practices it appears to be the Turkish state and its agencies such as the Ziraat Bankası or cooperatives that are activating agriculture through production, distribution, credit, and other schemes, in fact, international agencies like the World Bank, the FAO, and IFAD are the ones which hold the strings. These agencies do not lend money to governments unless they approve the projects suggested. It is quite often the experts of these agencies who have the final say in the use of the money lent (Payer, 1982; Hayter and Watson, 1985; and Williams, 1981). Through regular checks and controls, international agencies ensure that the money lent is spent in the areas agreed beforehand. In turn, local agencies such as cooperatives and the Agricultural Bank do their best to ensure that the credits and inputs provided to them are used in the desired areas.

World Bank lending to Turkish agriculture covers many diverse areas from infrastructural developments to production and distribution. Projects hope to improve dairy production through training, studies, and demonstration. Investments focus on ensuring increased production of fruits and vegetables, and the improvement of handling and marketing facilities. Farm credit goes to investment in imported and local livestock, farm buildings, pasture improvements, and foodstuff production as well as to improvements in poultry production and processing units. The state uses funds to develop and improve irrigation flood control facilities and to introduce intensive training and extension services to farmers. One important consequence of this has been the further integration and dependence of small producers on the market and a further increase in their vulnerability to market forces and state policies.

CHANGES IN TURKISH AGRICULTURE

Cash injection into rural areas from the 1950s onward has led to some notable changes in the Turkish countryside. Cultivated areas showed a significant increase between 1950 and 1960, but the trend since then has steadied. Even in recent years, however, agricultural production has shown a significant increase in a number of crops due to the use of improved technology and chemicals, the betterment of infrastructure, and increased use of agricultural machinery.

Both the increases in production and in agricultural machinery have resulted largely from the agricultural credits made available to a wide spectrum of farmers. Total credit, from the Agricultural Bank and credit cooperatives, sales cooperatives, or the General Directorate of Agriculture Supplies, reached the staggering amount of 1,360,550 million Turkish liras in 1986, while in 1977 the amount was 47,701 million Turkish liras (see Table 2).

The thrust of my agrument is that this credit policy, along with the agricultural price support policy followed by the Turkish state with the help and encouragement of the World Bank and similar international organizations, has enabled a specific type of transformation in the Turkish countryside. This transformation has been characterized by the integration of small, family-based agricultural units into market relations and their subordination to capital (for various regions and crops see Aydın, 1986; Ecevit, 1987; and Sirman, 1988). This particular form of subordination seems to defy the classical Marxist understanding of the transformation of the countryside under the effects of capitalism. In contrast to expectations of the emergence of dichotomous social classes–large agricultural capitalists and the proletariat–the countryside has a very large number of market-dependent (both for inputs and outputs) small producers. International capital has discovered that agriculture is capable of producing surpluses without the elimination of small producers and their substitution with large capitalist farmers (Vergopoulos, 1977a, 1977b, and 1978). Nonetheless, this does not mean that small producers are surviving without any change in their production, consumption, and distribution relations. Given the economic difficulties of small producers in Turkey today, their persistence, and their indirect subordination to capital, one wonders if the situation can best be explained as one in which capital has found ways of controlling the production of small producers without dundamentally changing their property relations in a short period of time.

Table 2
Agricultural Credits in Turkey (Million TL)

YEAR I	New Loans II	Loans Outstanding and not Overdue III	Overdue Credits IV	Credits under Litigation V	III+IV+V	IV+V III+IV+V
1977	47,701	52,560	13,776	1,742	68,078	22.8%
1978	64,177	58,957	20,780	1,803	81,540	27.7%
1979	119,643	113,252	18,119	1,841	133,212	15.0%
1980	184,957	190,445	24,270	1,843	216,558	12.0%
1981	267,206	329,281	31,415	2,186	362,882	36.0%
1982	229,255	336,935	30,915	3,954	371,084	9.3%
1983	335,562	485,984	58,291	9,599	553,874	12.3%
1984	445,676	489,631	76,650	15,622	581,903	15.8%
1985	692,296	883,099	110,464	30,309	1,023,872	13.7%
1986	1,360,551	1,430,805	305,165	48,113	1,784,083	19.8%

Source: Calculated from State Institute of Statistics publications (1977-1987).

It is clear that, after decades of encouragement policies, subsidies have been gradually withdrawn from the small producers, who are left with the dilemma of either defaulting on their debts or facing the confiscation of their means of production (land and tractors mostly). In other words, the differentiation of the peasantry has not stopped, as assumed by the Chayanovian school (Kerblay, 1971 and Shanin, 1972), but has taken a different course. Perhaps the penetration of banking capital in the form of credit has retarded the differentiation of the peasantry by several decades.

Between 1950 and 1979, the international organizations of the capitalists, such as the World Bank, attempted to commercialize rural areas of Turkey without creating sharp tension in these regions. However, the more recent needs of international capital have now overtuned. Cheap agricultural credits have been extended to producers in Turkey since the 1950s, but it is during the last eight years, in line with structural adjustment policies, that interest rates have gradually increased and subsidies have been gradually withdrawn from agricultural inputs without a corresponding rise in the prices of agricultural commodities. This has resulted in more and more farmers not being able to repay their debts to the Agricultural Bank and similar creditors. Agricultural Bank figures suggest that the amount of defaulted farmer debt has gradually increased from the early 1980s. For instance, the percentage of overdue credits and credits under litigation increased from 10.2 percent of the total loans outstanding in 1981 to 14 percent in 1983 and 24.6 percent in 1986 (Table 2). Turkish daily newspapers are full of stories of how small producers have been forced to part with their land because of their debts–be they official or private. For instance, the economy column of the daily *Milliyet* reported on 11 February 1986 that in Kaşlıca village (which consists of 140 households with a total population of 1,800) in Adana province in southern Turkey, only twelve tractors remained out of seventy; the rest had been confiscated by bailiffs' courts on behalf of creditors.

The withdrawal of subsidies from petroleum and chemical fertilizers especially has increased the cost of production to agricultural producers and therefore their inability to repay their debts. For example, the same article in *Milliyet* entitled "Bailiff Officer: The New Lord of the Peasants" reported that the Çelik family from Çakırtepe village in the Çukurova region lost their two tractors and 500 decares of land through confiscation because they were not able to pay their debts resulting from the purchase of chemicals and petroleum.

The weekly magazine *İkibine Doğru* in its edition of October 23, 1988, reports that about 1,500 small farmers from twenty villages in the Haymana district neighboring Ankara have been taken to court by the Agricultural Bank and Agricultural Credit Cooperatives for not being able to repay their debts. According to Turkish law, the ultimate penalty is the confiscation of the land. *İkibine Doğru* states that unpaid credits reached unprecedented dimensions after 1985. While in 1986 200,000 farmers were unable to pay their debts to

Agricultural Credit Cooperatives, this number had increased to 600,000 in 1988. This figure constitutes 40 percent of the total number of farmers who obtained credits from Agricultural Credit Cooperatives in 1988. The inability of farmers to pay their debts is quite often explained by unequal internal terms of trade working against the agricultural sector (see Table 3), by high interest rates and by the increase in the prices of inputs. Understanding why the internal terms of trade work against the agricultural sector necessitates an understanding of the state price support policies.

Table 3
Internal Terms of Trade Between Agriculture and Industry

Years	Terms of Trade	Years	Terms of Trade
1966	100.0	1976	100.4
1968	103.4	1978	87.9
1970	109.6	1980	62.9
1972	107.3	1982	65.7
1974	111.2	1984	59.3
		1985	56.6

Source: Akad (1987: 148); Boratav (1987:99)

The Turkish state has interfered in the formation of agricultural prices since the 1930s. Over the years, the number of crops included in the price policy has increased to include industrial crops, meat and dairy products, and almost every other agricultural product except citrus and other fruits and vegetables. Despite the rhetoric about improving the standard of living of the majority of farmers, the agricultural support policy has basically aimed to increase the market orientation of farmers and to encourage the production of certain crops for both the internal and external markets. At times, the desire to increase production of certain crops has led to the assignment of high prices for these crops and the provision of inputs at subsidized prices. These policies have quite often coincided with election years. Nonetheless, it is wrong to assume that the major concern of the government in offering high prices and subsidizing certain inputs was simply electoral popularity. These policies have to be analyzed as part and parcel of the general structuring of the economy.

The import-substituting industrialization of the 1960s and 1970s definitely necessitated a highly commercialized agriculture that could alleviate the foreign currency crisis of the industrial sector. However, the commercialization of agriculture in turn necessitated external funding, which matched the desires and intentions of international agencies like the World Bank. While multinational corporations penetrated the industrial sector through import-substituting industrialization policies, the state treasury met foreign currency requirements by external borrowing. The 1960s and 1970s saw the generation of externally dependent industrialization, for which the rural areas were gradually transformed. The state was able to pour resources into the countryside during this process of restructing it through external borrowing. This explains why there were favorable terms of trade for the agricultural sector until the middle of the 1970s. It is ironic that despite occasional grumbling about agricultural subsidies, international agencies such as the World Bank, the FAO, and the IMF turned a blind eye to these policies in the 1960s and 1970s, since they were necessary for the commercialization of agriculture and the integration of large numbers of owner-producers into the capitalist system.

Once the commercialization of agriculture had matured and producer market dependence had been achieved, these organizations, particularly the World Bank, insisted firmly on abolishing the subsidies and allowing large and very unorganized small producers to carry the cost. External lenders are not interested in pumping money into the Turkish countryside forever, nor are they interested in a Turkey unable to pay its debts to international financiers. Instead, they support countries which are able to pay their debts and, most importantly, their interest. An increase in exporting can achieve this. Subsidies to agriculture mean more state indebtedness and less capability to repay debts; therefore, subsidies should be stopped while the ability of agriculture to generate foreign currency must be retained. This occurred in the early 1980s with the structural adjustment policies. Upon the recommendations of the IMF and World Bank, subsidies for agricultural chemicals and machinery were abolished (Birdal, 1978:27), but the floor or support prices were not increased accordingly, nor was the high rate of inflation taken into consideration.

It is possible that individual governments and political parties in power want to follow populist policies and keep the rural masses happy by subsidizing agriculture in order to gain short-term advantages over rivaling political parties. However, governments of independent underdeveloped countries cannot act completely independently within the world capitalist system. The imposition of IMF and IBRD austerity and structural adjustment programs on Third World states is a testament to this. The IMF and the World Bank have often asked Turkey to accept certain measures that conflict with the populist intentions of governments (Sertel, 1988). The abolition of subsidies for agricultural chemicals and machinery in the 1980s is such an example. However, there is a limit to playing with the internal terms of trade between sectors. Once the producers pass this limit, they can passively react to government plans to increase the production of certain crops. In such a case, producers will simply limit or not use expensive, sophisticated inputs, which in turn will lead to a decrease in marketable surpluses. This has been happening in Turkish agriculture since the early 1980s (Gürkan and Kasnakoğlu, 1987). Another case in point is the Çorum-Çankırı Integrated Rural Development Project area. Small producers from the village of Demirşeyh in Sungurlu District of Çorum emphasized, in interviews conducted in the summer of 1989, that they had to decrease the amount of chemicals used in cultivation because of the soaring costs (for an evaluation of the Çorum-Çankırı Integrated Rural Development Project see Aydın, forthcoming, and Nott, 1983).

The results of unequal terms of trade working against agriculture until 1987 have been dramatic in certain cases as already meantioned. Muzaffer Ilhan Erdost (1987) examines the relationship between input prices and prices received by the farmers. He calculates that in 1979, for one litre of petroleum, producers had to grow 1.79 kg of wheat, while in 1985 they had to grow 2.92 kg of wheat; in addition, they exchanged 6.32 kg of sugar beet for one liter of petroleum in 1979, while in 1985 the amount was 14.21 kg. Erdost makes further calculations: Producers obtained 1 kg of fertilizer with 0.45 kg of wheat in 1979 and 1.70 kg of wheat in 1985; similarly, they obtained 1 kg of chemical products for 3.37 kg of wheat in 1979, and 17.63 kg in 1985. The imbalance of input and output prices in agriculture has reached such levels that producers can claim that state-declared prices do not cover their costs of production, let alone their labor.

Despite all these processes accelerating the commercialization of agriculture, •the differentiation of the producers has not yet gained sufficient momentum to lead to the disappearance of small producers and the concentration of land in a few hands; instead, a clear tendency of proletarianization has appeared along with the increasing number of farming families in rural areas. The latest available figures on landownership relate to 1981. An examination of the growth of landlessness in rural areas for various years shows the gradual increase of proletarianization in the Turkish countryside. Unfortunately, at the time of this writing, there are no figures for the late 1980s to enable us to see the degree of differentiation in the period characterized by the structural adjustment policies. However, reports referred to in this chapter for many areas in Turkey and my interviews with farmers in Sungurlu indicate that the tendency is toward increasing indebtedness and alienation from the means of production (tractors and land). The fact that petty commodity-producing household units will attempt to resist such a tendency of proletarianization does not invalidate my contention that the process of pauperization of household production units has quickened with their further integration into the capitalist market economy. In the short run, commodity-producing household production units may have recourse to "self-exploitation" by decreasing their consumption level and minimizing their expenditures on certain items and events. It is precisely these kinds of household strategies that are involved in the tendency of proletarianization in the countryside. Both Ecevit (n.d.) and Sirman (n.d.) refer to various household strategies of commodity producers (tobacco in Gökceağaç Village and cotton in Tuz Village) to face increasing prices of inputs and decreasing prices of crops. These "adjustment mechanisms" include enlargement of the area cultivated, decreases in the amount of consumption, changes in the composition of consumption, postponement of marriages and/or reduction of the content of goods purchased for marriages.

These measures themselves are not capable of ensuring the survivability of the household production unit but are indicators of the pauperization of small producers. There is a limit to how far a small producer can go by increasing her/his labor input and decreasing her/his consumption. Another countervailing tendency to the proletarianization suggested is to decrease the size of the household. This means that the individual who is pushed out of the production/reproduction unit of the household loses his access to land, and this is a good indication of proletarianization. Of course, in some cases proletarianization does not take such a direct form. The households that have reached the limits of "survival strategies" do lose their means of production, and it seems this process did accelerate in the early 1980s.

Tables 4 and 5 indicate the process of increasing landlessness. Clearly the proportion of landless farming families to total farming families increased from 14.5 percent in 1950 to 30.9 percent in 1981. The striking fact is that, between 1950 and 1981, the numbers and the proportion of landless and small landowning families have increased considerably among the Turkish farming population. Conversely, the numbers of large and medium-sized landowners have decreased considerably in the same period.

Table 4
Landlessness in Turkey

Years	Total Farming Families	Landowning Families	Landless Farming Families	% of Landless Families
1950	2,322,391	1,985,645	336,764	14.5
1968	2,737,431	2,257,710	479,721	17.5
1973	3,794,631	2,965,476	829,155	21.8
1981	5,563,110	3,844,861	1,718,244	30.9
1950-81 increase	140 %	94%		410%

Source: State Planning Organization.

Table 5
Land Distribution in Turkey in 1950 and 1981

		1950	
	No. of Families	%	Av. Amount of Land Owned (decares)
Landless	336,747	11.9	
0 - 50	1,550,397	55.2	25.0
51 - 100	547,790	19.5	70.9
101 - 200	263,844	9.4	150.0
201 - 500	110,564	3.9	316.9

			1981		
	No. of Families	%	Amount of Land Owned (decares)	%	Av. Amount of Land Owned (decars)
Landless	1,718,249	30.9	---	---	---
0 - 50	3,017,962	54.3	55,513,530	35.1	17.9
51 - 100	516,419	9.3	37,597,544	23.8	72.9
101 - 200	228,754	4.1	32,587,009	20.6	142.0
201-500	80,702	1.4	20,982,520	13.3	259.9

Sources: State Institute of Statistics (1956) and Köy Işleri Bakanlığı (1983), *Village Inventory Surveys* for 67 provinces.

Another striking fact is the general decrease in the average amount of land owned, except for the 51-100 decares category. This tendency of increasing landlessness and land fragmentation is undoubtedly related to population growth and the inheritance system. Nonetheless, these two factors alone do not provide a sufficiently plausible explanation for the decreasing size of holdings. The explanation lies in the use of agricultural technology (including machinery and chemicals), which has the effect of increasing productivity and therefore the reliability and viability of smaller holdings. In this respect, the World Bank and the state have played significant roles in creating the conditions for smaller landowners to proliferate and make a living from agriculture through more labor and other inputs. Also, the inability of industrialization to create sufficient jobs for the rural landless and of commercialized agriculture to create some employment opportunities (be it temporary or permanent wage labor, or sharecropping) in rural areas has contributed to the decision of some of the rural proletariat to stay in rural areas instead of migrating to urban areas. Tables 4 and 5 clearly illustrate the fact that the pace of increase in the number of landless farming families has far outstripped the pace of increase in total farming families and landowning families. While the number of landless farming families increased by 410 percent between 1950 and 1981, the relevant percentages for total farming families and landowning families were 140 percent and 94 percent in the same period.

INCREASING SUBORDINATION

A clear contradiction exists between the general policies the World Bank and IMF have imposed on the Third World and their aims for specific rural development projects. The austerity packages and structural adjustment policies, which include credit restrictions, emphasis on raw materials and agricultural production, decreasing government expenditures and subsidies, decreasing wages, and discouraging high tariffs and exchange controls and encouraging devaluation, all mean a deterioration in the standard of living for the poor; this trend is diametrically opposed to the aims expressed in the World Bank's Rural Development Sector Policy (World Bank, 1975). The attempts to increase the rate of interest, decrease wages, and devalue the local currency, in particular, have directly contributed to the decline in the standard of living of the urban and rural poor. On the one hand, promoters of rural development projects suggest that small producers should have access to cheap credit; on the other hand, the World Bank and the IMF insist that interest rates should be kept high to avoid inflation. While they insist that the income of the rural masses should rise, at the same time they force the local governments to devalue their currency. The net result for the rural producers is that their products are sold more cheaply in the world market, provided that they can find buyers.

Quite often, producers are encouraged to produce certain commodities with improved technology provided on credit, but a proper channel of marketing may not be established. This leaves the producers to dispose of their commodities at a loss (for an example, see the report by Kadir Can in *Cumhuriyet* June 14, 1985; also see *Cumhuriyet* June 14, 1985). Production increase does not automatically mean an increase in the living standards of producers. The effects of such overproduction can be extremely harmful for small producers, especially since they have little security in times of crisis. On the contary, large producers manage to survive the crisis by relying on savings from previous years.

Çorum-Çankırı Integrated Rural Development Project

Apart from the contradictory nature of austerity measures and the aims of specific rural development projects, the basic assumption underlying such projects may be at fault. A consequence of this would be that even if the project were implemented properly (as designed), it would not achieve the stated aims. To substantiate this point, I examine the first World Bank-supported Integrated Rural Development project in Turkey, the Çorum-Çankırı project. This project was intended to raise production, and thereby income, and to improve the rural infrastucture in Çorum and Çankırı provinces (World Bank, 1975). The basic goal of the project was "helping the rural poor and dampening the rate of urban migration" (World Bank, 1975:4). This was to be achieved through the construction of irrigation facilities and roads, provision of credit, and provision of water, electricity, public baths, and other social facilities (World Bank, 1975:11). For these purposes, the World Bank provided 75 million US dollars out of the total cost of 162 million US dollars. One important assumption of the project appraisal was that rural development projects would benefit everyone living in rural areas, regardless of socioeconomic differences among them.

In this way, poverty is isolated from its political and economic dimensions and seen as something that can be eliminated at will. The project also assumed that this benefit would be realized through the use of machinery, and improved seeds and inputs. Thus, the incomes of small producers would increase and they would retain some profits. The provision of credit in particular, as well as inputs, and the offer of extension services were seen as a panacea that would increase production as well as alleviate poverty.

Despite the placement of so much faith in credit, the distribution of credit and inputs created a serious bottleneck for the success of the stated aims of the project. Farmers had differential access to credits from the Agricultural Bank. To prove their creditworthiness, farmers had to provide real estate mortgages and guarantees of cosignatories before the advance of any loans. Most important, the exclusion of landless farmers from the project's credit system seems contrary to the general aim of the project to alleviate poverty. In an area where 33.26 percent of farming families (66,222 out of 199,097) are landless and where 49 percent of landowning farming families own twenty-five decares or less land (KIKB, 1983), it is impossible to discuss the alleviation of poverty without including the largest and poorest segment of society. In various reports based on a sample of credit applications, K. Heinz Grammelspacher, the agricultural extension adviser to the project, states that credit distribution was highly unequal and basically favored those with large farms (1978a, 1978b, 1978c, 1979). In particular, medium-term credit for the purchase of machinery and construction had gone to a very small proportion of farmers (3 percent).

As for short-term credit, his analysis of Çorum province reveals that small holders had little access to credit, although their proportion of shor-term credit acquisition was higher than that of the medium-term. However, the raising of short-term credit limits in July 1978 further increased the gap between large and small farmers in terms of their access to credit, since land titles were required as a guarantee. Grammelspacher (1978b) found that due to red tape, farmers who owned less than ten decares completely lost their access to credit; moreover, the proportion of credit borrowers among the owners of fifty or less decares of land was even lower. In his analysis of credit implementation in Çankırı (1978c), he also concluded that credit distribution favored large farmers.

It seems that the Agricultural Bank's credit regulations worked against the project's aims, since they presented difficulties for landless and small farmers. Also, the provision to farmers of agricultural inputs like fertilizers, seeds, and so on, by the Agricultural Bank encountered great difficulties during most of the project years. Owing to the economic difficulties and foreign currency shortages of Turkey in the late 1970s and early 1980s, the import and distribution of good seeds and chemicals was highly erratic and led to corruption and black marketing (Nott, 1983:232-233). Coupled with shortages and high prices of petroleum, the unavailability of good seeds and fertilizer in sufficient quantities seriously affected the productivity of farms.

The amount of credit given to farmers increased from 32,251 Turkish liras in 1977 to 4,758,361 liras in 1985, while the number of credit-receiving farmers increased from 3,938 to 74,278 between the same years (State Planning Organization, 1986:100). It is interesting to note that a sum of 3,977,825 Turkish liras was overdue, with legal action involving 31,316 farmers (42.2 percent of all borrowers). While in the first years of the credit program, farmers were able to repay their credit in time, in a few years the project farmers were highly indebted and not only unable to repay their debts to the bank, but even in danger of losing their land and machinery. Unfortunately, no information exists on how the distribution of credit occurred, on the relationship between size of holding and amount of credit, or on the relationship between size of holding and indebtedness. In almost all the published and unpublished reports concerning the Çorum-Çankırı project, facts are in aggregate figures without much indication as to their social context (State Planning Organization, 1986). These reports show production increase as the benefit received by the farmers without specifying how this benefit was distributed.

However, Grammelspacher's work indicates that the stated aims of the project could not be achieved by technocratically defined means. There is not much correspondence between the stated aims and the means used to achieve these aims. A general increase in production does not mean the alleviation of poverty, nor does it mean that poorer farmers will benefit from the project on a par with richer farmers. Taking Grammelspacher's arguments as criteria, one could easily argue that the Çorum-Çankırı project has failed to achieve its basic aim of helping the rural poor.

As for the productivity increase, nothing dramatic has happened. A simple comparison with the neighboring provinces where no Integrated Rural Development project has been implemented shows that in terms of the area of cultivation, neither Çorum nor Çankırı had a higher productivity level in the most significant four crops in 1986; in fact, both provinces exhibited productivity levels in wheat lower than the Turkish average, and lower than those of three out of the five neighboring provinces (Amasya, Ankara, and Bolu). Also, the productivity level in sugar beets in both provinces stayed well below the Turkish national average and that of the neighboring provinces. Observing the small size of productivity increases, one wonders about the significance of building sixty-three public baths in villages in Çorum and Çankırı to the alleviation of poverty and increase of production. One commentator concluded that the construction of sixty-three public baths, which are not used at all, had been a complete waste of resources (Nott, 1983).

One of the project's consequences is the increase in the number of items of agricultural machinery (State Planning Organization, 1986:44). Despite this, the increased mechanization of agriculture has actually worked against one of the aims of the project. Instead of dampening the rate of urban migration, it has reduced the number of employment opportunities in the affected areas. Migration from the area has continued more or less at the same pace. While net migration from the area was 32,134 between 1970 and 1975, the figure was 37,450 between 1975 and 1980 (State Planning Organization, 1986:75).

CONCLUSION

In conclusion, I would like to offer some theoretical observations. The predominance of small family-operated commodity producers in the Third World led some social scientists in the 1970s to explain why these producers had not disappeared or become proletarianized, as had been predicted by Marx. The answers offered varied from the inherent ability of peasant family farms to survive (Kerblay, 1971 and Shanin, 1972) to the characterization of these producers as disguised proletarians (Banaji, 1977 and Roseberry, 1989) and wage labor equivalents (Bernstein, 1977 and 1979). Whatever the term used to describe the small producers, the common belief was that they were here to stay.

Turkish social scientists also participated in these debates, bringing in empirical cases and macroanalysis to support their conclusion (Boratav, 1980; Sirman, 1988; Keyder, 1983; Aydın, 1986; and Ecevit, 1987). Their contributions reflected views developed for other parts of the world: the subordination of producers to capital, the viability and the resistance of household production, and so on. Again, the general contention was that small commodity producers characterized the Turkish countryside, and this was envisaged as a lasting feature. However, my foregoing analysis suggests that continued predominance of small producers in the Turkish countryside is a conjectural one and that the processes unleashed since the begining of the 1980s will prove to be very powerful in destroying the viability of petty commodity producers. In the wake of structural adjustment policies, social differentiation in the Turkish countryside has unprecedentedly accelerated.

However, these two seemingly contradictory processes, the entrenchment of small producers and their gradual elimination, are part and parcel of the strategies of international agencies for the Third World in general. The first process was completed in Turkey between the 1940s and the late 1970s, but the second process was not prompted until the early 1980s. The available data are insufficient to argue strongly for proletarianization, but a logical projection is that this process will further quicken if the current structural adjustment policies continue and if Turkey remains a weak partner in her relationship with the World Bank and IMF. One conclusion appears to be that the post-1980 period will mark a definite break with earlier trends. This fact necessitates further research and further evaluation of small commodity-producing household economies in order to establish a firmer basis in the search for the internal logic which ensures their resilience and survival. This new interpretation should consider the active role of the agencies of international capital in reshaping the Third World in accordance with the requirements of the new international division of labor.

REFERENCES

Akad, T. (1987). "Kırsal Kesime Devlet Müdahaleleri." *Onbirinci Tez.* No.7, pp. 142-157.

Alpar, C. (1980). *Çokuluslu Şirketler ve Ekonomik Gelişme.* Ankara: Turhan Kitapevi.

Arsevik, O. (1975). *The Agricultural Development of Turkey.* New York: Praeger.

Aydın, Z. (1986). *Underdevelopment and Rural Structures in Southeastern Turkey: The Household Economy in Gisgis and Kalhana.* London: Ithaca Press.

_____ (forthcoming). "The Çorum-Çankırı Development Project in Turkey and the World Bank." In M. Murdock and M. Horowitz, eds., *Anthropology and Development in the Middle East.* Boulder, Colo.: Westview Press.

Banaji, J. (1977). "Modes of Production in the Materialist Conception of History." *Capital and Class.* No. 3.

Berk, M. (1980). "Public Policies Affecting the Distribution of Income Among Cotton Producers in Turkey." In E. Özbudun and A. Ulusan, eds., *The Political Economy of Income Distribution in Turkey.* New York: Holmes and Meir.

Bernstein, H. (1977). "Notes on Capital and Peasantry." *Review of African Political Economy.* No. 10.

_____ (1979). "African Peasantry: A Theoretical Framework." *The Journal of Peasant Studies.* Vol. 6. No. 4.

Birdal, A. (1978). "Tarım Kooperatiflerinin Son 7 Yılı ve Özgürlük Paketi." *Bilim Sanat*. No. 78 (June).

Birtek, F., and Ç. Keyder (1975). "Agriculture and the State, an Inquiry into Agricultural Differentiation and Political Alliances: The Case of Turkey." *Journal of Peasant Societies*. Vol. 2. No. 4, pp. 446-467.

Boratav, K. (1980). *Tarımsal Yapılar ve Kapitalizm*. Ankara: Ankara Üniversitesi Siyasal Bilgiler Fakültesi.

Bulmuş, I. (1981). "Türkiye'de Tarımsal Taban Fiyat Politikası ve Etkileri." *METU Studies in Development*. Special Issue:573-641.

Chayanov, A.V. (1966). *The Theory of Peasant Economy* Homewood, Ill.: Irwin.

Chenery, H. (1974). *Redistribution with Growth*. Oxford: Oxford University Press.

Cumhuriyet (1985). June 12 and 14 .

Cumhuriyet (1989). September 11.

De Janvry, A. (1981). *The Agrarian Question and Reformism in Latin America*. Baltimore and London: The John Hopkins Press.

Ecevit, M. (1987). *Small Peasant Tobacco Production in a Blacksea Village*. Unpublished Ph.D. thesis. University of Kent.

_____ (n.d.). "A Report on the Post-1980 Adjustment Mechanisms and Strategies of Petty Commodity Producers in Gökceağaç Village." Mimeo.

Erdost, M. I. (1984). *Kapitalizm ve Tarım* . Ankara: Onur Yayınları.

_____ (1987). "Kırsal Alan: Yapısı ve Özellikleri." *Bilim Sanat*. No.78, June.

Ergüder, Ü. (1980). "Politics of Agricultural Price Policy in Turkey." In E. Özbudun and A. Ulusan, eds., *The Political Economy of Income Distribution in Turkey*. New York: Holmes and Meier.

Feder, E. (1977). "The World Bank Programme for Self Liquidation of the Third World Peasantry." *The Journal of Peasant Studies*. Vol. 6. No. 1.

_____ (1981). "The World Bank-FIRA Scheme in Action." In R. Galli, ed., *The Political Economy of Rural Development*. Albany: State University of New York Press.

Financial Times (1989). September 11.

Grammelspacher, K. Heinz (1978a). "The Implementation of Medium Term Credit in Çorum Province through the Çorum-Çankiri Rural Development Project." World Bank: Internal Project Report (October 31).

_____ (1978b). "The Implementation of Short Term Credit in Çorum Province through the Çorum-Çankiri Rural Development Project." World Bank: Internal Project Report (November 9).

_____ (1978c). "Credit Implementation in Çankiri Province through the Çorum-Çankiri Rural Development Project." World Bank: Internal Project Report (December 27).

_____ (1979). "Credit Implementation in Çorum and Çankiri Provinces through the Çorum-Çankiri Rural Development Project." World Bank: Internal Project Report (January).

Gürkan, A. Arslan, and H. Kasnakoğlu (1987). "Tarım Sektörünün Güncel Sorunları." *Bilim Sanat*. No. 78 (June).

Harris, L. (1988). "The IMF and Mechanisms of Integration." In B. Crow, ed., *Survival and Change in the Third World*. Cambridge and Oxford: Policy Press.

Hayter, T., and C. Watson (1985). *Aid: Rhetoric and Reality*. London: Pluto Press.

İkibine Doğru (1988). October 23.

Kazgan, G. (1988). *Ekonomide Dışa Açık Büyüme*. 2d ed. Istanbul: Altın Kitaplar Yayınevi.

Kerblay, B. (1971). "Chayanov and the Theory of Peasantry as a Specific Type of Economy." In T. Shanin, ed., *Peasants and Peasant Societies*. Harmondsworth: Penguin.

Keyder, Ç. (1983., "Paths of Rural Transformation in Turkey." *The Journal of Peasant Studies*. Vol. 11. No. 1, pp. 34-49.

_____ (1987). *State and Class in Turkey*. London: Verso Press.

KIKB (1983). *Village Inventory Surveys* (for 67 provinces). Ankara: KIKB Yayınları.

KIP, E. (1988). "Türkiye'de Taban Fiyatları, Destekleme Alımları ve İç Ticaret Hadleri." In Ş. Pamuk and Z. Toprak, eds., *Türkiye'de Tarımsal Yapılar (1923-2000)*. Ankara: Yurt Yayınları.

Mason, E. S., and R. E. Asher (1973). *The World Bank since Bretton Woods*. Washington: World Bank.

McNamara, R. (1968). *The Essence of Security*. New York:

_____ (1973). *Address to the Boards of Governors of the World Bank*. Washington: IBRD Publications.

Milliyet (1976). February 11.

Nott, G. A. (1983). *The Political Economy of Monitoring and Evaluation: The Case of the Çorum-Çankiri Development Project, Turkey*. Unpublished Ph.D. dissertation. University of East Anglia.

Payer, C. (1982). *The World Bank: A Critical Analysis*. New York: Monthly Review Press.

Sertel, Y. (1988). *Türkiye'de Dışa Dönük Ekonomi ve Çöküş*. Istanbul: Alan Yayıncılık.

Shanin, T. (1972). *The Awkward Class*. London: Oxford University Press.

Sirman, A. N. (1988). *Peasants and Family Farms: The Position of Households in Cotton Production in a Village of Western Turkey*. Unpublished Ph.D. dissertation. University of London.

_____ (n.d.). *Petty Commodity Production in Turkish Agriculture in the 1980s: The Case of Cotton and Wheat*. Mimeo.

State Institute of Statistics (1956). *Agricultural Census of 1950*. Ankara: SIS.

_____ (1950-1988). *Statistical Yearbook of Turkey*. Ankara: SIS.

State Planning Organization (1986). *Çorum-Çankırı Projesi*. Ankara: SPO.

Ulusan, A. (1980). "Public Policy toward Agriculture and its Redistributive Implications." In E. Özbudun and A. Ulusan, eds., *The Political Economy of Income Distribution in Turkey*. New York: Holmes and Meier.

Uras, T. Güngör (1979). *Türkiye'de Yabancı Sermaye Yatırımları*. Istanbul.

Vergopoulos, K. (1977a). "Capitalisme Difformé. Le Cas de l'Agriculture dans le Capitalisme." In S. Amin and K. Vergopoulos, eds., *La Question Paysanne et le Capitalisme*. Paris: Anthropos-Idep.

_____ (1977b). "La Productivité Social du Capital dans l'Agriculture Familiale." *L'Homme et Société*. Nos. 45-46.

_____ (1978). "Capitalism and Peasant Productivity." *The Journal of Peasant Studies*. Vol. 5. No. 4.

Williams, G. (1981). "The World Bank and the Peasant Problems." In H. Roberts and G. Williams, eds., *Rural Development in Tropical Africa*. London: Macmillan.

Wolff, P. (1987). *Stabilization Policy and Structural Adjustment in Turkey 1980-1985*. Berlin: German Development Institute.

World Bank (1975-1988). *The World Bank Annual Reports*. Washington: World Bank Publications.

_____ (1975). *Rural Development: Sector Policy Paper*. Washington: IBRD Publications.

_____ (1985). *World Development Report*. Baltimore: Johns Hopkins University Press.

Yağcı, F. (1985). "Structural Adjustment Lending: An Evaluation of Program Design." World Bank Staff Working Papers. No. 735. Washington: IBRD Publications.

Yıldırım, A. (1988). "Hesaplar Kabardı, Bacalar Tütmedi." *Cumhuriyet,* September. 11.

_____ (1989). "Sermaye Yerine Servet Birikimi." *Cumhuriyet*. September 12.

7

Trade Strategy in the 1980s

Canan Balkır

INTRODUCTION

Turkey's Stabilization Program of January 24, 1980, was designed to radically change its economic structure through the implementation of a more liberal and export-oriented policy. Turkey abandoned the model of import substitution and instead started to pursue the principles of an export oriented model of industrialization. This was intended to allow for appropriate structural change, with greater reliance on market forces and the private sector. In this changed mentality and environment, the success of the export drive became synonymous with the success of the Stabilization Program. The outward orientation of the economy through export promotion and trade liberalization resulted in the growth of exports and an improvement in the balance of payments and international creditworthiness, and these were accomplished under conditions of declining world trade.

Import liberalization helped reduce nominal tariff rates substantially, abolish quantitative restrictions, and reduce bureaucratic controls over imports. Direct control protection provided to domestic industry was partly replaced by other instruments such as import levies. The program focused on export support measures, mainly in the form of monetary subsidies, tax rebates, and exemption from certain taxes and duties. Exports grew rapidly, increasing from 2.9 billion dollars in 1980 to 11.7 billion dollars in 1988, and particularly noteworthy was the performance of industrial exports, whose share in total exports more than doubled.

The purpose of this chapter is to examine the Turkish export incentive system and to review the main export incentives and their significance in promoting exports, as well as to clarify the export sector's role in restructuring industry. The main question is whether export growth will continue in the face of declining incentives, since Turkey has modified its incentive system toward a more internationally accepted one. Ideally, the answer will be affirmative, but Turkish evidence does not suggest that the incentives, especially direct incentives, can be safely withdrawn without a decline in the volume of exports. This chapter is composed of seven sections. After the introduction, the second section presents a brief review of the export performance of Turkey in the 1980s and the internal and external factors which contributed to it. The third, fourth, and fifth sections examine the export incentive system and its modification over time. Then the sixth section discusses how manufacturing industry faced the challenge created by the change in trade and industrialization strategy. In the concluding section, I present my general assessment of Turkish trade strategy in the 1980s.

EXPORT PERFORMANCE

Turkey's export performance after 1980 was amazing, especially in the first three years, during which the annual increase in exports was 28.7 percent (1980), 61.6 percent (1981) and 22.2 percent (1982). During 1980-1987, total exports grew at an average annual rate of 22.3 percent, while industrial exports increased in current dollars at an average annual rate of 38.2 percent. The share of agriculture and livestock in total exports decreased from 57.4 percent in 1980 to 20.1 percent, while the share of industrial exports in the total increased from 36 percent in 1980 to 79.1 percent in 1987 and then decreased to 76.7 percent. When we subtract processed agricultural products, whose share is about 7.6 percent, the share of manufactured products is 69.1 percent, with the most important category being textiles and clothing (27.5 percent), followed by iron and steel (12.5 percent), metal products and machinery (3.3 percent), hides and leather (4.4 percent) and chemicals (6.3 percent). As to geographical distribution, about 42 percent of Turkey's exports goes to four countries. The Federal Republic of Germany (18.4 percent), Iraq (8.5 percent), Italy, (8.2 percent) and US (6.5 percent). The fect that certain products and countries accounting for a large portion of exports has caused problems from time to time. Nonetheless, Turkey's satisfactory export performance in comparison with other developing countries led to an increase in Turkey's share in overall exports of developing countries from 0.86 percent in 1980 to 2.27 percent in 1987 (see Table 1).

The internal factors important for this growth of exports include increased export incentives, depressed domestic demand, exchange rate policy, and the government's strong commitment to exports. For the first time, the prime minister and other ministers involved in economics led trade missions to many countries to promote Turkish exporters and Turkish contractors. Turkish contractors received large bids in the Middle East, reaching contract volumes of over twenty billion dollars by the mid-1980s.

Table 1
Turkey's Exports in Comparison with Other Developing Countries (billions US$)

	1980	1981	1982	1983	1984	1985	1986	1987
Turkey	2.91	4.72	5.73	5.71	7.14	7.95	7.45	10.19
Developing Countries[1]	335.26	343.73	329.00	336.87	368.65	364.89	370.92	444.45
Share of Turkey (%)	0.86	1.36	1.74	1.69	1.93	2.18	2.01	2.27

1. Excluding oil producers.
Source: Undersecretariat of Treasury and Foreign Trade.

External factors contributed to this performance. The Iranian revolution isolated Iran from its major suppliers. Furthermore, the Iran-Iraq war increased demand for Turkish exports by both countries due to their geographical proximity. Although the share of Middle Eastern countries and North Africa increased from 22.3 percent to 30.3 percent, the major customers of Turkish exports were still the EC countries, whose share was 47.8 percent in 1987. Awareness of the unpredictability of Middle Eastern markets led members of the private sector to revive relations with the EC. The share of the Eastern bloc decreased from 16.9 percent to 3.3 percent. The improvement of Turkish macroeconomic performance lasted until the end of 1985; the rate of inflation began to decline from its peak at the beginning of 1980s and reached a level as low as 25 percent. Starting in 1986, however, due to a number of reasons including budget deficits, expansionary monetary policy, and the price increases of the State Economic Enterprises, the rate of inflation increased, reaching 80 percent in late 1988.

As the acceleration of prices became evident, beginning with the end of 1987, a series of demand-tightening measures were taken. In spite of these measures, inflationary expectations accelerated the shift out of local currency and real assets. By late January 1988, the premium over the official rate of exchange in the parallel market had increased to about 25 percent, which caused the announcement of a package of economic measures on February 4, 1988. These measures were aimed at tightening the money supply and motivating exporters to accelerate the return of export earnings. Interest rates on lira deposits significantly increased, while interest earnings on foreign deposits were made subject to a 5 percent withholding tax, and interest paid to banks on foreign exchange reserve requirements was reduced. In order to encourage the early remittance of foreign exchange, support subsidies were granted on a graduated scale. These measures produced the expected results and the demand for Turkish lira deposits increased. Also, the spread between official and black market exchange rates was almost eliminated by April 1988.

However, at the end of September the spread once again increased considerably over the official rate, which gave rise to the measures of October 13, 1986, when the interest rates on lira deposits were deregulated. As part of the measures taken in February 1988, the government adjusted the tax rebate, and the Support and Price Stabilization Fund (SPSF) subsidy systems, to encourage faster repatriation of export earnings. As the economy moved into 1989, inflation remained high and exports declined in volume.

EXPORT INCENTIVE SYSTEM

The introduction of an extensive export incentive system definitely changed the mentality of Turkish industrialists who, for the first time, looked seriously at foreign markets. This orientation intensified as they grew aware of the preferential treatment of exports and the perception that government commitment was not transitory. The administration of these incentives was centralized within the State Planning Organization under the Directorate of Incentives and Implementation (Teşvik ve Uygulama Dairesi-TUD). The name later became Teşvik ve Uygulama Başkanlığı–TUB–in 1984.

The 1980-1983 period was the heyday of direct export incentives mainly tax rebates, preferential export credit, exchange allocation, and import permits.[1] Actually, all of these measures were present before 1980. However, the overvaluation of the Turkish lira limited their impact. The following section reviews briefly the main incentives and their significance for the expansion of exports.

Tax Rebates

One of the most extensively used export incentives has been tax rebates. The system was designed to compensate exporters for taxes levied at earlier stages of production. Although this system existed before 1980, tax rebates were raised in May 1981, and the products eligible for tax rebates were allocated into ten lists with rates varying between 20 percent (on list 1) and 0 percent (on list 9), with list 10 including specific export tax rebates. The criteria for list placement were based on the estimated amount of indirect taxes paid in the stages of production as well as the share of the domestic value added and the encouragement of the export of certain products. The decision about the shift of products from one list to another rested with the TUB and the Undersecretariat of Treasury and Foreign Trade.

Tax rebates were the crucial element of the export incentive system of the 1980s. Research indicates that manufactured exports have been positively correlated with tax rebates, and the elasticity of exports with respect to tax rebate ratios was higher than that with respect to prices (SIAR, 1987). According to the figures in Table 2, as an increasing proportion of exports was granted rebates, the share of exports receiving tax rebates in total exports increased from 24.84 percent in 1980 to 60.71 percent in 1984, and later declined to 47.84 percent in 1988. The amount of average tax rebates also rose from 8.91 percent to 22.31 percent in 1984, then declined to 8.54 percent in 1988.

The average rebate rate in 1980 was 8.91 percent, which was supposed to compensate only for the indirect taxes paid and not include a subsidy component. Thus, the difference between the average tax rebate rates in the years 1981-1988 and the tax rebate rate in 1980 is the subsidy rate (see Table 3).

TABLE 2
Export Tax Rebates (TL million and %)

Year	Total Exports (1)	Exports Receiving Rebates (2)	Amount of Rebates (3)	Rebates as % Total Exp (4 = 3/1)	Share of Exports Receiving Rebates (5 = 2/1, %)	Ave. Rebate (%)
1949-79	327,525	106,151	17,955	5.48	32.41	16.91
1980	221,498	55,031	4,905	2.21	24.84	8.91
1981	530,716	174,220	24,653	4.64	32.83	14.15
1982	967,311	412,612	86,816	9.25	44.03	21.01
1983	1,298,945	667,931	148,990	11.47	51.42	22.31
1984	2,608,332	1,583,506	329,059	12.61	60.71	20.78
1985	4,152,927	2,268,406	287,238	6.92	54.65	12.66
1986	5,012,345	2,761,536	281,960	5.62	55.09	10.20
1987	8,884,331	5,183,997	438,475	4.95	58.61	8.46
1988	16,519,248	7,902,033	674,802	4.08	47.84	8.54

Source: Calculated from figures of the Undersecreteriat of Treasury and Foreign Trade.

Table   3
Subsidy   Rates   (in   TL   billion)

Years	Tax Rebate Base	Subsidy Tax Rebates	Subsidy Rate (%)
1980	8.91	0.00	0.00
1981	8.91	5.24	9.16
1982	8.91	12.10	49.93
1983	8.91	13.40	89.50
1984	8.91	11.87	187.95
1985	8.91	3.75	85.10
1986	8.91	1.29	35.62
1987	8.91	-0.45	- 2.33
1988	8.91	-0.37	- 2.92

Source: Calculated from figures of the Undersecretariat of Treasury
 and Foreign Trade

Since the tax rebates in excess of the indirect taxes constituted the subsidy component, the subsidy rate jumped in 1982, 1983, and 1984, and then declined to negative figures in 1987 and 1988.   As for the average tax rebates and the coverage, capital goods enjoyed the highest average as well as coverage (see Table 4).   However, consumer goods enjoyed the highest tax rebate payments first, and intermediate goods afterward, as these were the two categories with highest export realization, as shown in Table 5.

Table 4
Average Tax Rebates (in TL billion)

Years	Consumer Goods	Intermediate Goods	Capital Goods
1980	9.5	6.6	14.9
1981	12.8	14.7	19.2
1982	20.9	20.5	23.2
1983	22.3	22.7	23.6
1984	20.6	22.2	18.4
1985	12.2	12.9	15.2
1986	9.8	12.9	13.1
1987	6.6	11.7	11.8

Source: Calculated from the figures of the Undersecretariat of Treasury
and Foreign Trade.

The allocation of tax rebates as a percentage of export value, however, shows that this percentage had a declining trend in the case of consumer goods and an increasing trend in the case of intermediate goods and capital goods. The figures, in Table 5 show that in all subsectors, the subsidy components were highest between 1982 and 1984, the heyday of export tax rebates.

Export Credits

Export credits until 1985 consisted of four kinds: general export credits, export credits for packing and delivery, export credits for fresh fruits and vegetables, and credits for foreign trading companies. The last two were channeled through the Export Promotion Fund.

The interest differential between the interest rate charged on short-term export credits extended by commercial banks and export discount credits was the export credit subsidy. The data in Table 6 show that the subsidy component was high between 1980 and 1983, declined between 1984 and 1986, and increased after 1987, parallel to the modifications in the export incentive system, discussed later in this chapter.

Table 5
Allocation of Tax Rebates and Subsidy Component (% of Export Value)

Years	Consumer Goods		Intermediate Goods		Capital Goods	
	Tax Rebates	Subsidy Tax Component	Rebates	Subsidy Tax Component	Rebates	Subsidy Component
1980	64.3	1.4	19.5	0.4	13.3	0.3
1981	44.7	2.1	35.9	1.7	17.3	0.8
1982	44.4	4.2	36.0	3.3	14.8	1.4
1983	50.6	5.8	31.9	3.7	10.6	1.2
1984	51.3	6.5	36.1	4.5	8.0	1.0
1985	35.7	2.5	46.3	3.2	12.6	0.8
1986	25.6	1.4	48.0	2.7	11.3	0.6
1987	33.0	1.6	36.4	1.9	19.6	1.0

Source: SPO, the Central Bank.

Table 6
Interest Charged for Short-Term Export Credits and Subsidy Component

Year	Rediscount Credits (TL billion)	Interest[1] by Commercial Banks (%)	Interest Rediscount Credits (%)	Interest Differential	Credit Subsidy[2] (TL billion)	% of Total Exports
1980	48.1	18.5	14.7	3.8	182.8	0.8
1981	113.2	27.0	20.1	6.9	781.1	1.5
1982	100.6	29.2	24.0	5.2	523.1	0.5
1983	181.6	29.0	26.5	2.5	454.0	0.5
1984	33.6	44.0	42.3	1.7	57.1	0.3
1985	7.0	60.0	52.0	8.0	56.0	0.0
1986	3.9	57.0	38.0	19.0	74.1	0.0
1987	54.6	51.0	35.0	16.0	573.6	0.0
1988	342.7					

1. Interest rates are yearly averages.
2. The subsidy is calculated as interest rate differential times export credits.
Source: Central Bank.

The share of credits extended by the Central Bank and the commercial banks was also high between 1980 and 1983, after which it declined until 1988. Central Bank export credits were always below the volume of commercial bank export credits, because commercial banks were able to hold smaller required reserves on export credits. There was also the expectation that the export firm receiving the credit would deposit the foreign exchange earnings with the financing bank.

The export credit system underwent modification in 1984. Rebates to export credits from the Interest Differential Fund were discontinued, and credits given to exports from Central Bank resources were frozen from April 1984 through November 1986. Table 7 provides data reflecting this modification.

Between January 1985 and November 1986, no specific export credit was given, and beginning with December 1986 export rediscount credit and credit against documents were used. Then after April 1988, Eximbank export credits became available. Turkey's Export-Import Bank (Eximbank) was founded by reorganizing the State Investment Bank with the objective of financing exports and imports through long-;medium-; and short-term credits, as well as providing insurance and other guarantees.

There are four general export finance facilities available through the Turkish Eximbank, namely the special Export Rediscount Credit, preshipment export credit, postshipment export credit, and wholeturnover insurance. The special Export Rediscount Credit is available to exporters with annual sales above 100 million US dollars, the main recipients being Foreign Trade Corporate Companies (FTCCs). Thus, this facility provides the working capital for these large exporters. The special Export Rediscount Credit and postshipment credits in 1988 totaled 129.3 billion TL. Intermediary banks extend preshipment export credit, while Eximbank provides the funding. As commercial banks prefer to lend money to the least risky firms, this type of credit does not go to indirect exporters or small firms. Postshipment export credits are issued by the Turkish Eximbank through intermediary banks. The purpose of this type of credit is to ease the financial difficulties encountered by exporters during the period after shipment but before payment is made. Short-term wholeturnover insurance covers 80 percent of political and commercial risks of all shipment affected within a year on credit terms of up to 180 days per shipment. The premium rate is determined according to the terms and conditions of payment, the buyer, and the country. The purpose is to encourage exporting to new markets and customers and also to find new payment methods. The system is used by small and medium-sized firms or new firms which have difficulty in gaining access otherwise to preshipment financing from commercial banks. In addition, Eximbank acts as an intermediary in implementing the Islamic Development Bank longer-term trade financing schemes available to exporters of goods under the Organization for Islamic Countries (OIC). There are also credit lines to specific countries such as Algeria.

Table 7
Export Credits (TL billion)

Year	Credits by CB (1)	Share in Exports (%)	Credits by Commercial Banks (2)	Share in Exports (%)	Total Export Credits (1)+(2)	Total Share in Exports (%)	Share of CB Credits in Total (1/(1+2))
1980	48.1	21.70	43.2	18.64	91.3	39.39	52.7
1981	113.2	21.11	93.7	17.48	206.9	38.59	54.7
1982	100.6	10.62	379.2	40.03	479.8	50.65	21.0
1983	181.6	13.74	547.2	41.41	728.8	55.15	24.9
1984	33.6	1.29	560.9	22.52	594.5	23.87	5.7
1985	7.0	0.17	716.5	17.25	723.5	17.42	1.0
1986	3.9	0.09	1690.7	33.70	1695.4	33.82	0.2
1987	54.6	0.62	2142.1	24.22	2196.7	24.84	2.5
1988	1985.6		2970.9		4956.5		

Source: Central Bank Bulletins.

Much of these export credits have leaked into nonexport-related activities. Generally, holding groups that have an export trading company taking advantage of export subsidies can do this. The trading company gets an export loan at a subsidized rate by giving guarantees to export a certain volume of products. The loan is made available to a group company which uses it to retire a local loan or meet a local financing requirement. The management of the trading company in turn seeks an individual company that is producing for export but is not utilizing export financing, and convinces this company to export its products through the trading company by offering a premium in exchange. In this way the trading company fulfills its export obligation and uses the export loan until such time that the proceeds of the exports can come to Turkey. At that time, either the loan is substituted with a local loan, or similar new arrangements are created with the same or similar companies. The process is a short-term solution if the export loan is paid back; it is a longer-term solution if similar arrangements are formulated perpetually whenever an export obligation is fulfilled.

The unequal access to credits by smaller-scale firms and new exporters was due to insufficient information, as well as the failure of financial intermediaries to develop risk evaluation techniques for firms of different sizes. Since the demand for export credits always exceeded the supply, commercial banks preferred the least risky firms in credit rationing.

To get a preferential export credit, the producers sometimes accepted very low export prices just to fulfill their export obligations. This in turn led to decreasing export prices. Thus, export credits were sometimes subsidizing importers in the importing country and not the domestic exporters. As to credit financing with respect to industry groups, capital goods industries had the highest share, while consumer goods industries had the lowest.

Foreign Exchange Allocations

Exporters are allowed to import duty-free the raw materials and packaging materials used in the production of the goods they export, the rate of subsidy depending on the amount of imports and the tariffs on the imported materials. Under Temporary Import Permits, exporters with an Export Promotion Certificate can import duty-free raw, intermediate, and packing materials in the production of exports, provided these materials are reexported within the specified time period. Exporters with Export Promotion Certificates are also allowed to retain part of their foreign exchange earnings as coverage for office and maintenance expenses incurred abroad.

The subsidy of the foreign exchange allocation system is twofold. First, there is a right to duty-free import of intermediate and raw materials used in the production of export products. Second, foreign currency has a premium over the official rate, which can be appropriated by the exporters. As the overvaluation of the Turkish lira decreased during 1980-1986 the premium declined, as indicated by the data in Table 8.

Table 8
Foreign Exchange Allocations

Year	Official Exchange Rate (TL/$)	Subsidy through Parallel Market Exchange Rate (TL/$)	Subsidy per $ Allocated (TL/$)	Foreign Exchange Allocations (TL billion)
1980	76.04	84.5	8.46	1.451
1981	111.20	124.9	13.68	4.875
1982	162.55	182.2	20.25	11.006
1983	225.46	259.1	33.64	29.348
1984	366.68	383.9	17.22	21.696
1985	521.98	536.3	14.32	26.051
1986	674.51	703.7	29.19	76.304

Source: Undersecretariat of Treasury and Foreign Trade.

Furthermore, foreign exchange distribution seems to concentrate on consumer goods and intermediate goods as shown in Table 9. This is due to higher tariffs on inputs used by capital goods industries which make the subsidy component greater in this group (World Bank, 1988).

Moreover, as Table 10 demonstrates, the foreign exchange allocated as a proportion of exports increased from 5.8 percent in 1980 to 27.2 percent in 1988, but the subsidy element declined during the period due to import liberalization, which lowered tariff rates, so the value of duty saved was much smaller.

Table 9
Distribution of Foreign Exchange Allocations (%)

Year	Consumer Goods	Intermediate Goods	Capital Goods
1980	33.2	31.4	34.3
1981	31.8	35.1	18.7
1982	26.8	50.6	20.4
1983	27.9	53.1	17.5
1984	16.7	35.5	10.4
1985	18.0	41.3	20.5
1986	22.0	33.0	8.9
1987	20.1	38.1	14.5

Source: Undersecretariat of Treasury and Foreign Trade.

Table 10
Foreign Exchange Allocations (thousands US$)

Year	FE Allocations	Exports	FE Allocations % of Exports
1980	171,518	2,910,100	5.8
1981	356,358	4,702,900	7.6
1982	543,504	5,245,900	10.4
1983	872,401	5,727,700	15.2
1984	1,259,917	7,133,600	17.7
1985	1,819,206	7,958,100	22.9
1986	2,614,041	7,456,800	35.1
1987	2,585,559	10,190,100	25.4
1988	3,058,340	11,662,071	27.2

Source: Calculated from figures of Undersecreteriat of Treasury and Foreign Trade.

Exchange Rates

Exchange rates became one of the main policy tools after 1980. Prior to 1980 a devaluation would have occurred only prior to a major foreign exchange crisis. After 1980 exchange rates continuously adjusted according to developments in related prices and in the balance of payments. Thus, the lira was not only devaluated in line with domestic inflation, but also with a margin for competitiveness, resulting in a real depreciation of around 5 percent annually. The very fast depreciation starting with the austerity measures of January 1980 devaluated the lira much faster than the rate of inflation in the early years of 1980s, but since 1985, on the average, devaluations have been slower than the rate of inflation. In periods when devaluation surpassed the rate of inflation, companies with foreign loans and foreign investments, and firms using substantial amounts of imported raw materials, felt the squeeze. In those periods some firms tried to shift out foreign currency loans into Turkish lira loans. Although the depreciation of the lira improved the competitiveness of Turkish goods abroad, the counterpart of this real depreciation has been a substantial capital loss on Turkey's external debt. In 1988, in order to slow down the impact of imported inflation on the domestic price level and the foreign debt, the Central Bank intervened in foreign exchange markets to counteract currency speculation, thereby achieving a lower rate of depreciation of the lira.

ASSESSMENT OF THE INCENTIVE SYSTEM

The total export subsidy is the sum of the subsidies granted through export tax rebates, export credits, foreign exchange allocations, foreign exchange transferred under the retention scheme, temporary import permits, exemption from corporate income tax, and the Resource Utilization and Support Fund.[2] The share of direct export subsidies in total exports was 2.2 percent in 1980, increased up to 12.6 percent in 1984, and declined afterward, although the absolute figure for the total subsidy increased. Table 11 provides the data for these observations. Besides the few exceptional years (1980-1984), the incentive followed a seasonal pattern. It was high in the first quarter of the year when exports were sluggish, and low in the last quarter of the year when exports were highest. The Central Bank's efforts to remain within the credit ceilings at the end of the year and the shortage of funds for tax rebates all affected the low level of subsidy in the last quarter of the year. As to the exchange rate policy, the depreciation of the lira tended to accelerate toward the end of the year, leading to an increase in the lira value of exports.

Table 11
Direct Export Incentives

Year	Tax Rebates (TL million)	SPSF[1] (TL million)	RUSP[2] (TL million)	Total Incentives (TL mil)	Total Incentives 1000$	Total Exports 1000$	Incentives/ Exports (%)
1980	4,905			4,905			2.2
1981	24,653			24,653			4.6
1982	86,716			86,716	539,413	5,746,000	9.4
1983	148,990			148,990	665,045	5,727,700	11.6
1984	329,060			329,060	901,905	7,133,600	12.6
1985	287,387		45,530	332,908	642,258	7,958,100	8.0
1986	281,602	8,102	146,029	435,913	651,200	7,456,800	8.7
1987	437,207	145,500	78,220	660,927	772,400	10,190,100	7.6
1988	674,802	330,347	11,546	1,016,695	717,757	11,662,071	6.2

1. Premium from Support and Price Stabilization Fund.
2. Resource Utilization and Support premium (includes freight premium).
Source: Calculated from SPO figures.

The other prominent characteristic of the Turkish export incentive system was that the subsidy component was inversely proportional to the importance of the type of the goods in total manufactured exports. Thus, it favored the exporters of capital goods over the exporters of intermediate and particularly consumer goods. The effect was very pronounced during 1980-1983 when subsidies were highest. After 1984 the subsidies declined, but the ranking between the types of goods remained unchanged. This differential treatment of goods was successful in many cases, promoting those industries with an export potential to enter into foreign markets. However, in the long run, it encouraged rent-seeking activities and distortions in the allocation system.

The export promotion system adversely affected the small exporters by giving special incentives to large exporters, especially with the introduction of the concept of Foreign Trade Corporate Companies. The eligibility criteria for the export incentive program provided in the appendix to this chapter support this view. By a decree issued in July 1980, Turkish exporters who realized an annual export volume of 15 million US dollars or more, of which at least 50 percent consisted of manufactured and processed goods, were granted the title of Exporter Corporate Companies (İhracatçı Sermaye Şirketleri). The title was later replaced by a more comprehensive one including importing, offshore and counter-trading–Foreign Trade Corporate Companies, or FTCCs (DIS. Ticaret Sermaye Şirketleri). These companies had a working capital of a maximum of 500 million TL and an export obligation of at least 30 million US dollars, of which 75 percent had to be manufactured items.

The main groups establishing FTCCs were: (1) big industrial groups (Koç, Sabancı, Çukurova, Yaşar), (2) big contracting groups (STFA, Enka, Tekfen, Doğuş), (3) Iron and steel producers (Çolakoğlu, Ekinciler, Metaş, Özdaş, Borusan), (4) textile groups (Akın, Dinçkök), and (5) general trade and industrial groups (Okan, Menteşoğlu, Sözer).

Thirteen of the FTCCs concentrated exports in textiles, nine in iron and steel, and seven in ready-made clothing. These three subsectors constituted about 67 percent of the manufactured exports of the FTCCs. The question here is to see if these companies would have realized nearly the same amount of exports without the special incentives given during the period. However, this should not lead to underestimation of the specialization in export activities gained by the FTCCs over time, as well as in import activities, mostly originating from COMECON countries.

The FTCCs enjoyed special incentives and privileges, not only in the area of exports, but also the privilege of being the sole importers from the COMECON countries (1984) and additional tax rebates for exports exceeding a set volume of exports. The FTCCs were also the sole beneficiaries of Eximbank's Special Rediscounting Credit due to its minimum eligibility requirement. A recent decision (1989) to initiate marketing premium payments of 2 percent by Eximbank was aimed to offset the loss of the tax rebate subsidy by the FTCCs.

Given all these special incentives, the FTCCs began to play a crucial role in the foreign trade of Turkey, especially in certain subsectors, as can be observed from Table 12.

The Turkish FTCCs were established after the Japanese model, but unlike their Japanese counterparst (Sogo Shosa), the Turkish FTCCs were not successful in financing small and medium-sized producers and exporters. In addition, as most of the FTCCs were not vertically integrated with the productive sectors, the profits accrued could not trickle down to the producers. Thus, the distributional aspects of the incentive system has been of serious concern.

Credit allocations to FTCCs were made separately and additional tax rebates caused these firms to prey on small export firms. The small exporters sold goods to the FTCCs, which then exported them, and split the additional tax rebate. Although both sides benefited from this transaction, the FTCCs at that time appeared as companies receiving commissions for no work and as a symbol of the government's inequity in incentive policies.

The high level of tax rebates in the incentive system also seemed to cause fictitious exports. For the so-called fictitious exports, business partners abroad transferred foreign exchange from the country of destination of the exports, although the actual transfer of goods never occurred or goods of much less value than stated in documents were exported. The transfer of foreign currency entitled the exporter to ask for tax rebates (see Table 13). Afterward, the exporter then sold the foreign currency at a premium that the exporter and partner abroad split.

The fictitious exports were estimated to be around 14 percent of total exports in 1984. According to IMF statistics, disturbing amount of Turkish exports during 1984-1987 are fictitious as demonstrated by figures in Table 14. The difference between the figures of the IMF and the export figures given by the Turkish authorities is greatest in the cases of Germany and Switzerland.

Table 12
Exports of FTCCs

Subsectors	Share of FTCCs ManufacturedExports in Total Exports (%)	Share of Subsector in Total Manufactured Exports of Turkey (%)
Chemical fertilizer	98.7	2.4
Cement	92.4	0.1
Glass, ceramics	91.1	1.8
Iron and steel	85.5	13.9
Plastics	83.8	0.9
Flour products	81.8	0.6
Paper	80.8	0.6
Vegetable oil, animal fats	74.4	1.4
Clothing	71.5	14.2
Hides, leather prod.	70.2	0.3
Textiles	69.5	25.0
Metal products	68.6	2.0
Footwear	56.0	0.2
Motor vehicles	53.4	1.2
Others	27.5	34.7
Total	58.7	100.0

Source: Calculated from figures of the Undersecreteriat of Treasury and Foreign Trade.

Table 13
Extra Tax Rebate Ratios in Exports (%)

1975-1986

Annual Export Limits ($ million)	From April 1981	From April 1984	From September 1984	From February 1986	From April 1986
2-10	6.0	4.8	3.3	3.4	3.2
10-30	12.0	9.6	6.6	6.8	6.3
30 and above	10.0*	10.0	11.0**	5.7	5.3

Annual Export Limits ($ million)	From June 1986	From August 1986	From October 1986	From December 1986
2-10	3.0	2.8	2.6	2.4
10-30	6.0	5.6	5.2	4.8
30 and above	5.0	4.7	4.4	4.0

(Table 13 continued)

1987-1988

Annual Export Limits ($ million)	From Jan. 1987	From April 1988	From May 1988	From June 1988	From July 1988
2-10	2.0	1.8	1.6	1.4	1.2
10-30	4.0	3.6	3.2	2.8	2.4
30-50	4.0	3.6	3.2	2.8	2.4
50 and more	6.0	5.4	4.6	4.2	3.6

Annual Export Limits ($ million)	From Aug. 1988	From Sept. 1988	From October 1988	From Nov. 1988	From Dec. 1988
2-10	1.0	0.8	0.6	0.4	0.2
10-30	2.0	1.6	1.2	0.8	0.4
30-50	2.0	1.6	1.2	0.8	0.4
50 and more	3.0	2.4	1.8	1.2	0.6

1. If annual exports exceed 30 million dollars, the 10% extra rebate rate would be applied to all exports starting from the beginning of the year and including all the tax rebate-related exports. The new ratios would be applied to all exports when the limits are reached.

2. A ratio of 6% was applied starting with July 27, 1985. (See *Official Gazette* no. 18824, July 27, 1985, decree no. 85/9716.)

Source: Turkish Eximbank.

Table 14
Fictitious Exports (millions US$)

Countries	1984	1985	1986	1987	Total
Germany					
IMF	794.3	899.3	1904.3	1921.4	4919.7
Turkey	1279.7	1391.0	1444.0	2183.6	6298.3
Difference	-485.4	-491.7	-139.3	-262.2	-1378.6
Italy					
IMF	492.5	419.5	467.7	662.9	2042.6
Turkey	501.2	502.2	579.8	850.6	2433.8
Luxembourg					
IMF	98.7	101.4	150.4	168.3	518.8
Turkey	190.2	161.8	195.1	318.5	865.6
Difference	-91.5	-60.4	-44.7	-150.2	-346.8
Austria					
IMF	57.0	66.9	91.3	---	215.3
Turkey	126.8	122.5	111.2	---	360.5
Difference	-69.8	-55.6	-19.9	---	-145.2
Switzerland					
IMF	53.7	73.9	117.5	123.3	368.4
Turkey	358.2	128.4	162.3	355.9	1004.8
Difference	-304.5	-54.5	-44.8	-232.6	-636.4
Netherlands					
IMF	107.9	141.9	164.9	246.0	655.3
Turkey	181.1	213.2	222.4	280.2	896.9
Difference	-73.2	-711.3	-57.5	-34.2	-241.6
Total					
IMF	1604.1	1702.9	2296.5	3116.5	8720.0
Turkey	2637.2	2519.1	2714.8	3988.8	11860.0
Diffeence	-1033.1	-816.2	-418.3	-872.3	-3139.9

Source: IMF, *Foreign Trade Statistics.*

MODIFICATION OF THE SYSTEM

The adverse effects of promoting exports with financial incentives such as overinvoicing and fictitious exports led to the modification of the system in 1984. However, this was not the sole reason for modification. Turkey's decision to join the agreement concerning the implementation of Articles 6, 16, and 23 of GATT required a revision of export incentives. The most important revision was to pledge to eliminate tax rebates to exports by the end of 1988. The rebates to exports from the Resource Utilization and Support Fund were first reduced and then dismantled in November 1986. Turkey also pledged to eliminate by 1989 the corporate income tax reduction privileges granted to firms with an export value of a minimum of 250,000 US dollars. Thus, on April 1, 1984, all rebates were lowered by 20 percent. In September 1984, a further reduction of 25 percent of the original amount took place. The coverage of the tax rebate scheme increased to about 87 percent in 1984, lessening the decrease in the tax rebate rate and leaving the subsidy almost unchanged.

During the period 1984-1986 the government attempted to reduce the reliance on direct export incentives and to place importance on real exchange rate depreciation. The decrease of exports in response to gradual reductions of direct incentives showed the sensitivity of exports to such measures: The export growth rate in 1984 was 24.5 percent, declined to 11.6 percent in 1985 and to -6.3 percnet in 1986. In 1986 the decrease in oil prices reduced the Middle Eastern countries' ability to impor,t and Turkish exports faced an unprecedented decline, while imports increased during the same period. Due to pressure from exporters and the fear that the reduction in financial incentives would affect exports adversely, a preferential export credit scheme was reinstated in November 1986. The Support and Price Stabilization Fund (SPSF) financed a new export subsidy scheme which replaced the Resource Utilization and Support Fund (RUSF) subsidy scheme. Granting different rates of subsidies to a limited number of products allowed this new scheme to be more selective.

With the difficulties associated with the export-oriented strategy, the industrialists, the political parties in opposition, and the public began to criticize the export incentives, accusing them of favoring fictitious exports. As the industrialists asked for the extension of export incentives to producers, incentives shifted to the production level. Eximbank's preferential credit scheme and the reduction in the expense of electricity, fuel oil, and coal used in export-oriented production changed the direction of incentives at the production level. However, the decline in the performance of exports since 1986 is indicative of the insufficiency of incentives at the production level. They did not compensate for the loss of financial incentives at the export stage. The change of incentives from the final stage to the production stage was the first step toward diminishing the extra incentives given to FTCCs, whose share in total exports increased 46 percent in 1986.

Although Turkey has modified the system, there are still some export incentives, such as subsidized export credits, corporate income tax exemptions and the Support Price and Stabilization Fund, which do not comply with GATT rules. The total export subsidy for 1988 is shown in Table 15.

Table 15
Export Subsidies (1988)

	Subsidies ($ million)	S/x[1] (%)
1. Corporate income tax exemption	772.2	6.65
2. Dut- free imports	467.6	4.00
3. Tax rebates	480.8	4.10
4. SPSF	223.8	1.90
5. Export credits (commercial banks)	197.0	1.70
6. Rediscount credits (Central Bank)	28.2	0.25
7. Eximbank	92.8	0.80

1. S/x = Ratio of subsidies to exports. Export value in 1988
was US$ 11,662 million.
Source: Eximbank.

EXPORT PERFORMANCE OF MANUFACTURING INDUSTRY AND COMPETITIVENESS

Turkish industry was able to met the challenge of the outward orientation of the economy following the stabilization measures. Industry grew at an average rate of 8 percent per annum during 1981-1986, a rate below plan targets but high enough to supply the domestic market and support the increase of manufactured goods. The share of manufacturing industry products in total exports rose from 35.9 percent in 1980 to 79.1 percent in 1987, and later declined to 77 percent in 1988.

Thus, the very foundations of the Turkish industry were transformed. Through state support, import-substituting industrialists became export-oriented industrialists. Export promotion favored large capital- and holding-based companies which could easily move to export. This transformation required some companies to change management, some to alter production, and some to go bankrupt. Unfortunately, no reliable statistics exist on company failures, but the names of some of the blue-chip companies that closed, went bankrupt, or sold subsidiaries or substantial assets to banks and other parties make an impressive list. On the other hand, some sectors experienced rapid growth and a good degree of comfort and prosperity. These companies were either able to foresee the basic elements of the post-1980 Turkish economy and restructured themselves accordingly, or just happened to be in sectors which enjoyed rapid growth. Some predicted that the new economic policices designed to shift the emphasis of growth and industrialization from import substitution to a major export boost would require (1) direct subsidies and exchange rate policies to support exports, (2) an accelerated devaluation of the Turkish lira, (3) liberalization of imports to make the Turkish economy a more competitive environment, (4) an increase in deposit interest rates to curb savings from shifting over to foreign currencies, and (5) an increase in loan interest.

Changes in exchange rates seemed to exert mainly the following influences on companies. First, expatriate companies felt the squeeze on their capital. Also, companies that had borrowed foreign currency had difficulty in debt servicing. Third, export companies had trouble matching sales revenues in foreign currency with domestic production costs. Moreover, companies importing raw materials had to match raw material costs quoted in foreign currency with domestic sales prices (revenues).

During the early 1980s, when devaluation far surpassed the rate of inflation, companies with foreign loans, foreign investments, and substantial amounts of imported materials had difficulties. The measures to neutralize the effect of exchange rate changes or even to use them to the companies' advantage were in many instances not understood or available in Turkey. Consequently, only a little forward purchasing or selling of foreign currency occurred informally between banks and their import or export customers. The purpose of most hedging to avoid equity erosion by companies using foreign capital was to use this imported capital to buy fixed assets. As assets seemed to appreciate faster than devaluation, a type of guarantee was provided against equity erosion.

Companies trying to restructure their loans between the lira and foreign currency based their expectations on devaluation and the availability of lira and foreign currency loans. Companies suffered substantial losses from foreign currency loans due to the acceleration of the devaluation of the lira. In those periods, companies tired to shift away from foreign currency loans to TL loans. In the last couple of years, however, local interest rates have increased to such levels that companies do not shift their loan portfolios toward foreign currency loans.

The rate of capacity utilization in manufacturing industry was low before 1980 due to a foreign currency bottleneck, an energy shortage, and disturbances in industrial relations. The solution of most of these problems increased the rate of capacity utilization up to 70-80 percent in the large establishments and around 50 percent for small establishments. Full capacity utilization in Turkish industry is considered to be 75 percent and by 1987 most of the industrial sectors that weighed heavily in exports were above this level.

However, what is alarming at this point is that Turkey's manufacturing industry was still based on the production capacity of investments realized before

1980. At a time when manufacturing needed a new capacity to improve its competitiveness, it was deprived of this because of various reasons. The diversion of loanable funds from directly productive investments to public infrastructure, import competition, the absorption of a subtantial portion of funds by the foreign trade sector, and the high domestic real interest rate all contributed to a decline in total fixed investment as a percentage of GNP, with the lowest rate being 18.1 percent in 1984. It rose to 22.3 percent of GNP in 1986 and 24.9 percent in 1987 due to the rise in public infrastructure investments.

The total investment in manufacturing fell from 4.8 percent of GNP in 1983 to 3.7 percent in 1987. This decline affected productivity negatively by retarding the growth of capital stock and the incorporation of new technologies. The rate of capacity utilization also fell at the end of 1988 because of stagnant domestic demand and financial difficulties concerning working capital. The shifting composition of investments is also disconcerting in line with the spirit of the program. The share of manufacturing in public investments declined steadily from 18.6 percent in 1983 to 6.5 percent in 1987, but there was no compensatory increase in private investment.

The decline in private investment in manufacturing has been at the expense of investment in housing. P. Conway (1988) states that during the 1980s, the financial liberalization and the increase in public investment both encouraged private investment while nominal depreciation discouraged it. As housing investments were relatively less susceptible to these factors, they acted as a "safe haven" for private investors in uncertain times (Conway, 1988). As to the sector orientation in investments and exports, investment in recent years in electrical machinery, electronics and transport equipment was stimulated not by export demand but by domestic demand. Although business circles cite insufficient domestic demand as a rationale for postponing investment, in reality investment was weakest in sectors with high international demand. The export boom was not successful in creating an investment climate in export industries, and there was no significant structural change in the manufacturing sector favoring export orientation.

The relative profitability of exports over the domestic market was questionable during the 1980s. The export incentives plus the tariff revisions in 1984 reducing nominal protection raised the profitability of production for exports over the domestic market (Togan et al., 1987). The World Bank estimated ratio of the effective exchange rate for exports to imports (EERx/EERm) as 0.79 for 1987. This indicated that in spite of the incentive system, there was still a bias toward production for the domestic market.[3] This level of protection enabled the continuation of high profits in the domestic market in 1986; the average profit ratio for 100 large firms in Turkey was 5.96 percent while for FTCCs the ratio was only 0.82 percent.

The high level of protection and the lack of regulation concerning competition in the domestic market affected the sectoral distribution of foreign capital invested in Turkey. A comparison of the respective shares of foreign investment in 1983 and 1988 shows that the expectation of an increase in foreign investment in export-oriented industries was not fulfilled and that foreign firms were reluctant to invest in these branches. The share of foreign investment in manufacturing declined from 67.9 percent (1983) to 53.4 percent (1988).

The subsectoral breakdown in the manufacturing sector shows that foreign investors prefer import-substituting industries which have a monopolistic tendency in the domestic market. Thus, foreign firms did not make any significant contribution to the diversification of exports. Foreign investors were more interested in services, especially tourism and banking, with high profits. Out of 1,050 foreign firms in 1986, 686 were in the services sector. Not only the sectoral distribution of foreign investment was disappointing, but also the actual inflow of foreign capital, even though the basic orientation of the 1980 Program implied that international capital flows would have a greater say in Turkey's economy. For this purpose, various decrees and directives were issued in order to clarify and simplify procedures and provide additional incentives to foreign capital. The Free Trade Zone (Law 3226, passed on June 28, 1985) and the establishment of a Foreign Capital Department within the framework of the prime minister's office are examples of this.

Therefore, export orientation was not successful in encouraging the investments in industries in which Turkey enjoys an international comparative advantage. Oktar Türel, with the use of revealed comparative advantage as an indicator, concludes in chapter 4 of this volume that Turkish trade orientation has not changed much in quantitative terms, but that specialization in some subsectors has taken place, which has led Turkey to focus on nondurable consumer goods in a few relatively unsophisticated intermediates which have a bias for using natural resources as inputs. This conclusion is backed by other studies related to the competitive power of industrial products (SIAR, 1987 and Togan et al., 1987). However, the representation of true competitiveness by these studies is questionable since incentives have helped the exports of most of these products.

The competitiveness of Turkish industry would have really been challenged by import liberalization, had it not been for the import levies. In other words, the protection provided to domestic industry by direct controls has been replaced by another instrument, import levies. The import levies not only provided protection from competition abroad, but also modified the composition of imports. The frequent alterations of levies responded to pressure from import-competing firms, as when tariffs were lowered.

In restructuring the nominal tariffs, the final products of natural resource-based sectors enjoying a high comparative advantage were assigned low tariff rates. However, the effects of nominal tariffs on inputs with respect to effective protection rates on final products has been ignored. There were various exemptions from import taxes and levies; for example, imports under investment promotion certificates were free of taxes and levies. The elimination of quotas in 1981 precipitated structural changes in 1983 and 1984. Furthermore, the replacement of quantitative restrictions (QRs) by taxes was the most important step in import liberalization. The number of items subject to QRs was cut from 450 to 33 as shown in Table 16. Given the large reduction of QRs, further increases in levies cannot be justified on the grounds that they are replacing QRs. This will also affect the competitiveness of import-competing firms.

In January 1988 a series of measures were taken. A ceiling of 50 percent was set on all statutory tariffs and large tariff, cuts on imports of raw materials were implemented. Despite all of these measures, nominal protection remained very high and rose between 1985 and 1987 (World Bank, 1989). The nominal protection rate (combined tariff and levies) decreased from 57.0 percent (1987) to 38.4 percent (1988); the greatest decline was in consumer goods, the lowest in capital goods. Levies are highest in the case of consumer goods.

Table 16
Quantitative Restrictions (QRs)

	1980	1981	1982	1983	
Liberation list #1	71	935	959	972	
Liberation list #2	870	813	798	821	
Quota list	330				
	1984	1985	1986	1987	1988
Imports under permission	450	520	111	111	33
Items whose import					
not permitted	224	127	4	4	4

Source: SPO.

The nominal protection rate across subsectors in 1986 was 64 percent in consumer goods, 17.1 percent in intermediate goods, and 46 percent in capital goods. The most astonishing figures are 82.5 percent for textile and leather, 43.9 percent in food, beverages and tobacco, and 43.6 percent for wood products, with all three being regarded as the subsectors with highest comparative advantage. The low level of protection provided to agriculture (22.0 percent in 1988) is in line with the philosophy of the 1980s.

CONCLUSION

The increase in exports constituted the basis of the claim that the Turkish experiment has been one of the successful cases of stablization programs. This chapter has attempted to review the growth of exports and the factors contributing to this growth, mainly the export incentive system. Tax rebates, preferential export credits, foreign exchange allocations, and the exchange rate system were reviewed in detail, as they constituted the main incentives duing the 1980s.

As discussed above, the export drive heavily correlated with the incentive system, and especially with direct incentives. These export-specific measures gave a strong initial boost to exports, but were not likely to achieve sustained growth without fundamental restructuring of the productive sectors. Also, with the decline of the direct incentives, export growth decreased substantially. The depreciation of the real exchange rate was the main incentive after the decline of tax rebate rates, but the intention to reduce inflation and debt burden after 1986 indicated the limits of depreciation.

Rapid export growth has occurred primarily by exporting the available stock of idle capacity rather than by additional investment in export industries. Although the increased investment in manufacturing is necessary for further export growth, the flow of funds has been diverted away from manufacturing into sectors such as construction, tourism, and other subsectors of service industries. The structure of foreign trade toward the end of the 1980s indicates that Turkey is specializing in sectors with lower skills and technology intensity, although the expectation was that it would move into more capital-oriented branches reflecting a higher stage in comparative advantage. Türel, in his contribution to this volume, states that "the relative share of engineering industries in total gross output has not significantly increased over the last eleven years." Thus, Turkey is entering the 1990s with a weaker base for engineering industries in contrast to the experience of large, semi-industrialized middle-income LDCs.

Since Turkey continued to specialize in sectors which are labor-intensive and less technology-intensive, the decline in real wages in manufacturing was a prerequisite for the competitiveness of export-oriented industry. As export industries were heavily based on agricultural inputs, which make up about 45 percent of exported manufactures, the deterioration of the domestic terms of trade against agriculture suited the objectives of the program. Therefore, the social cost of the Stabilization Program was a significant transfer of income toward exporters, large export-oriented firms, and financial intermediaries. Small firms oriented toward the internal market, wage earners, and agricultural income earners were the losers.

The export receipts accrued to social classes who invested them in speculative areas. Thus, they did not contribute to a higher propensity to save and to invest in productive areas. These classes also had the tendency to consume imported goods, which import liberalization promoted. As a result, their spending affected the economy of the exporting country rather than the Turkish economy.

The expansion of the export sector absorbed most of the available resources, such as domestic and external finance, qualified labor, and entrepreneurial capacity, depriving the rest of the economy of these qualities. The real devaluations and the increase in real interest rates also contributed to the decrease of investment in other economic sectors. Paradoxically, although everything favored exporters in the final stage, production for the domestic market was still profitable, especially if the producing firm had a monopoly in the market.

Trade policy adjustments in 1988 are estimated to have reduced the bias against production for exports. In the coming years, Turkey's trade policy will center on domestic demand management, with import liberalization policy lowering protection on imported goods favored in the domestic market and diverting investment into exportable goods. As a result exports are expected to reach 22.477 million US dollars by 1994, with 90.5 percent of this being industrial products.

The major outlet in the 1980s for Turkey's export products was the European Community, which raised hopes about her potential performance under the Community rules. The likely adverse effect of the second and third enlargement of the Community on Turkish exports contributed to Turkey's application for full membership on April 14, 1987. The success of Turkey's commitment to full membership will be decided by her abililiy to adapt her agricultural and industrial structure to that of the EC.

Within a decade, Turkey has covered a considerable distance in various fields, shifting from a quota system to an almost fully liberalized import regime, from very strict foreign exchange control mechanisms to almost complete freedom in foreign transactions. Despite this substantial progress, Turkey has much to accomplish in the coming years to improve her foreign trade policy. The first step may be the reduction of the uncertainty of the exporter with respect to the timing of changes in foreign trade strategy. Moreover, the quantitative effects of the changes vis-à-vis the whole economy must be carefully analyzed before any public announcements.

Since Turkey cannot favor direct export incentives anymore, the delay in the receipt of payments through the internationally more acceptable incentive system must be eliminated, since such delays reduce the subsidy rate due to the inflationary environment. The new incentive mechanism must promote backward linkages in the economy so that the export value added at each stage of production can be examined, and so that incentives can be passed to output- and/or input-supplying indirect exporters also. Such a policy will depend not only on what is economically feasible but also on what is socially desirable.

NOTES

1. The incentive measures for exports can be listed as follows: tax rebates on exports, payments from the Export Subsidy and Price Stabilization Fund, low-cost export rediscount credit, exemption from taxes, duties, and fees, advance payment of tax rebate on exports, exemption from the value added tax (VAT) on exports, exemption from corporate and income tax, incentive to freight, exemption of imports from customs duty, retention and utilization abroad of the foreign exchange earned from exports, allocation of global amounts of exchange for imports, importation of goods and packing materials under the temporary admission regime, designation of sales and deliveries as exports benefiting from the incentives, and Eximbank pre- and postshipment credits.

2. There are a number of minor subsidies such as the following: (1) Exporters of over 1 million US dollars per year may deduct 20 percent of their export earnings from their taxable profits if they are manufacturers and 5 percent if they are traders. In the case of exports of fresh fruit and vegetables and cut flowers, exporters of over 250,000 US dollars per year may benefit from a 20 percent deduction from taxable profits. For foreign exchange proceeds from freight, all export earnings are tax deductible. (2) Firms which guarantee to export a certain percentage of their production are exempted from taxes, duties, and charges on the TL credits that they use. (3) Since April 1986, freight subsidies are given, ranging from three dollars per ton for Africa to twelve dollars per ton for West Coast America and the Far East. These are the rates for Turkish flag vessels. Half rates apply to foreign flags.

3. The term *EERx* is defined as the TL equivalent of a dollar's worth of exports, taking into account export subsidies, input subsidies related to exports and other financial and tax measures that affect the price of exports. The term *EERm* is defined as the TL equivalent that would be paid for a dollar's worth of imports, taking into account tariffs, levies, interest on advance deposits, and other measures that affect the price of imports.

APPENDIX

ELIGIBILITY CRITERIA	EXPORT INCENTIVE PROGRAMS	RESTRICTIONS
EXPORT VOLUME BASED	Eximbank special rediscounting credit	Firm's previous twelve months' exports exceed 100 m dollars.
	Central Bank L/C and C/D credits	Firm's previous three years' exports > $5 m and > $10 m each year.
	Eximbank post-shipment credit	FOB value of export shipment > $25,000.
	Corporate income tax	Firm's export > $250,000 .
	Export tax rebate system[1]	Rates vary according to export value. 6 percent for firms with annual exports > $50 m.
	Advance tax rebate payments	Firm's annual exports exceed $12 m.
PRODUCT BASED	Eximbank preshipment /postshipment credits	Industrial products[2].
	SPSF fund subsidy	Selected products, different rates of subsidies by product, import content of exports > 40 percent.
	Corporate income tax concession	Low minimum export requirement for fresh fruits and vegetables.
	Freight Incentives	Textile products to distant places; to bc transported by the Turkish Airlines.

1. Abolished.
2. Specifically excluded (U = Unprocessed, P = Processed): U agricultural products, U/P cotton, U/P tobacco, U animal products, U marine products, U forestry products, U mineral products.

Source: P. Lazonde and H. Kozanoğlu, "A Review of Turkish Eximbank's Export Credit Strategies," mimeo.

REFERENCES

Balkır, C. (1988). "Structural Adjustment of Turkish Agriculture and Industry in the Light of Turkey's Accession to the EC." *The Political Economy of Turkey in the 1980s.* Harvard University Conference. Cambridge, Mass.: Harvard University Press.

Baysan, T., and C. Blitzer (1988). "Turkey's Trade Liberalization in the 1980s and Prospects for Its Sustainability." Mimeo.

Central Bank (selected years). *Bulletins.* Ankara: Central Bank Publications.

Conway, P. (1988). "The Record on Private Investment in Turkey. " *The Political Economy of Turkey in the 1980s.* Harvard University Conference. Cambridge, Mass.: Harvard University Press.

Ersel H., and A. Temel (1984). "Türkiye'nin Dışsatım Başarısının Değerlendirmesi." *Toplum ve Bilim,* No. 27.

Ibrahimhakkıoğlu, N. (1986). *Planlı Dönemde İhracatı Teşvik Politikası.* Ankara: IGEME Yayını.

Lasonde, P., and H. Kozanoğlu (1989). "A Review of Turkish Eximbank's Export Credit Strategies." mimeo.

Milanovic, B. (1985). "Export Incentives and Turkish Manufactured Exports, 1980-1984." World Bank Staff Paper. Washington, DC: World Bank.

NCM Associates Ltd (1989). "Some Practical Measures Used by Turkish Businesses to Manage Under High Interest, Inflation and Devaluation of the Turkish Lira." Special project report.

SIAR (1987). "Prospects for Turkey's Accession to the Community." mimeo.

Togan, S., H. Olgun, and H. Akder (1987). *Report on Development in External Economic Relations of Turkey.* Istanbul: Turktrade.

World Bank (1989). *Country Report: Turkey 1988.* Washington: World Bank Publications.

_____ (1988). *Turkey: Country Economic Memorandum Towards Sustainable Growth.* Washington: World Bank Publications.

8

Turkish Foreign Policy toward the Middle East

Birol A. Yeşilada

INTRODUCTION

Despite the crucial and pioneering works of Frank Tachau (1984), Dankwart Rustow (1987), and Philip Robins (1991), there has been a serious lack of academic research on Turkey's important role in Middle Eastern affairs. In the light of its geographical location, sizable population, economic reforms in the 1980s, and membership in NATO, this observation may seem unrealistic. Nevertheless, works on Turkey from an international studies perspective place scholars of Turkish studies at a disadvantage. Their works focus primarily on Turkey's relations to its Western neighbors on the basis of specific issues, for example, Cyprus, the European Community, and the United States. Turkey's relations with the Middle East, in a broader perspective, are ignored. As Philip Robins noted (1991:1):

Even in Turkey itself the subject is largely neglected, partly because resources are not available within the country and partly because there is little interest among Turkish academics. Both reasons are indicative of the Kemalist view of Turkey's foreign policy priorities, and the values of the Kemalist cadres inside the republic. And both go some way to explaining the lack of understanding which Turkey periodically displays for its Middle Eastern neighbors, and the policy problems which result.

Recent developments in the Middle East and Central Asia will undoubtedly lead academics and officials alike both in Turkey and abroad to a major reconsideration of this subject. Furthermore, the growing significance of Turkey in the Middle East is a product of developments occurring over the last few decades. Over the last thirty years, Turkish foreign policy toward the Middle East has changed singnificantly. What began as unquestioned support of US interests in the region in the 1950s became a cautious foreign policy in the 1960s and 1970s. In effect, various events persuaded Turkish officials to distance Turkey's interests in the region, as much as possible, from those of the US and NATO, and to relate better with their southern neighbors. In this regard, the efforts of Turkish leaders to gain acceptance as a friend of the Arab world was a calculated strategy aimed at understanding their country's heritage and security needs in the region (Sezer, 1984:78-79).

These attempts were crucial due to the previous pro-Greek Arab stance during the Cyprus crisis of 1963. As Duygu Sezer (1984:78) and George Lenczowski (1980:160-166) explain, the Arab advocacy of the Greek position was a reaction to Turkey's support of US foreign policy in the Middle East during 1949-1963. However, Turkish officials did not decide to strengthen their ties to the Arab world simply because of Arab support for the Greeks. The United States punishment of Turkey for its intervention in the Cyprus crisis also influenced their decision. First, on June 4, 1964, President Johnson issued a warning to Turkey's Prime Minister Ismet Inönü not to invade Cyprus and not to expect American assistance in case of Soviet aggression against Turkey. And second, following Turkey's intervention in Cyprus to prevent Greek annexation of the island in June 1974, Congress imposed an arms embargo on Turkey that lasted until August 1, 1978. Therefore, the Turkish leaders became convinced that they needed to distinguish their country's interests in the Middle East independently from those of the US in order to mend their country's relations with the Arab states. Another factor playing a crucial role in this Turkish-Arab rapprochement was Islamic ideology. This influence in political policies began following the International Sharia Congress in Pakistan in 1976 (Yeşilada, 1988a). As explained later, this congress, funded by the Saudi Arabian institution *Rabıtat al-Alam al-İslami* (the World Muslim League), passed crucial decisions that called for increased interaction among the Muslim countries.

However, despite the lessons of the previous two decades, the leaders of the September coup in 1980 and the subsequent civilian governments pursued a dual strategy in outlining Turkey's foreign policy toward the Middle East that did not significantly oppose US interests in the region. First, due to their desperate need for American approval of the military government (known as the National Security Council [NSC]), the generals gave high priority to US strategic demands in the Middle East. And second, Turkey's domestic economic requirements further pushed the NSC toward increasing the country's ties with the Islamic world in a manner closely reflecting the *Rabıtat* decisions of 1976. In a move supporting this second factor, but contradicting the previous concern with US interests, the Turks also reduced their diplomatic relations with the state of Israel. Considering these crucial developments, this chapter examines the domestic and external factors that are responsible for Turkey's foreign policy objectives in the Middle East during the 1980s.

MODELS OF FOREIGN POLICY MAKING

As T. B. Millar (Rosenau, 1969:58) explains, there are "no immutable or absolute factors in foreign policy." The most significant determinants of foreign policy are still those contained in daily diplomatic contacts and national decision-making circles. Therefore, it is difficult to theorize about foreign policy in general terms. To find the basis for the foreign policy of a country it is essential to ascertain why and how decisions are actually made. This entails examining the thinking of the decision makers, their images of the world and their own environment, and how they consider certain factors.

These analytic difficulties are also reflected in the attempts of James Rosenau (1966, 1976, 1980, and 1984) to develop a pre-theory for the analysis of foreign policy. According to Rosenau (1980), "there can be no real flourishing of theory until the materials of the field are processed, i.e., rendered comparable, through the use of pre-theories of foreign policy." In order to accomplish this task, Rosenau developed a pre-theory based on five sets of independent and explanatory variables: (1) the individual factor, relating to all those aspects of the decision maker that distinguish his policy choices or behavior from those of other decision makers; (2) the role factors, the external behavior of officials that is generated by the roles they occupy; (3) the governmental factors that enhance or limit the foreign policy choices made by the decision makers; (4) the societal factors; and (5) the systemic factors. As Bahgat Korany (1986:44) explains, Rosenau exceeded this list of factors and tried to establish the "relative potencies" of each independent variable according to some specific classificatory criteria: size (large or small country), state of the economy (developed or underdeveloped), type of political system (open or closed), extent of penetration or non-penetration of, and issue area (status, territorial, human and nonhuman resources).

The above attempts of Rosenau led to other works on foreign policy theory building (Brecher, 1972, 1974, 1979; Azar and Sloan, 1975; Burgress and Lawton, 1972; and Munton, 1978). Among these, Brecher's has been the most comprehensive in listing explanatory variables, within the context of individual-psychological factors, that influence decision making. Many scholars regard this approach as one of the most successful endeavors in explaining foreign policy processes.

Over the last two decades, the analysis of foreign policy-making through different decision-making models has helped define the nature of and identify the factors responsible for decision making processes. These models generally fall into four categories: the rational choice model, the bounded rationality approach, the bureaucratic-organizational model, and game theory. However, despite the initial enthusiasm over these models and their explanatory powers, this approach has not succeeded in developing a scientific theory of foreign policy decision making. Extensive research in foreign policy decision making and crisis bargaining situations by Robert Axelrod (1976), Robert Jervis (1976), John Steinbrunner (1974), and Glenn Snyder and Paul Diesing (1977) demonstrated that a combination of two models, bounded rationality and game theory, was a more appropriate approach to the analysis of foreign policy decision making. The bounded rationality model explains the individual-specific factors that include perceptions, motivations, images, beliefs, attitudes, personality traits, and cognitive attributes. These factors determine how decision makers evaluate information and choose policy from a set of alternatives. Game theory, on the other hand, explains how decision makers select strategies in crisis bargaining situations.

However, there are additional elements in the study of foreign policy decision making. The techniques and practices of decision making in democratic systems differ significantly from those of authoritarian regimes (Gharaybeh, 1987:18-19). Decision making in democratic systems is more complicated due to the sharing of decision-making powers between the executive and legislative branches of the government. Parliamentary consent in these systems is highly advisable, because the legislature often has the ability to overrule the executive branch. In contrast, authoritarian regimes make foreign policy decisions with less difficulty. The concentration of decision making powers in the hands of one person or a few individuals characterizes the operational milieu of authoritarian regimes. Thus, in accordance with the role, governmental, and systemic variables of Rosenau, decision makers in authoritarian regimes enjoy more freedom in making policy decisions than elected officials of democratic governments. This last factor particularly applies to the post-1980 governments of Turkey. The NSC certainly practiced authoritarian rule during its reign of three years. The new constitution adopted during this period presented the state as an "iron fist in a velvet glove," with extensive powers given to government officials and numerous restrictions imposed on individuals' civil and political rights (Yeşilada, 1988b). The civilian administrations of Turgut Özal that followed the NSC continued to govern the country through highly authoritarian practices. Therefore, two individuals played key roles in shaping the country's foreign policy profile during these times: General Kenan Evren and Turgut Özal.

Despite the great freedom authoritarian decision makers enjoy in making foreign policy, they are still very human. Not only are they affected by domestic and foreign pressures, they are also influenced by their own belief systems. Their decisions are reflections or embodiments of both personal and environmental factors. In line with the views of Snyder, Bruck, and Sapin (1962) and others discussed above, these two categories of factors will be referred to in this chapter as the microsetting and macrosetting of decision making respectively. They comprise the independent variables shaping or affecting the foreign policy of Turkey.

The microsetting refers to the human dimension of foreign policy. It includes personality and role variables. The personality variable basically involves childhood experiences, social background, and the education and religion and/or ideology of the decision maker. Such attributes distinguish the individual's behavior from those of other decision makers. Role variables, on the other hand, pertain to the external behavior of leaders generated by the position they occupy and likely to occur regardless of the personal characteristics of decision makers.

The second set of independent variables, the macrosetting, refers to the environmental and circumstantial factors confronting the decision maker. These determinants come from the domestic and external environment. The domestic variables include the social structure, national character, level of economic development, and the degree of political institutionalization. The external variables, on the other hand, contain all policies and/or actions occurring outside a country's national borders that shape or otherwise affect the choice of its decision makers. A simple model combining the micro- and macrosettings of foreign policy is given in Figure 1.

Figure 1
Factors Affecting Foreign Policy

Source: Adopted from works by Gharaybeh (1987), Rosenau (1966, 1976, 1980), Brecher (1979), and Snyder, Bruck, and Sapin (1962).

AN EVALUATION OF TURKEY'S FOREIGN POLICY TOWARD THE MIDDLE EAST

As explained in the introduction, the leaders of the military regime of 1980–1983 and the subsequent civilian governments decided to follow a dual strategy in Turkey's foreign policy toward the Middle East in the 1980s. On the one hand, Turkish-American relations entered a new period of closeness during which US concerns crucially influenced the foreign policy profile of Turkey. On the other hand, Turkey's domestic economic needs further pushed the NSC and the governments of Turgut Özal toward increasing Turkey's connections with the Islamic world in consonance with the *Rabıtat* agreements of 1976. Thus, the Turkish lessening of diplomatic ties to Israel is not surprising. This last development indicated the lack of confidence Turkish leaders had in US policies toward the region. Moreover, Turkish officials wanted to keep some distance between themselves and the Americans regarding the Arab-Israeli problem (Karaosmanoğlu, 1983:169). In the meantime, however, Turkey's rapprochement with the Arab world was anything but harmonious. While relations with Iraq, Saudi Arabia, Egypt, and other North African and Gulf states improved during the 1980s, the same cannot be said about relations with Syria. Today, Syria still provides a safe haven for the Kurdish separatists who carry out guerrilla attacks deep inside Turkey (Yeşilada, 1990). Furthermore, Syria sells SAM antiaircraft missiles to Greek Cypriots (*Cumhuriyet,* May 3, 1990). While the Kurds initiated these attacks into Turkey from Iraq, the Turkish and Iraqi officials reached an agreement that permitted the Turkish military to pursue these terrorists inside Iraq. Since the Gulf crisis, however, this option is no longer available. Finally, Turkey's relations with Iran were also turbulent. During the 1980s, partly because of the Iran-Iraq war, Turkey's trade with this country improved dramatically. Yet, at the same time, the Iranians continued to condemn the secular Turkish republic and supported the fundamentalists' efforts in this country. Within this complex framework, two important individuals, General Kenan Evren and Turgut Özal, helped determine Turkey's foreign policy toward the region. This chaapter's analysis of the overall picture must first look at the microsetting and then examine the macrosetting of foreign policy making.

Microsetting: Personal and Role Variables

Following the 1980 coup, foreign policy making became highly personalized under the authoritarian government of General Kenan Evren, who later became the civilian president of the country. Kenan Evren viewed himself as the "Second Atatürk," this feeling often being reinforced by those around him (Ludington and Spain, 1983:159-163). Thus, given his personal view of himself as the second savior of Turkey, coupled with the rigid authoritarian rule of the NSC, General Evren quickly moved to construct the country's foreign policy objectives. Under these circumstances, no one could challenge Evren's policy decisions. Accordingly, the Evren regime decided to strengthen Turkey's ties to the West while at the same time improving the country's relations with its Muslim neighbors.

Evren's attitude towards the US and Islamic countries was influenced by the support of these states for his regime. First, the US was the only major NATO ally not critical of the NSC's political decisions. While the European allies of Turkey criticized the NSC's violation of democratic norms, the US viewed the following changes as necessary for stabilizing the democratic system: the replacement of the country's constitution with a more authoritarian document restricting individual civil and political rights, the abolition of all political parties, and the establishment of a state corporatist political system. Thus, in order to secure continued American support for the NSC and assistance for military modernization and economic development, General Evren and his aides decided to provide the US with added military facilities in eastern Turkey.

While US assistance was needed, the economic difficulties of Turkey provided the basis for improved relations with the Arab world, resulting in an influx of Saudi Arabian and other oil-rich Arab states' capital into the country. Furthermore, the election of Kenan Evren as the chairman of the Islamic Standing Committee for Economic and Commercial Cooperation (ISEDAK in Turkish acronym) necessitated closer financial and political relations with these Muslim countries.

The ISEDAK was established under the auspices of the Islamic Conference during the Third Islamic Summit Conference in 1981 as part of three such committees that would undertake specific steps to realize the original goals specified in the Sharia Congress of 1976. The three committees were (1) the Permanent Committee for Scientific and Technological Cooperation, (2) the Permanent Committee for Cultural and Informational Cooperation, and (3) the ISEDAK. Furthermore, three national presidents became permanent directors of these committees. The late President Zia Ul Hak of Pakistan became the director of the Permanent Committee for Cultural and Scientific Cooperation. The president of Senegal, Abdu Diuf, was elected as the director of the Permanent Committee for Cultural and Informational Cooperation. And at the Fourth Islamic Summit Conference, the then President Kenan Evren of Turkey became the director of ISEDAK (Yakış, 1987:77). Furthermore, conference participants agreed that the directorship of these committees will remain with these three countries. In accordance with this agreement, Turgut Özal replaced Kenan Evren as director of ISEDAK upon becoming the president of Turkey in November 1989 (Yeşilada, 1989).

The election of Evren to this post was important for several reasons. His official ties in this all-Muslim organization provoked two interesting questions concerning Turkey's political future. First, how could a secular state like Turkey maintain a membership in a nonsecular political network without endangering her own political order? And second, was Evren's willingness to participate in this all-Muslim organization an indication of Turkish officials' desire to change secularism in Turkey? Notably, prior to this time, Turkish leaders including even the right-wing prime ministers, the late Adnan Menderes and Süleyman Demirel, were cautious in their dealings with the fundamentalist Arab states.

In an interview with the Turkish daily *Milliyet* (April 30-May 1, 1990), Evren stated that he had good intentions in establishing such ties with the Arab states because these countries provided much needed financial assistance to Turkey. He also explained that he did not foresee any danger in such a relationship. This last point is quite remarkable, since Saudi Arabia continuously denounced the secular Turkish republic and its founder Atatürk (as an enemy of Islam) in its radio programs broadcast in Turkish. From the perspective of Figure 1, it is important to note that a strong general had a definite worldview about Turkey's position in the Muslim world with improved ties with the US. As explained in the next section, the macrosetting reinforced Evren's conceptions, just as it did for his successor Özal, and dramatically shaped the country's foreign policy. Such personalized decision making, in which the National Assembly and the political opposition had virtually no influence on the foreign policy profile of the state, continued to characterize Turkish foreign policy making following the transition to civilian rule in November 1983.

From the election victory of the Motherland party (MP) in 1983 until the October 1991 national elections, when this party was voted out of office, former Prime Minister, now President, Turgut Özal personally outlined the domestic and foreign policy objectives of Turkey. Furthermore, due to his party's substantial majority in the National Assembly, Özal virtually eliminated the opposition parties' input into decision making. Practices such as running the everyday affairs of the state through governmental decrees with the power of law, rather than passage of specific laws in the National Assembly, demonstrated an authoritarian political atmosphere in Turkey (Yeşilada, 1988b:364-372). Furthermore, Özal's prominent position within the MP canceled any successful opposition to his policy preferences, because he approved most of the MP parliamentarians prior to national elections by review of the list of candidates.

In fact, following his election to the presidency by the National Assembly, when the opposition parties walked out, Özal chose his replacement for prime minister with total disregard for the views of the other MP leaders. Those individuals who chose to oppose any policy preferences of Özal lost their battles and either resigned from the party or experienced a decline in their position of strength within the organization. The close followers of Özal who unsuccessfully disagreed with his policies and subsequently resigned from their posts include Finance Minister Vural Arıkan (also resigned from the party), Mayor of Istanbul Bedrettin Dalan (also resigned from the party), Minister of Education Hasan Celal Güzel, Finance Minister Kaya Erdem, Minister of Finance and Customs Ekrem Pakdemirli, Foreign Minister Mesut Yılmaz, Foreign Minister Ali Bozer, Defense Minister Safa Giray, and Defense Minister Hüsnü Doğan. The resignations of Pakdemirli, Yılmaz, Giray, and Doğan occurred after Özal became president.

According to the Turkish constitution, the president does not have the power to determine the policies of the government. This duty lies within the Cabinet and the National Assembly. Furthermore, the president is supposed to keep no loyalties to any political party and serve as a neutral head of state. Despite these facts, Özal continued to make policy statements, gave directives to former Prime Minister Yıldırım Akbulut, and interfered with the daily affairs of the Cabinet ministers. Upon his resignation, for example, Yılmaz made it quite clear that, under these circumstances, he could not carry out his duties (*Cumhuriyet*, February 21-22, 1990).

In terms of the microsetting, Turgut Özal's perception of his role as Turkey's leader is important. He saw himself as a unique alternative leader to pre-1980 politicians and one who could bring together individuals from different ideological persuasions. In forming the MP, Özal originally tried to form a coalition of pre-1980 liberals, fundamentalists, and nationalists (Yeşilada, 1988b:355-364). However, due to the establishment of the liberal oriented *Doğru Yol Partisi*, the True Path party (TPP), by the traditional leader of the liberals, Süleyman Demirel, the fundamentalists and nationalists occupied the key administrative positions in the MP. It is also significant that the fundamentalists and nationalists who were supporters of the pre-1980 National Salvation party and Nationalist Action party respectively had been at odds with one another over many issues throughout the 1970s. Thus, the future of the MP undoubtedly depended on how these groups compromised to make key policy choices and maintain their coalition (Yeşilada, 1988b).

As explained in my earlier study of post-1980 political developments in Turkey (Yeşilada, ibid.), Turgut Özal embraced the Turkish-Islamic Synthesis of the *İlim Yayma Cemiyeti* as the dominant party position in order to balance and strengthen the coalition between the fundamentalists and nationalists. This "ideology" emphasizes joining Turkish nationalism and Islam as the only viable channel for creating a strong Turkey. It views the golden age of the Ottoman Empire as its reference point (Aydınlar Ocağı, 1973). Other tenets of this ideology include (1) the union of religion and state, (2) a society built on Islamic foundations, (3) a coalition between government and military, and (4) the rule of the religious law, the Sharia. In addition, the Synthesis identifies various enemies of the social culture, who need to be eliminated. They are (1) atheists, (2) separatists and Western humanists, (3) members of other religions, (4) those who blame Islam for the collapse of the Ottoman Empire, and (5) leftist, elitist, and etatist intellectuals (Güvenç et al., 1987 and Yeşilada, 1988b). As I discuss in the next section, the above principles and goals of the Turkish-Islamic Synthesis reflect the objectives of the International Sharia Congress held in Pakistan in 1976.

The Turkish fundamentalists' call for a coalition between the government and the military is significant. The capture of the government alone in Turkey is no guarantee of the success of fundamentalist goals. The military, as guardian of the secular republic, could stop the fundamentalists' plans. Thus, the Synthesis also envisions a coalition of fundamentalists and the military. Within this organizational network, Turgut Özal saw himself as the one person who could strengthen Turkey's relations with the Islamic world and promote fundamentalism in the country while maintaining a good working atmosphere with the military. It is no surprise then, that once in power, he passed governmental decrees in the National Assembly that gave preferential investment opportunities to Saudi Arabian finance houses. He also prevented the appointment of General Necdet Öztorun as chief of staff (head of the Turkish armed forces) and appointed his own candidate Necip Torumtay to this position. Özal's action was unprecedented in Turkish politics.

Özal also has a good relationship with the World Bank and the IMF-something that the former Turkish leaders lacked. During the 1970s he was trained in the World Bank and his American associates helped persuade Kenan Evren to appoint him the Assistant Prime Minister responsible for the economic affairs of the state during the NSC rule (Çölaşan, 1989:159-161). His main responsibility was to carry out the January 24, 1980 Stabilization Program of the IMF.

One last observation concerning Turgut Özal's ideological orientation is his connection with a fundamentalist religious order known as the *Nakşibendi Tarikatı* (Çölaşan, 1989; Velidedeoğlu, 1990; Cemal, 1990; Mumcu, 1987a; and Yeşilada, 1989). Turgut Özal's association with religious organizations dates back to the 1960s and 1970s. In fact, during the 1977 national elections, Turgut Özal was the National Salvation party's candidate from Izmir. As Mumcu (1987a:182-183) explains, Özal also participated in the *İlim Yayma Cemiyeti* (the Society to Propagate *İlim* [the Islamic science of religion as contrasted to worldly knowledge]). This society is one of the most important organizations behind the spread of the Turkish-Islamic Synthesis in Turkey. Thus, it is not surprising that once elected to the prime ministry, Özal strengthened Turkey's ties with the fundamentalist Arab states in the Middle East.

The Macrosetting

With regard to the macrosetting, Turkey's relations with the US and NATO in the region and her connections with the Islamic countries need a separate examination. The former refers to the security commitments of Turkey within the NATO framework. However, as stated above, Turkey's relations with the individual Middle Eastern countries were influenced by her financial needs and the ideological orientation of her present leaders.

Strategic Commitments within NATO

The decision of the Turkish leaders to improve Turkish-American cooperation was designed to strengthen NATO's capabilities in the region. Since the signing of the Turkish-American Defense and Economic Cooperation Agreement in 1980, and the revised version in 1987, Turkey's relations with the US have improved significantly. In December 1981, the two governments agreed to establish a high-level joint military group to improve defense cooperation. At the same time, the two sides agreed to modernize the Turkish armed forces and to improve NATO's posture in the region. In accordance with these agreements, Turkey became the third largest recipient of American foreign aid following Israel and Egypt. According to US Senate hearings, the bulk of American assistance to Turkey was in the form of concessional credits, followed by map grants and treasury-rate credits.

Renewed American interest in the modernization of the Turkish armed forces was not without US strategic interests. Currently, there are seven US bases and an additional twenty-one US installations in Turkey with 7,000 US personnel are stationed at these sites (Yeşilada, 1988c:52-53). These facilities are capable of spying on the former Soviet Union republics' nuclear tests and shipping in the Black Sea, Central Asia, and Ukraine. In addition, American officials wanted to install fifty-four new underground storage facilities in Turkey and replace those aging nuclear weapons deployed on F-16, F-4, and F-104 fighter bombers and land-based missiles. This modernization program, which originally was part of the Montebello Agreement of 1983, further included the deployment of additional US F-16s at Incirlik and perhaps the giving of nuclear capabilities to the Turkish-built F-16s. These plans temporarily gained more importance following the signing of the INF treaty between the US and USSR. However, the dramatic developments in Eastern Europe and the START treaty between the US, Belarus, Russia, Ukraine, and Kazakhistan will most likely cause a revision of these objectives.

Besides US strategic concerns in Eastern Europe, the Americans have also used the Turkish bases for military operations in the Middle East. In December 1983, the US was permitted to use Incirlik Air Base near Adana as a stopping-off point for American troops moving into and out of Lebanon (Barchard, 1985:55). This exceptional case differed from previous Arab-Israeli conflicts, in which Turkey did not allow the US to use these bases. The only other times when Incirlik or any other bases in Turkey saw the movement of American troops into the Middle East was during the 1957 civil war in Lebanon and the most recent Gulf war. A final change in US-Turkish relations is that the US Sixth Fleet can now make frequent port calls to Turkey–something it could not do during the 1968-1980 period.

As a result of these developments, the US embarked on an expensive program of modernizing the Turkish armed forces with the direct participation of Turkish and American businesses in the joint production of various weapons systems. Among these ventures, the production of the F-16 fighter plane by General Dynamics and TUSAŞ (Türkiye Uçak Sanayi Anonim Şirketi) is the most significant. According to the offset agreement between the two countries, General Dynamics obtained direct and indirect profits from this undertaking. The indirect profits included a complex arrangement in which the company was required to sell Turkish export products in international markets (*Cumhuriyet*, November 7, 1987).

In addition to the F-16 project, Turkish Military Electronics Industries Inc. (ASELSAN) obtained licenses from Litton (US) for production of tactical communications equipment, scramblers, and digital message devices (Karasapan, 1987:29). The army also reached a separate agreement with the Americans to overhaul helicopters in a facility in Ankara. According to Ömer Karasapan (1987:29), this facility started to assembly UH-1 helicopters, and delivered the initial batch of fifteen helicopters in late 1985. Furthermore, the Machinery and Chemical Industries Establishment (MKE) now produces air-to-ground FFAR rockets under a US license. More programs, including the joint production of an armored personnel carrier, missiles, and multi-rocket launchers are under negotiation between the two countries.

In return for these military-industrial joint ventures, the US and Turkey concluded a "Memorandum of Understanding" that provided for the construction, improvement, and joint use of some airfields in the eastern provinces of Turkey. This document and the efforts made toward implementation aroused speculation among Turkey's southern neighbors about the possible use of such airfields by the Rapid Deployment Force (RDF) of the US. Actually, these fears were not unfounded. While the RDF, which has been renamed as the Rapid Deployment Joint Task Force (RDJTF–or the 82nd Airborne Division), is designed to increase the US capability to respond to Soviet aggression in the Middle East, congressional reports indicate that the response to lesser threats is also a function of this force. According to a report of the Congressional Research Service by Ellen Laipson (1981:14), "the planned Rapid Deployment Joint Task Force will be sized to fight against the most serious threat, a direct Soviet aggression into the region, apparently assuming that some part of the force will be able to cope with any lesser threat arising out of regional conflict or internal stability." Thus, most Arab states and Iran were inclined to view the RDJTF as a possible threat to themselves , rather than as a protector against the Soviets.

An incident in 1982 confirmed the fears of Turkey's southern neighbors that the Evren regime was indeed providing new base facilities and headquarters for the RDJTF and that the operation was quite large. In April 1982 a US transport plane crash in eastern Turkey resulted in the death of twenty-seven officials working on the projects: two Air Force colonels from Colorado, together with junior officers, and NCO and civilian Air Force employees, who were officially described as a "contract performance evaluation team," and a team from the headquarters of the US Strategic Air Command (SAC) in Omaha, Nebraska (*New Statesman*, May 14, 1982). Congressional documents indicated that construction of runways, hangars, and barracks for American airmen were completed at bases in Diyarbakır and Incirlik. Furthermore, similar projects were continuing at Erzurum, where there is a NATO nuclear storage site. Similar construction also occurred at airfields at Bitlis and Van, east and southeast of Erzurum, and at a base close to the Soviet border, now Georgia, north of Kars. These new bases are capable of serving two units of B-52H bombers.

It is important to note that after the September coup, the Turkish armed forces exercised in this area, frequently joined by British, American, and other troops from the NATO ACE (Allied Command Europe). According to NATO officials, the major aim of these exercises was the preparation for a possible Soviet intervention in the region. The writings of Professor Albert Wohlstetter (1981:174-188) also argued that aircraft flying from bases in Turkey could intercept Soviet lines of communication in case of a Soviet attack south through Iran.

While these maneuvers seemed to reflect NATO's general concern over the Soviet Union's intentions in the region, they also raised questions in Iran. The Iranians were wary of the possible use of NATO forces for intervention in the Iran-Iraq war, yet the real threat was the desire of some key Turkish officers to exploit the situation in northern Iraq. General Haydar Saltık, the first secretary-general of the NSC, advocated military intervention in northern Iraq to regain Turkish territory (the oil-rich Kirkuk and Mosul regions, where a sizable Turkish minority is located) lost at the end of World War I. According to *New Statesman* (May 14, 1982), some American officials also supported the plan. These Americans, led by former National Security Adviser William Clark, argued that if the Iranians were to push into Iraq on several fronts, the Iraqi regime would collapse. At that time, it would become necessary for pro-Western forces to secure the strategic northern oilfields of Iraq. Thus, the Turkish armed forces could enter the region and the US would position the RDJTS and the Sixth Fleet to deter any Soviet intervention against Turkey. Iran's fears were further fueled when Turkish forces crossed over into Iraqi territory in May 1983 in pursuit of Kurdish terrorists who had carried out separatist activities in southeastern Turkey. While Turkish officials maintained that the operation was small-scale, the Western media described it as a major operation. Apparently, a mechanized brigade of crack Turkish commandos penetrated seventy-five miles into Iraq and carried out "seek and destroy" missions against the Kurdish guerrillas for three weeks. This action, however, was not without the permission of the Iraqi government. As explained above, the two governments agreed on such operations. Moreover, the Iraqis welcomed the Turkish intervention because they themselves could not control the anti-Iraqi Kurds in the region.

This operation and the apparent mutual understanding between the NSC and Iraqi leaders, coupled with the explicit criticism by the Iranians over the Turkish action, led to the abandonment of Turkey's military intervention in northern Iraq. Instead, General Saltık was eased out of the NSC and given a less powerful position, with his retirement following. Since that time Turkish officials have pursued an active policy of neutrality in the Iran-Iraq conflict. Furthermore, this neutrality paid off in the form of improved trade between Turkey and her two neighbors. However, Turkey's neutrality in this war did not mean that the Turkish leaders abandoned the greater American concern over Gulf security. With new base facilities in eastern Turkey, and forces already present at Incirlik, American officials could enact the Air Land Battle doctrine for intervention in the Gulf.

Events following Iraq's invasion of Kuwait on August 2, 1990, proved this to be correct. Turkey not only joined the economic embargo on Iraq by shutting down the Iraqi oil pipeline that passed through this country but also allowed US aircraft to use Turkish airbases to operate bombing missions to Iraq. President Özal single-handedly decided Turkey's policy. His close ties to the American administration and to the oil-rich Saudis seem to be the causal factors behind this policy choice. This is despite the fact that the overwhelming majority of Turkish citizens and the armed forces general staff opposed Turkey's active involvement in the Gulf War (Turkish dailies, August-December 1990). Özal's total disregard of these views led to the resignation of the armed forces commander General Necip Torumtay.

In another Middle East issue, the Arab-Israeli conflict, the Turkish attitude has continued to deviate from the Americans' since the September coup. In order to win Arab support for Turkey, Turkish officials have been conducting a low-key policy toward Israel. Turkey continued to oppose Israeli occupation of Arab territories, and in December 1980 it decided to withdraw all its embassy staff from Tel Aviv, except for a second secretary acting as chargé d'affaires. At the same time, the Israeli government was asked to lower its diplomatic representation in Ankara. Finally, during autumn 1988 the Turkish government recognized the PLO's declaration of a Palestinian state in exile. While these decisions support Sezer's arguments (1984:78-79) that Turkey has wanted a friendly relationship with the Arab world since the 1960s, an additional factor compels Turkish leaders to move closer to the conservative Arab states. This factor is the increasing fundamentalist connection between Turkish rightist leaders and their Saudi supporters.

The Closer Financial Relationship With the Islamic World

The ideological factors discussed under the microsetting, as well as an official desire to integrate this country's economy with global capitalism, led to the decision to have closer ties with the Islamic countries. In order to understand this complex situation, one needs to look briefly at the economic difficulties this country faced in the 1970s and the policies adopted over the last fifteen years.

Turkey's severe economic problems began with the 1973 oil crisis, which caused a drastic increase in petroleum import expenditures. While the total oil import bill in 1973 was about 17 percent of export earnings, this figure reached 76 percent, or a total of 1.4 billion dollars by 1979. Starting in 1974, Turkish officials financed the resulting budget deficit through short-term commercial credits known as Convertible Turkish Lira Deposits (CTLD) which became impossible to service by the end of the 1970s.

In an attempt to combat deteriorating economic conditions, the weak Nationalist Coalition government of Süleyman Demirel in 1978 and the Republican People's party government of Bülent Ecevit in 1979 adopted two IMF-based economic stabilization programs. They implemented several devaluations of the national currency and tried to enforce tight monetary policies. Both measures failed due to increasing political violence in the country and the weaknesses of the government coalitions. The IMF survey of the Turkish economy in October 1979 found the tight monetary policies heavily relaxed and standby agreements violated (OECD, 1980:25). To counter these developments, Demirel's Justice party government adopted a new IMF austerity package in 1980, known as the January 24 Measures (OECD, 1980:32-35). Through these measures, Turkey embarked on a new policy designed not only as a comprehensive program of economic stabilization but also as a basic reorientation of economic programs away from detailed government regulation and control toward greater reliance on market forces, foreign competition, and foreign investments. All of these factors simply signaled the sharp acceleration of Turkey's economic integration with global capitalism (Yeşilada and Fisunoğlu, 1992).

One of the key features of this economic austerity program was foreign investment. In fact, further liberalization of the laws occurred in February 1986. The new policy gave foreign capital the same rights and obligations as domestic capital, with guarantees in transferring profits, fees, and royalties. It also recognized the Foreign Investment Directorate as the single authority in Turkey which could guide, receive, review, and negotiate all foreign investment applications (Togan, Olgun, and Akder, 1987:43). Furthermore, during the 1980s, the growing number of agreements for bilateral reciprocal protection, promotion of investment, and avoidance of double taxation increased confidence in the stability of the investment environment in Turkey. The results of these efforts were encouraging. While the cumulative foreign capital inflow into Turkey was 228 million dollars during 1954-1980, the amount for the 1980-1986 period was 874.1 million dollars (State Planning Organization, 1988:62). Thus, policies aimed at economic integration with global capitalism were relatively successful in terms of attracting foreign capital to Turkey. It is in this context of Turkey's economic integration with global capitalism, through liberalization of trade and investment regimes, that Saudi Arabian and other "Islamic" capital entered this country.

In this context the Saudis, who had close ties to government circles in Turkey, saw ample opportunities to invest in this country. While the flow of money into Turkey coincides with post-1980 economic reforms, Saudi attention to Turkish politics dates back to the previous decade. Certain key developments since the mid-1970s illustrate how and why Saudi capital entered Turkey.

First, an Islamic conference that occurred in Pakistan in 1976 demonstrated increasing Islamic influence. This conference, known as the International Sharia Congress, was organized by a Saudi Arabian institution, the *Rabıtat al-Alam al-İslami*. Representatives of Islamic states attended the conference to increase ties between their respective countries. At this meeting the Turkish Minister of State Hasan Aksay, a NSP member of Süleyman Demirel's first Nationalist Coalition government, represented Turkey. Following tens days of discussion, the participants adopted the following goals and principles:

1. The constitutional frameworks of the Islamic countries should be restructured according to Islamic principles and the Arabic language should be spread among the people.
2. Civil laws should be replaced by the Sharia (Islamic legal code).
3. Women should obey Islamic restrictions.
4. Necessary economic and political steps should be taken to establish modern Islamic states based on the Sharia.
5. At every level of educational training, Islam should be taught as a mandatory subject.
6. The five principles of Islam should be memorized by all primary school students.
7. Secondary school students must learn the entire Koran.
8. In order to promote these goals, Islamic educational institutions must be established in each country.
9. In order to recreate Islamic Unity, all Muslim states should first recognize and accept their Islamic attributes and then establish a confederation under the guidance of a commonly elected Caliph. (Mumcu, 1987a:174-175)

These principles and goals show that the *Rabıtat's* main concern is the revival of Islam in the social, economic, and political affairs of all Muslim countries. Obviously then, the Sharia Congress threatens the secular nature of the Turkish republic. When this conference occurred, the Turkish Chief Prosecutor's Office questioned Aksay's participation in this meeting. However, due to political intrigues and Demirel's need to maintain his coalition government at that time, this issue "was swept under the proverbial carpet." Most importantly, *Rabıtat's* objectives laid the foundation for the subsequent entry of Saudi Arabian capital into Turkey. The January 24 Stabilization Program simply provided an additional economic incentive for this process.

In a related development at the Third Islamic Summit of the Organization of the Islamic Conference, the member states agreed to joint investments and cooperation in trade, industry, food and agriculture, transportation, telecommunications, tourism, science and technology, energy, labor, social issues, money and finance, population and health care, and information. The three permanent committees, including the ISEDAK, administered these issue areas. Basically, the ISEDAK was designed to promote economic and commercial cooperation among the members of the Organization of the Islamic Conference. It is important to note that while Turkey joined the ISEDAK, it did not sign the political agreements pertaining to the Islamic reforms of the institutional framework of the member states.

The ISEDAK first adopted policy recommendations in each subsector of commerce and economy. The member states could then make necessary adjustments in their domestic spheres to effect these recommendations. In this context, needed financial assistance could be obtained from Islamic financial centers like the Islamic Development Bank. Furthermore, the concerned mimisters of each member state evaluated the activities of the organization at annual meetings. In accordance with these functions, the ISEDAK members met in Istanbul during November 14-16, 1984 and adopted the following additional decisions:

1. To establish a financial mechanism for medium-term foreign trade loans through the Islamic Development Bank.
2. To standardize trade regulations between the members.
3. To create an information network for trade among the members.
4. To establish a preference system for trade among the members.
5. To promote joint investment ventures for industrial development of the member states (Yeşilada, 1989:7).

These decisions clearly demonstrate that the original goal of promoting economic and political ties among Islamic countries had begun notwithstanding Turkey's "official nonparticipation" in the political agreements of the organization. Industrial projects and increased trade links between the member states started the process. Moreover, the Islamic Development Bank, which heavily depends on Saudi Arabia's contributions, provided the necessary capital. In the subsequent meetings of ISEDAK, the member states increased their areas of cooperation. At the second ISEDAK meeting during March 14-16, 1986, the agriculture ministers agreed to increase joint activities in agriculture. Further decisions included the transportation, energy, and communications sectors at the third (1987), fourth (1988), fifth (1989), and sixth (1990) ISEDAK meetings.

After ISEDAK members agreed to economic cooperation the next step involved changing government regulations on foreign investment to facilitate joint financial dealings. In Turkey, this phase coincided with the transition from military to civilian rule following the Motherland party (MP) victory in the 1983 national elections and continued until the 1991 national elections, when the True Path party of Süleyman Demirel won. Turgut Özal's key role in accomplishing the necessary policy changes concerning foreign investment is obvious. First, as soon as Özal became the prime minister in November 1983, he revised the regulations on private financial institutions through a series of governmental decrees. As described below, other related decisions followed.

First, Özal allowed the establishment of the Faisal Finance and Al Baraka Turkish Finance houses and provided them with special exemptions from Turkish bankruptcy laws (Republic of Turkey, 1984). Interestingly enough, this happened shortly after the elections, on December 16, 1983, before the new government of Özal received a vote of confidence in the National Assembly. Second, the government extended tax exemptions to the Islamic Development Bank in order to allow capital flows in accordance with the ISEDAK agreements. As Mumcu (1987a:183) explains, the second development occurred soon after Korkut Özal, the younger brother of Turgut Özal, became a consultant for the Islamic Development Bank. These two decisions are significant because they provide major governmental benefits to Islamic financial institutions. No other foreign company presently operating in Turkey enjoys such a wide range of exemptions from Turkish laws. In fact, the Foreign Investments Laws (Nos. 5821 and 6224) and their revised versions of February 1986 provided foreign companies operating in Turkey with only the same rights as Turkish companies under the Turkish commercial and penal codes (Yeşilada, 1989). Thus, decrees in favor of these Saudi companies contradict this legislation. Table 1 provides figures on these investments in Turkey. It is crucial to emphasize that the privileges given to the Saudi firms are equivalent to the capitulations made to the European powers by the Ottomans. Just as capitulations made Ottoman firms second-class companies in their own country, so too did Saudi privileges undermine their Turkish competitors. As these figures indicate, Saudi Arabian and Iranian investments in Turkey increased dramatically during the second half of the 1980s. Among these investments, the most crucial are the Islamic finance houses that started an alternate form of banking, known as "interest-free banking," in Turkey.

The first such finance house was Faisal Finance of Turkey, which is a joint investment between Turkish businessmen and the Saudis. Its foreign founders include the *Maasaraf Faisal al-Islami* in Bahrain , the *Dar-al Maal Islami* Trust , the Faisal Islamic Banks of Egypt and Sudan, and the *Faisal Tekafül* Association. These companies are affiliates of the giant Saudi-based finance house, the *Dar al-Maal al-Islami*, which is the parent organization of fifty-five Islamic banks around the world and maintains its headquarters in Geneva, Switzerland (Mumcu, 1987a, 1987b and Yeşilada, 1989).

Table 1
Foreign Investments in Turkey (1984-1986)

Country of Origin	Number of firms 1984	1985	% Change 1986	1984-86
USA	37	61	74	100
West Germany	47	59	92	92
France	6	7	9	50
Great Britain	20	33	43	110
Holland	10	18	24	140
Switzerland	51	63	77	39
Italy	7	11	11	56
Austria	5	8	8	60
Consortium	23	37	50	115
Saudi Arabia	1	28	46	4500
Iran	1	10	22	2100

Source: State Planning Organization.

The second major Saudi-based international finance institution that invested in Turkey is the *Al Baraka* Group. This group includes *Al Baraka* Inc. of Saudi Arabia, *Al Baraka* Inc. Co. in London, *Al Baraka* International Ltd. in London, Best Bank of Tunisia, *Al Baraka* Islamic Insurance Bank of Saudi Arabia, *Al Baraka* Bank of Sudan, Arabian Thai International of Bangkok, *Al Baraka* Islamic Bank of Mauritania, *Al Baraka* Bank of Bangladesh, Jordanian Islamic Finance and Investment, and International Islamic Investment in Denmark. The *Al Baraka Türk* Private Finance House is a partnership between the international Saudi-based group and Turkish investors that include Korkut Özal.

Finally, the Islamic Development Bank, founded by forty-four Islamic countries (including Turkey), among which Saudi Arabia is the most influential member, benefitted from changes in the investment laws. According to the by-laws of the Islamic Development Bank, the purpose of this institution is "to enhance the individual or collective social and economic development of the Islamic countries in accordance with the principles of *Sharia*." (*Milliyet*, October 27, 1989). While being a member of the bank, Turkey did not sign the by-laws of this institution. Nevertheless, its membership in a Sharia-influenced bank does raise important questions over Turkey's commitment to the secular reforms of Atatürk. In an interview with the Turkish daily *Milliyet* (March 25, 1987), President of the Islamic Development Bank Ahmad Mohammad Ali explained that the bank works closely with *Rabıtat* in order to achieve its goals. The major task of the Islamic Development Bank in Turkey is to provide financial credits for development projects through "interest-free" banking. However, as its president stated, this bank has a close relationship with *Rabıtat* which financed the International Sharia Congress in 1976.

Rabıtat is a pan-Islamic organization that has been actively involved in spreading anti-secular ideas in Turkey by financing religious projects and maintaining contacts with political figures in the country (Mumcu, 1987a:171-196). Most of these individuals are key members of more than one of the following organizations in Turkey: the executive boards of the Saudi Arabian finance houses in Turkey, partners in the Turkish firms that have joint investments with the Saudi Arabian companies, the Motherland party, and the boards of the various religious pious foundations known as *Wakf*s (Yeşilada, 1989 and Mumcu, 1987b). In order to appreciate *Rabıtat'*s hidden threat to the secular Turkish republic, a brief examination of its history is helpful.

Originally, Saudi Prince Faisal (the late king of Saudi Arabia) established the *Rabıtat* in 1962 in order to check the spread of Egyptian President Abdul Nasser's ideas in the Muslim world. During that time, pro-Nasserite theologians dominated the Al-Azhar in Cairo, the most important center for Islamic theology, and taught Islamic socialism to its students. These student, in turn, spread the message throughout the Arab world. Prince Faisal's strategy was to limit Arab socialism by spreading the Saudi version of Islam. Such a strategy required strong financial backing, which came from the Saudi Arabian government and ARAMCO (Mumcu, 1987a). Turkey fit well into the operational arena of *Rabıtat* because, like Nasserism, the success of Kemalism could undermine fundamentalism in Muslim states.

Among its operations in Turkey, *Rabıtat* helped financially support the fundamentalist Eastern Turkestan Refugee Association, the Nationalist Turkish Students Union, and the Institute of Islamic Studies at Istanbul University. Furthermore, *Rabıtat* provided funds for mosque building throughout Turkey and paid the salaries of Turkish *imam*s (Muslim prayer leaders) in West Germany between 1982-1984 with the permission of former President of Turkey Kenan Evren (*Cumhuriyet,* March, 18, 1987 and Reed, 1988:3-4).

In essence, the influx of Islamic fundamentalist institutions into the Turkish economy occurred through a complex network of relationships. First of all, these investments began as a result of the changes, which Kenan Evren initiated and Turgut Özal consolidated, in Turkey's foreign policy toward the Islamic world. However, what seems to be a simple business venture between the Saudis and their Turkish partners carries with it the seeds of the destruction of the secular Turkish Republic. As several scholars explain (Mumcu, 1987a and b; Cemal, 1989; Yeşilada, 1989; and Velidedeoğlu, 1990) there is a dangerous relationship between these finance houses and *Rabıtat* and fundamentalist forces in Turkey. In these groups, the connection among these firms and members of the Nakşibendi order are crucial and require further research. Importantly, the members of this religious order have continuously opposed Kemalist principles and instigated several rebellions in the past against the secular state. It seems that the generals of the NSC opened the "Pandora's box" of fundamentalist forces in the country by allowing the blatant enemies of Atatürk to invest in the country. Turgut Özal and the MP simply continued where the generals had stopped, intensifying Turkey's ties to the fundamentalist Islamic countries.

CONCLUSIONS

On the basis of the above observations, it can be concluded that Turkey's foreign policy toward the Middle East in the 1980s was a product of the complex interaction between the micro- and macrosetting shown in Figure 1. In the microsetting, the authoritarian personalities of Kenan Evren and Turgut Özal, coupled with their respective worldviews, were the crucial variables. General Evren wanted to strengthen Turkey's position within the Western alliance and bring it closer to the Islamic world. Turgut Özal, on the other hand, wanted to integrate the Turkish economy with world capitalism, with assistance from Saudi Arabian and other Islamic investors, and to promote Islam in the country. To these ends, they expanded Turkey's commitments to NATO/American security interests in the region and increased financial, as well as political, ties with conservative Islamic states. While the former development resembles the US-Turkish relations of the 1950s, the latter has no parallel in the Turkish republic's history. In this sense, rapprochement with Islamic states truly opened a new chapter in Turkish foreign policy.

These changes in foreign policy could not have been achieved without the significant macrosetting: economic difficulties, the transition from military to civilian rule, support from Turkey's key allies, and the desire of the Islamic world to increase its ties with this country. In this environment, Turkish officials followed a dual strategy to satisfy US and NATO interests in the region and win Arab support for Turkey in its relations with Greece. The outcome of these actions, however, proved dangerous to Turkey's domestic security. While improved relations with the US resulted in the joint production of military hardware, the expansion of American military facilities in eastern Anatolia raised serious concerns among Turkey's neighbors. At the same time, the flow of Saudi Arabian capital into the Turkish economy strengthened the power position of Islamic fundamentalists.

REFERENCES

Axelrod, R., ed. (1976). *Structure of Decision: The Cognitive Maps of Political Elites.* Princeton: Princeton University Press.

Aydınlar Ocağı (1973). *Aydınlar Ocağı'nın Görüşü* [View of the Guild of Enlightened: Current Problems of Turkey]. Istanbul.

Azar, E., and T. Sloan (1975). *Dimensions of Interactions.* Pittsburgh: International Studies Association.

Barchard, D. (1985). *Turkey and the West.* London: The Royal Institute of International Affairs.

Brecher, M.(1972). *The Foreign Policy System of Israel.* London: Oxford University Press.

_____ (1974) *Decisions in Israel's Foreign Policy.* London: Oxford University Press.

_____ (1979). "State Behavior in International Crisis: A Model." *Journal of Conflict Resolution.* Vol. 23, pp. 446-480.

Burgress, P., and R. Lawton (1972). *Indicators of International Behavior.* Beverly Hills, Calif.: Sage Publications.

Cemal, H. (1990). *Özal Hikayesi* [The Özal History]. Ankara: Bilgi Yayınevi.

Converse, P. (1964). "The Nature of Belief Systems in Mass Public." In David Apter, ed., *Ideology and Discontent.* New York: Free Press.

Cumhuriyet. (Turkish daily). November 7, 1989 and May 3, 1990.

Çölaşan, E. (1989). *Turgut Nereden Koşuyor?* [Where Is Turgut Running From?] Istanbul: Tekin Yayınları.

Gharaybeh, M. H. (1987). *Determinants of Foreign Policy Decision-Making in an Unincorporated Authoritarian System: Sadat's Decision to Visit Jerusalem as a Case Study.* Unpublished Ph.D. dissertation. Department of Political Science, University of Missouri.

Güvenç, B., G. Şaylan, İ. Tekeli, and S. Turan (1987). "Türk-İslam Sentezi" *Cumhuriyet,* April 19.

Jervis, R. (1976). *Perceptions and Misperceptions in International Relations.* Princeton: Princeton University Press.

Karaosmanoğlu, A. (1983). "Turkey's Security and the Middle East." *Foreign Affairs.* Vol. 62. No. 1 (Fall):157-175.

Karasapan, Ö. (1987). "Turkey's Armament Industries." *Middle East Report.* No. 144. (January-February): 27-31.

Korany, B. (1986). *How Foreign Policy Decisions Are Made in the Third World.* Boulder, Colo.: Westview Press.

Laipson, E. (1981). *Turkey and U.S. Interests.* Washington: Congressional Research Service.

Lenczowski, G. (1980). *The Middle East in World Affairs.* 4th ed. Ithaca, New York: Cornell University Press.

Ludington, N. S., and J. W. Spain (1983). "Dateline Turkey: The Case for Patience." *Foreign Policy.* Vol. 50 (Spring): 150-168.

Millar, T. B. (1969). "On Writing About Foreign Policy." In James Rosenau, ed. *International Politics and Foreign Policy.* 2d ed. New York: Free Press.

Milliyet. (Turkish daily). October 27, 1989.

Mumcu, U. (1987a). *Rabıta.* Istanbul: Tekin Yayınevi.

_____ (1987b). "Islamcı Örgütler ve Paralar." *Cumhuriyet,* March 13.

Munton, D. ed., (1978). *Measuring International Behavior: Public Sources, Events and Validity.* Halifax: Center for Foreign Policy Studies.

New Statesman (May 14, 1982).

OECD (1980). *Country Surveys: Turkey.* Paris: OECD Publications.

Reed, H. A. (1988). "Islam and Education in Turkey: Their Roles in National Development." *Turkish Studies Association Bulletin.* Vol. 12. No. 1 (March):3-4.

Republic of Turkey (1984). *The Bankruptcy Law.* Ankara.

Robins, P. (1991). *Turkey and the Middle East.* New York: Council on Foreign Relations.

Rosenau, J. (1966). "Pre-Theories and Theories of Foreign Policy." In B. Farrell, ed., *Approaches to Comparative and International Politics.* Evanston, Ill.: Northwestern University Press.

_____ (1976). "Restlessness, Change, and Foreign Policy Analysis." In J. Rosenau, ed., *In Search of Global Patterns.* New York: Free Press.

_____ (1980). *The Scientific Study of Foreign Policy.* London: Francis Pinter.

_____ (1984). "A Pre-Theory Revisited: World Politics in an Era of Cascading Interdependence." *International Studies Quarterly,* Vol. 23. No. 3 (September): 245-305.

Rustow, D. A. (1987). *Turkey: America's Forgotten Ally.* New York: Council on Foreign Relations.

Sezer, D. (1984). "Turkey's Security Policies." In Jonathan Alford, ed., *Greece and Turkey: Adversity in Alliance.* New York: St. Martin's Press for the IISS.

Snyder, G., and P. Diesing (1977). *Conflict Among Nations.* Princeton: Princeton University Press.

Snyder, R., H. Bruck, and B. Sapin (1962). *Foreign Policy Decision-Making.* New York: Free Press.

State Planning Organization (1988). *1988 Yılı Programı* [The 1988 Program]. Ankara: State Planning Organization of the Prime Ministry of Turkey.

Steinbrunner, J. (1974). *The Cybernetic Theory of Decision.* Princeton: Princeton University Press.

Tachau, F. (1984). *Turkey: Authority, Democracy, and Development.* New York: Praeger.

Togan, S., H. Olgun, and H. Akder (1987). *External Economic Relations of Turkey.* Istanbul: Turktrade Research Center.

Velidedeoğlu, H. V. (1990). *12 Eylül: Karşı Devrim* [September 12: The Counter-revolution]. Istanbul: Evrim Yayınları.

Wohlstetter, A. (1981). "Meeting the Threat in the Persian Gulf." *Survey.* Vol. 25. No. 2, pp. 174-188.

Yakış, Y. (1987). "Türkiye-AET İlişkileri Karşısında Türkiye-IKO Ekonomik İlişkileri." In Ö. Bozkurt, ed., *Avrupa Topluluğu ve Türkiye* [The EC and Turkey]. Ankara: TODAIE.

Yeni Gündem. February 15, 1987.

Yeşilada, B. A. (1988a). "Türkiye'de İslamcı Akımlar ve Suudi Bağlantısı." *Bilim ve Sanat*. June: 22-25.

_____ (1988b). " Problems of Political Development in the Third Turkish Republic." *Polity*. Vol. 21. No. 2 (Winter): 345-372.

_____ (1988c). "INF Anlaşması ve Türkiye Üzerinde Artan Diplomatik Girişimler." *Panorama* (Ankara). Vol. 3. No. 25 (June):52-54.

_____ (1989). " Islam, Dollars, and Politics: Political Economy of the Saudi Capital in Turkey." Paper delivered at the 1989 Annual Conference of the Middle East Studies Association in Toronto, Canada, during November 15-18, 1989.

_____ (1990). "Turkey." In Richard F. Staar, ed.,*Yearbook on International Communist Affairs 1990: Parties and Revolutionary Movements*. Stanford, Calif.: Hoover Institution Press.

Yeşilada, B. A., and M. Fisunoğlu (1992). "Assessing the January 24 1980 Economic Stabilization Program in Turkey." In H. J. Barkey, ed., *The Political Economy of Stabilization Measures in the Middle East*. New York: St. Martin's Press.

9

Turkey and the European Community: Prospects for a New Relationship

Atila Eralp

INTRODUCTION

The application of Turkey in 1987 to the European Community for full membership surprised many observers. This application was greeted with mixed feelings both at home and abroad. The immediate reaction in Europe was one of extreme skepticism, while in Turkey tabloids reminded their readers of previous (Ottoman) forays into Europe. However, debates among the Turkish public as well as news of European discomfort dispelled the initial euphoria rather quickly. Instead, governmental and private institutions began a long-term process of preparation for a union with Europe that they saw as an inescapable eventuality. Frantic efforts to train the personnel needed to deal with European legal and economic institutions swelled the numbers of graduates applying to European Community departments newly established in the larger universities and state offices. As both the government and the public began to realize that union with Europe required a serious reorganization of the economy and society, Europe indicated that such a union would take even longer than the worst estimation.

Although Turkey has maintained close ties with Europe ever since the 1950s, it was only in the late 1980s that it defined this relationship once and for all. This decision ended the equivocations marking Turkey's attitude toward Europe during much of the 1960s and 1970s. The aim of this chapter is to analyze the factors that account for this change of policy and to suggest possible explanations for the timing of such a decision. To this end, first, Turkey-EEC relations will be analyzed over a period of thirty years; then a more detailed analysis of the changing conditions in the 1980s will be presented. The chapter will conclude by offering some reflections on the future prospects of Turkey's admission to the European Community.

TOWARD ASSOCIATION WITH THE
EUROPEAN COMMUNITY

The history of Turkey-EEC relations began with Turkey's application for associate membership on July 31, 1959, approximately two years after the signing of the Treaty of Rome on March 25, 1957. Two important political considerations prompted this decision: Turkey's determined efforts to be part of the Western world and her concern over Greek influence in Western-dominated international platforms. To these two ostensibly foreign policy considerations we should also add specific internal policy issues that placed importance on association with Europe at specific conjunctures. By examination of the convergence of these factors, this section attempts to explain the timing and form of Turkish moves towards the EEC.

Ever since its inception, officials in the Turkish republic had followed a policy of Westernization, with which they hoped to reorganize their society and their relations with the outside world (Ülman and Sander, 1972). Numerous factors, including the Depression and the Second World War, prevented the forging of multiple exchange relations with the West that would have very much aided this project. Then the postwar international system for the first time offered Turkish policymakers a fertile ground for instituting organic links with the West. At this point, the division of Europe into two rival blocs and the position of Turkey as a "frontline state" in the emerging Cold War atmosphere eased Turkey's entry into the nascent Western alliance. In the Cold War climate, the West created a united front from which Turkish policymakers did not wish to be excluded. It is with such considerations in mind that Turkey's leaders applied for membership in almost all the institutions created in the process of forging the Western alliance: The Marshall Plan, the OEEC (later OECD) the Council of Europe, and NATO (Gönlübol and Ülman, 1987).[1]

Turkish officials were specifically interested in two benefits they hoped inclusion in the Western alliance would provide. First and foremost in their estimation came security considerations. They did not believe Turkey could survive the Cold War alone and hoped to enter into larger and more secure alliances. In support of their application to the Western military alliance, Turkish policymakers emphasized the geopolitical importance of their country, a position which coincided with the US Cold War strategy of containment. The second benefit of association with the West centered on the material resources necessary for the country's economic development. Indeed, the Marshall Plan and economic and military aid received by Turkey after the Second World War did turn out to be important channels of credit as well as much needed machinery. In the four years following the end of the war, Turkey began to enter the different organizations designed to increase economic cooperation between Europe and the US. Inclusion in the Western military alliance did not come until 1952, after Turkey had displayed her allegiance by sending troops to fight in Korea (Sander, 1979:74).

According to Turkish policymakers, membership in the new European Community was a logical extension of Turkey's inclusion in the other Western organizations since the Community provided an economic dimension supplementing and cementing the Western alliance.[2] Nonetheless, absence of the US from the European Community did not conflict with Turkey's efforts to maintain intimate relations with the US. Turkish policymakers believed (and perhaps rightly) that the US strongly supported the creation of a community based on the premise of Western unity. Such a community also suited different groups in Turkey. These included a small number of industrialists organized in the Istanbul Chamber of Commerce and a few government functionaries working in the Ministry of Foreign Affairs. Both groups stressed not only the trade benefits, but also the "civilizing mission" that association with the West would have. However, rather than regarding membership in the EEC as posing a problem, Turkish decisionmakers adopted a holistic approach in which relations with Europe were considered as one aspect of the more encompassing issue of relations with the West.

Apart from the concern with inclusion in the Western alliance, the so-called "Greek factor" stood as another important consideration in Turkey's application for membership in the EEC. Turkey's application to the Community on July 31, 1959, was mainly in response to a similar application made by Greece two months earlier and can be understood in terms of the long-standing conflict between the two countries. Turkish policymakers, especially those in the Ministry of Foreign Affairs, believed that Turkey had to be present in each and every platform where the Greeks figured. However, to many in Turkey, the EEC was an unknown entity and the implications of Turkey's membership were not clear. What mattered most was the possible harm Greece could bring to Turkey in the Western alliance if it was able to monopolize the European arena. Officials felt that this would be an important site for the Turkish-Greek rivalry. (Birand, 1985:56-57).

The severe economic and political difficulties at the time were among the more critical factors serving to expedite Turkey's application to the EEC. The Democrat party (DP) government, which came to power in 1950, at first followed liberal trade policies and received large sums of credit from the US and international institutions. This easy access to foreign funds created a dependence on external finance which in turn caused a rising debt problem. As international terms of trade turned against agricultural commodities after the mid-1950s, balance of payments difficulties prompted the government to adopt protectionist policies. Already faltering under these pressures, the DP was also squeezed by rampant inflation caused by its strategy of investing in extensive infrastructure projects such as the building of roads. These economic difficulties finally forced the government to agree to an extremely unpopular IMF Stabilization Program in 1958. As the electoral strength of the Democrat party also began to erode, the party experienced increasing competition from its rival, the Republican People's party. In this climate, the DP regarded the EEC not only as a new source of credit and aid, but also as a means of boosting its political morale and credibility at home. Moreover, by the late 1950s, Turkey's stance in the international arena, especially its relations with the US, was more problematic than it was at the beginning of the decade. In this context, a successful association with Europe became necessary.

The European Community, for its part, viewed Turkey's inclusion cautiously. Europeans believed that Turkey's level of economic development would hinder European economic integration, since the latter was premised on advanced levels of industrialization. They thus planned to offer Turkey economic assistance as well as certain trade and tariff concessions (Turan, 1989:35-56). However, after signing a treaty of association with Greece (the Athens Treaty), such a posture became difficult to maintain. Aware of the competition between Greece and Turkey, European policymakers carefully balanced their relations with the two countries. Furthermore, since the European Community was still in its infancy and welcomed the application of new members, there were many in the Community who regarded both Greece and Turkey's membership favorably. The Cold War prompted the members of the European Community to act with strategic considerations in mind. Because Turkey and Greece were frontline states, their economic strength, crucial for political stability in the context of the Cold War, needed bolstering. Drawing their lessons from the Cuban crisis, NATO leaders began to stress what they called their "flexible response strategy" relying on conventional forces. This move reinforced the strategic position of Turkey and Greece within the alliance. The increased importance of security concerns caused the EEC to consider waving economic objections to Turkey's admission.

THE ANKARA AGREEMENT AND ITS AFTERMATH

Turkey and the European Economic Community signed the Ankara Agreement regulating Turkey's association with the Community on September 12, 1963, two years after the Athens Treaty established the terms of Greek association with the EEC. The delay in Turkey's move was caused by prolonged negotiations between the signatories after the 1960 military coup in Turkey suspended parliamentary politics for about eighteen months. Although the EEC has signed several association agreements with countries such as Malta and Cyprus, it was only in the case of Turkey and Greece that a clause was included in the agreements to specify the ultimate full membership of both countries at a future unspecified date. Thus, both Turkey and Greece viewed their admission to the EEC as a legal right.

The Ankara Agreement envisioned three stages of association between Turkey and the EEC. A preparatory stage with the extension of financial support to Turkey was supposed to ease Turkish integration into Europe. This support was mainly in the form of loans worth 175 million dollars extended by the European Investment Bank for Turkish infrastructure projects, especially the construction of the Keban hydroelectric project. Furthermore, the Community agreed to preferential treatment in its markets for Turkish agricultural exports. The second stage was to be a transitional period which set a timetable toward the establishment of a customs union between Europe and Turkey. A final period harmonizing and coordinating economic policies was supposed to finalize the steps necessary for eventual Turkish accession to the Community. The agreement also stipulated the establishment of certain institutions designed to supervise relations between the signatories. Foremost among these was the EEC-Turkey Association Council which was both an executive and a policy-making body charged with the implementation of the Association Agreement and was composed of members of the Council of Ministers and the Commission of the EEC and representatives of the Turkish government. A thirty-six member joint European-Turkish Parliamentary Committee composed of eighteen members from each parliament was to function as a consultative body whose main goal was to increase the number of high-level contacts between Turkey and the EEC.

The preparatory stage proceeded smoothly enough, and Turkish policymakers took the necessary steps to initiate the second stage of the Association Agreement by applying to the Community in May 1967. However, the issue of a customs union proved to be problematic, and it was not until July 1970 that the EEC-Turkey Association Council agreed on a Supplementary Protocol setting a revised timetable. It was signed the following November. Ratification of the Agreement took even longer and had to weather not only misgivings felt by both parties, but also the military intervention in Turkey in March 1971. According to the Protocol, which came into effect on January 1, 1973, members of the Community lifted all customs duties (excluding cotton yarn, cotton textiles, and machine-woven carpets) following the signing of the Agreement. Furthermore, Turkey was allowed a longer period of adjustment; duties on some commodities imported from Europe were to be abolished over a twelve year period, or a twenty-two-year span for some others. The same timetable was to followed for the adoption of the Community's common external tariff. The adoption of the Common Agricultural Policy was also to take a twenty-two year period during which the EEC would grant preferences to agricultural imports from Turkey. Financial assistance to Turkey was to continue in order to ease the transition to a customs union.[3] On the question of the free movement of labor, the Community agreed to a phased process that would culminate in the lifting of all restrictions on the free movement in Europe of Turkish workers by December 1, 1986.

As I have argued elsewhere (Eralp, 1990), the issue of a customs union became the bone of contention between Turkey and the EEC. Relations that went smoothly until then changed in the early 1970s as Turkish policymakers increasingly began to see association with Europe in terms of economic development strategies rather than a matter of foreign policy. Industrialists also began to fear the possible negative impact of EEC membership on Turkey's own industrialization. Although industrialists generally supported the spirit of the Ankara Agreement, they were skeptical of the terms and the timing of a customs union stipulated in the Supplementary Protocol. As balance of payments difficulties began to squeeze industrial profits, especially after the 1973 oil crisis, industrialists complained that the Protocol's transition period was too short to effect the necessary restructuring of the Turkish industry. Even in the originally pro-Europe institutions such as the Istanbul Chamber of Industry and the Economic Development Foundation, [4] strong opposition mounted to the idea of a customs union. Industrialists went as far as to ask the government to abandon the idea of a customs union altogether and seek ways of formulating a new association with the EEC.

Not all government agencies shared the emphasis on economic issues in relations with the EEC. The Ministry of Foreign Affairs had, throughout the 1960s and much of the 1970s, followed their initial assessment of Turkey's acdmission to the EEC by arguing for the primacy of political rather than economic considerations. In contrast, the State Planning Organization, in line with the industrialists' demands, emphasized the detrimental effects of a customs union on Turkey's industrialization. It would not be unfair to say that the 1970s witnessed the emergence of a tension between two of Turkey's basic national projects, Westernization and development, which had hitherto seemed quite compatible.

In October 1978 the difficulties involved in implementing tariff reductions finally compelled then Prime Minister Ecevit to freeze the terms of the Association Agreement in an effort to gain time. Although Turkey had already enacted the two phases of the tariff reduction scheme, a third set of cuts to take effect by January 1978 was increasingly pressuring the Ecevit government which had just acceded to power. Beyond this, other issues dissatisfied Turkish policymakers. They argued that the value of agricultural preferences given to Turkey was undermined by the extension of similar concessions to other Mediterranean countries as a result of the EEC's Global Mediterranean Policy. Moreover, in their view, the level of Community aid extended to Turkey inadequately prepared for the customs union stage. The Ecevit government thus presented a plan to revise the dictates of the Association Agreement and asked for a five-year period in which to honor its tariff reduction obligations.

One close observer of Turkish relations with the EEC argues that rather than trying to finalize Turkey's application to the EEC, Ecevit's primary concern was to secure the Turkish economy, ailing under the US-imposed arms embargo, with foreign credit urgently needed for economic revitalization. Therefore, Ecevit approached both the IMF and the EEC (Birand, 1985:364-387). At a time when the EEC was embroiled in its own economic difficulties, Ecevit's request for an 8-billion-dollar aid package was not met favorably. Furthermore, Turkey's inability to extricate itself from the Cyprus quagmire perhaps provided Europe a suitable excuse to refuse this request in spite of its support of a social democratic government in Turkey. Whatever the cause, Europe finally offered the Ecevit government 600 million dollars under the aegis of a fourth financial protocol already envisaged in the initial Protocol.

While Turkey was trying to cope with its economic troubles by freezing relations with the EEC, Greece applied to the Community for full membership in 1975 after the fall of the military regime. Although the Greek prime minister shared Ecevit's misgivings over the terms of the Association Agreement, Karamanlis's response, contrary to the latter's, was to apply for full membership. Due to the erosion of Greece's international standing as a consequence of Europe's Global Mediterranean Policy, Karamanlis assumed that Greek participation in community decisionmaking was the only way to improve his country's position (Verney, 1987:258). The primacy of political issues in Greece at that time as well as a different attitude toward the problem of industrialization meant that Karamanlis did not have the opposition from industrialists that Ecevit faced.

Greek moves toward the EEC alarmed only a small section of Turkish officials in spite of the latter's sensitivity toward Greek foreign policy. Still, in order to stem the possible negative effects for Turkey of Greek accession to the EEC in January 1981, Hayrettin Erkmen, the minister of foreign affairs in the minority Demirel government (which had succeeded the Ecevit government in 1979), announced Turkey's intention to follow Greece's example in the Association Council meeting held on February 6, 1980. Nonetheless, this last-minute attempt not to be outmaneuvered by Greece in Europe had little import even in the minister's own government.[5] Many observers have argued with hindsight that Turkey had missed a historic opportunity to join the EEC (Ceyhan, 1988). Few, if any, carefully considered the effect of Greek membership on Turkey's chances to follow suit. Concern with other issues such as increasing street violence at home, the urgency of economic problems, and the Cyprus imbroglio diverted attention from Europe.

European attitudes toward Turkey's association with the EEC during the 1970s were very much colored by Turkey's economic difficulties resulting from the energy crisis. As Turkey continued to regard the EEC as an organization to help meet Turkey's economic needs, the Community coolly viewed Turkey's requests. Moreover, during the 1970s, political issues increasingly concerned the Community. Economic considerations were not completely absent from this shift in emphasis as Europe, in an effort to buttress its economic strength vis-à-vis the US and Japan, began to open up to its southern neighbors. The Global

Mediterranean Policy and the Lomé Conventions are important indications of Europe's endeavors to find new markets and investment outlets. As these policies failed to produce the desired impact, Europe gradually began to consider the inclusion of some Mediterranean countries within the structure of the Community. However, in looking at certain Mediterranean countries new political attitudes, including the promotion of democracy, arose as foreign policy issues. Such considerations were very much apparent in the Greek case, as Europe froze all relations with that country as long as the Junta was in power. The belief that membership in the Community would strengthen democratic regimes guided European responses to the Portuguese and Spanish applications as well (Tsoukalis, 1981). This greater emphasis on political issues outweighed the economic burdens that the inclusion of these countries in the Community would bring (Eralp, 1988a).

This shift in emphasis in Europe allowed Greek policymakers to forge ahead with their bid for full membership once the Junta was gone. In contrast, the Turkish leaders' emphasis on economic parameters created a gulf among the southern Mediterranean countries that sought to establish closer links with the European Community. The 1980 military intervention in Turkey exacerbated this divergence and further complicated Turkish bids for incorporation into Europe, thus ushering a new and tense phase in Turkish-EEC relations.

MOUNTING TENSIONS IN TURKEY-EC RELATIONS IN THE 1980s

While Turkey shifted the orientation of her economy from inward to a greater integration with world markets, her relations with the EEC suffered a serious setback. This was in spite of widespread expectation in Turkey that an outward-looking economic policy would also improve her relations with the EEC. As it turned out, greater integration with world markets bypassed Europe as the volume of Turkey's trade with Europe began to dwindle dramatically. This decline in trade was accompanied by a similar reduction in the financial assistance of Europe to Turkey. Moreover, the souring of economic relations paralleled the appearance of a serious rift between Turkey and the EEC on political issues as well. The geopolitical considerations of the 1950s and 1960s gradually lost their importance as Europe began to emphasizze democracy and foreign policy issues. While the military intervention posed a problem for democracy, Turkey's increasing rapprochement with the US created a serious rift in foreign policy between her and a Europe which was trying to distance itself from its powerful ally.[6]

Immediately after the military intervention, the European Community adopted a wait-and-see attitude in its relations with Turkey. In the first few months, the Council of Europe, traditionally concerned with the issues of democracy and human rights, emerged as the main institution to oversee Europe's negotiations with Turkey. The Council's Parliamentary Assembly suspended Turkey's membership and refused to invite Turkish parliamentarians to its sessions but did not advise the expulsion of Turkey from the Committee of Ministers (Birand, 1985:434). Relations with the European Community continued even at a time when the Council of Europe distanced itself from Turkey, and it was in this early period (June 19, 1981) that the fourth financial protocol was ratified. However, the Community's attitude to Turkey began to harden in the fall of that year following the National Security Council's decree dissolving all political parties (October 15, 1981), as well as other measures deemed to be antidemocratic (Birand, 1985:422-423). Among the many indications of this was the Commission's decision to delay the implementation of the fourth financial protocol. The mission to Turkey in March 1982 by the Belgian Foreign Minister Tindemans as the president in office of the EEC Council of Ministers produced a critical report voicing serious concern over human rights in Turkey. Furthermore, the European Parliament passed a resolution on January 22, 1982, suspending the joint Community-Turkey Parliamentary Committee, and the Association Council did not call for another meeting. The 1983 elections did not change EEC attitudes in spite of the Council of Europe's resumption of relations with the Turkish Parliament in the spring of 1984.

The military government and Özal interpreted a number of European reports attesting to inhumane practices in Turkish courts and jails as unwarranted interference in a sovereign country's internal affairs. This demonstrated another serious divergence between Europe and Turkey. While the former regarded democracy as a *sine qua non* of inclusion into Europe, Turkey's leaders considered democracy an internal problem. Furthermore, Turkish leaders viewed democracy in relative rather than absolute terms and believed that relations with Europe would stabilize once Turkey announced a timetable of transition to its version of democracy. The inability of Turkish policymakers to assess correctly the importance placed by Europe on the question of democracy even in view of the Greek, Spanish, and Portuguese examples served to escalate tensions between Turkey and the EEC.

TURKEY'S APPLICATION FOR FULL MEMBERSHIP

The relationship between Turkey and Europe during much of the 1980s continued to revolve around competing definitions of democracy. Rather than regarding the 1983 general election as the transition to democratic rule (as the Turks depicted then), the European Community considered the 1984 local elections as the first steps toward the establishment of a parliamentary democracy in Turkey. It wasn't until these local elections that those parties banned from competition in the general election were first allowed to take part.

The Özal government elected to power in 1983 attempted to normalize relations with the EEC, but several issues continued to plague the EEC-Turkey dialogue. Among these, the question of human rights figured strongly, but other unresolved issues such as the volume of Turkish textile exports to the Community, the resumption of the financial aid blocked in 1981, and the free circulation of Turkish workers in Community countries as of December 1986 remained central. Added to these was the obstruction of the Greek lobby which, since Greece was now full member of the Community, became increasingly effective.

In spite of such problems, the EEC reversed its earlier stance and started a process of reactivating the Association Agreement, albeit without easing the pressure on the question of democracy. Thus, on February 17, 1986, the Community foreign ministers agreed to convene a special meeting of the EEC-Turkey Association Council which was eventually held on September 16, 1986 after Turkey's call for the reactivation of the agreement. After this meeting (from which the Greeks were significantly absent) the normalization of relations with Turkey resumed. Nonetheless, reactivation of the Association Agreement and the implementation of the fourth financial protocol took much longer as a result of later Greek opposition. In any case, one step that facilitated better relations was Turkey's agreement to grant the right of individual petition to her citizens at the Council of Europe in the winter of 1987. This action prompted five European countries to drop their charges of violation of human rights against Turkey at the Council of Europe. Association institutions, however, didn't begin to function until 1989: The joint Turkey-EEC Parliamentary Committee met for the first time in January 1989. Even so, two attempts to convene the EEC-Turkey Association Council failed due to Greek efforts to introduce the Cyprus question.

While the normalization of Turkey-EEC relations were still being debated, Prime Minister Özal's decision to apply to the European Community for full membership on April 14, 1987 surprised many observers inside and outside Turkey. Two traditional factors shaping Turkish foreign policy, (Westernization and Greek international action) contributed greatly to this decision. The Turkish officials involved in the decision-making process openly stressed the importance they attached to the issue of Westernization, and the minister of foreign affairs went as far as declaring that Turkey's membership in all Western institutions prevented its exclusion from the European Community (Yılmaz, 1988). Nevertheless, Turkey's commitment to Westernization became weaker than its founders hoped it would be. Instead, Islam became a political force and, at least according to one observer (Mardin, 1989:177), was transformed into a potent ideology capable of contesting Turkey's traditional adherence to Westernization.[7] The ruling party itself, squeezed by the demands to accord greater expression of Islamic identity, had to adopt a pragmatic policy which combined pro-Islamic and pro-Western tendencies. Mardin sees the success of Özal's party as lying in its ability to articulate a society that can accommodate the aspirations of and create the space needed by a Turkish "provincial" and "bazaar" population bred on Islamic precepts (Mardin, 1989:177 and 183).

These diverse internal pressures increasingly impinged on foreign policy decisions in the 1980s, while closer links emerged with the Middle Eastern countries both at the governmental and private level. Thus, Turkey's role in the Islamic Conference and its ties with the Islamic world increased. In 1981 Turkey assumed the chair of a standing Committee for Economic and Commercial Cooperation, established at the third summit meeting of the organization. The decline in volume of trade with the EEC was accompanied in the early 1980s by an increase in trade with the Middle East, while the government encouraged the proliferation of joint Turkish-Arab banks and trading companies. Prominent Turkish businessmen including the prime minister's brother actively forged such links, especially with Saudi Arabia. Against such an economic backdrop, Turkey's foreign policy also showed greater cooperation with Arab and other Islamic states. Hence, Turkey adopted what its policymakers called an attitude of "active neutrality" in the Iran-Iraq war, which effectively meant that, contrary to the US, it did not pursue either an overt or a covert anti-Iran foreign policy. Furthermore, Turkey strengthened relations with the PLO, by being among the first countries to recognize the newly declared independent Palestine state.

Despite the significance of this rapprochement between Turkey and the Arab world, both international and external considerations circumscribed it. First, trade with the Middle East suffered a severe setback by the mid-1980s, mainly as a result of the decline in oil revenues. This volatility in Middle Eastern markets caused entrepreneurs to turn once again to the comparatively more stable and thus reliable European markets. Second, the Turkish pro-Arab stance increasingly strained its more traditional alliances. For example, Turkey's almost immediate recognition of Palestine created grave tensions with the US and marked the country's first overtly anti-Israel governmental decision. These tensions were exacerbated by Turkey's refusal to follow the US policy of isolating Libya. The policy of forging stronger ties with the Arab world also met strong opposition within Turkey itself. Economic and political links with Saudi Arabia and other Islamic countries caused increasing extreme concern and suspicion in the country's secularist intelligentsia and press. In addition, the revelation that the government had obtained funds from a Saudi organization in order to pay wages to Turkish religious officials in Europe created a scandal that even implicated the president of the republic.

Lastly, the changes undergone in the nature of the Western alliance within the last decades complicate Turkish attempts at Western institutional participation. Turkish perceptions of an undifferentiated Western unity weakened as economic and political rivalries undermined European-US cooperation. As Turkey applies for full membership in the European Community, the difficulties of reconciling greater participation in Western institutions with deeper insertion in the Islamic world will be matched with those faced in defining a new role for Turkey within the changing Western alliance itself.

As Turkey's hurried application for full membership shows, the Turkish government seems to have realized belatedly the significance of the "Greek factor." That Greece would have a definite advantage over Turkey in furthering its policies in Cyprus and the Aegean by being inside the Community only became apparent to Turkish policymakers after the fact. Moreover, these political advantages have been accompanied by economic gains that Greece obtained as a result of full membership. Greece not only receives assistance through the Community's regional and social funds, but also gained a competitive edge over Turkey, with whom she shares a similar export portfolio. Furthermore, Turkey's trade difficulties in European markets are exacerbated by the admission of Spain and Portugal, since they too export similar agricultural products and textiles. The admission of countries that are exporters of textiles severely curtails Turkey's chances of success in her efforts at having the European quotas on its textile exports increased. Under such conditions, full membership appears to both policymakers and industrialists in Turkey as the only way of securing Turkish exporting capability to Europe.

Turkish policymakers, drawing on the experiences of Greece, Portugal, and Spain, finally realized that mere association with the European Community was no longer meaningful. According to Turkish Minister of Foreign Affairs Mesut Yılmaz (1988), Greece had stopped association procedures in favor of full membership because association only brought heavy economic burdens without providing corresponding advantages. In Yılmaz's estimation, the same calculation had prompted Spain and Portugal to negotiate for full membership directly. In all three cases the issue of a customs union appeared to Yılmaz as the source of gravest concern. If Europe's Global Mediterranean Policy eroded the advantages that Greece hoped to obtain from association with Europe, Turkey was suffering mainly from the presence within the European Community of southern European countries with similar export portfolios. The only way to outweigh the disadvantages brought by a customs union would be to obtain access to the financial benefits that membership to the European Community could provide. This view was also shared by Turkey's leading industrialists, whose apprehensions of a customs union in the past had been quite effective in stalling the Association Agreement (Eczacıbaşı, 1988; Koç, 1988).

Still, the truthfulness of the above does not suffice to explain the timing of Turkey's application to the European Community for full membership. The decline in Turkey's economic profile in recent years also accounts for this seemingly abrupt decision. After the mid-1980s, the earlier optimism generated by Özal's economic policies disappeared in the face of rising inflation and increasing debt problems. This rather bleak economic picture, reminiscent of the late Democratic party years, forced the Özal government to seek new sources of aid and credit. The prime minister thus relied on longer-term credits than available through the European Community to ease the pressure created by the short-term loans under which the Turkish economy operates. Leading industrialists agreed with the prime minister, arguing that Turkey should be able to use the same funds available to Turkey's international competitors. One such industrialist calculates that membership in the European Community would provide an inflow of foreign funds to the value of 6 billion ECUs, a sum which would also be useful in curbing inflation (IKV, 1989).

Becoming part of Europe furthers Özal's stated aim of improving Turkey's present standing in the international system. Ever since the military intervention (if not before), Turkey's isolation on many international platforms had pushed toward greater dependence on US political as well as financial backing. The questions raised about the nature of Turkish democracy both at home and abroad, and the uneven performance of Turkey's economy had significantly contributed to this isolation. Another widely recognized fact is that disputes with Greece, and especially Turkish policy in Cyprus, have significantly added to this isolation (Sezer, 1989:96). Reversing this situation and retrieving Turkey's political and economic respectability had been one of Özal's election tickets. In fact, a look at the Mediterranean countries' foreign policies shows that while Greece, Spain, and Portugal adopted a multidimensional stance in their policy orientations, the Turkish government in the early 1980s closely supported US policies. The US administration, for its part, did not, after the mid-1980s, maintain its earlier pro-Turkish attitude. The decline in US military assistance to Turkey as of 1984, as well as the increasing importance of the Cyprus issue in considerations of aid to Turkey in the US Congress, attests to this change in US policy (Sezer, 1989:91).[8] One wonders whether the reactivation of links with the EEC is one way of counterbalancing the effects of this shift in US policy toward Turkey.[9]

DOMESTIC ATTITUDES TOWARD FULL MEMBERSHIP

Within Turkey, the business community has most strongly supported Turkey's application for full membership. Some of the economic problems mentioned above, especially the unpredictability of Middle Eastern markets, have been among the main factors accounting for this support. The new export-oriented economic policy reduced the importance of the customs union issue for industrialists and instead stressed the question of foreign investments. The attraction of foreign investments to Turkey was an integral part of Özal's policies of export promotion; it was in partnership with foreign companies that Turkey could acquire not only the technology to produce competitive commodities, but also the information needed to trade in world markets. Capital erosion sustained by large firms within the last few years as a result of inflation and high interest rates has discouraged industrialists from insisting on the production of Turkish technology and forced them to seek European partners to access expensive European technology. Full membership, it is thought, will facilitate the entry into Turkey of foreign capital and technology, which, despite progressively more favorable regulations, remained extremely cautious in the past (IKV, 1987). Unsatisfactory levels of foreign investment in Turkey have led industrialists to argue that European investors would be more attracted to Turkey if, as a full member of the EEC, she could act as a bridge between the Middle East and Europe. Indeed, the increased activity within Turkey of Japanese and other Far Eastern firms strengthens the possibility of such a development. Asian countries further afield may also try to use Turkey as a base for economic operations within Europe.

However, economic factors alone do not sufficiently explain the importance of the EEC for certain sections of the private sector. During the 1960s, relations with the EEC concerned mainly a relatively small and homogeneous group of Istanbul-based traders who shared a pro-European attitude. In the intervening twenty years, the politicization and debate regarding Turkey's relations with Europe introduced many divisions within the Turkish private sector itself. The rising political potency of an Islamist discourse exacerbated these debates, as indicated above. Those secularist members of the private sector view policies that accommodate Islamic demands with increasing alarm. These range from the increasing role in the economy of charitable foundations and funds outside the supervision of the national parliament, sanctioned by the government, to the greater importance attached to improving economic relations with the Middle East. In particular, the increased visibility within the Turkish economy of Arab finance corporations promising the average citizen large economic returns without interest, and the role played in some of these by the prime minister's brother, are seen as ways of disseminating Islamic ideologies. Membership in the European Community therefore appears to many Istanbul-based industrialists as a force to hold these currents in check. In contrast, a majority of traders and industrialists who emerged within the 1960s and 1970s as holders of small but significant portions of capital in Anatolia regard membership in the EC rather suspiciously. For them, becoming part of an Islamic Economic Community and the operation of non-interest finance corporations within Turkey would be a better way to realize economic development, since it would also align economic practices with the dictates of Islam on a national scale (Eralp, 1990). Such conflicts erupt periodically within the umbrella organization of the private sector, the Union of Chambers which, in the event, has had to adopt an equivocal stance on the question of EC membership (TOBB, 1987).

In contrast to the diversity of attitudes within the private sector, Turkey's political parties that were represented in the parliament unanimously supported Turkey's application to the EC for full membership. The main opposition at the level of party organizations came from smaller parties on the right that have not overcome the 10 percent national barrier and thus remained outside the parliament. The Welfare party, heir to the banned National Salvation party, most vigorously opposed Turkey's accession to the EC. The leader of the party, also ex-leader of the NSP, depicted the EC as a Christian community organized to undermine the Islamic world's rise to prominence and denounced the pro-EC lobby in Turkey as part of a Zionist plot to sow the seeds of dissent among Islamic countries.

Crucial differences between the ruling party and the main opposition party also exist in their approaches to the EC question. The Motherland party (MP) regarded membership in the EC primarily as a way to further integrate Turkey in the world markets. In line with the expectations of the private sector, the MP viewed the EC as a stable market for Turkish exports as well as a source of foreign funds and technology. Politically speaking, the MP was apprehensive of European definitions of democracy and insistence on human rights and free speech. In the words of one observer (Turan, 1988:85), the MP was concerned that

European understanding of political democracy might accord legitimacy to political viewpoints and organizations which have not been viewed with favor by groups such as the business community, small businessmen, wealthy farmers, and some other groups which count heavily among the electorate of the center right.

Thus, in response to the European Community's emphasis on full democracy, the MP government tried to advance the thesis that full democracy is something to be achieved gradually, and after incorporation into the Community. In sum, democracy becomes a point of negotiation rather than an essential requirement.

In contrast to the ruling party of the 1980s the main opposition party, the Social Democratic Populist party (SDPP), approached the EC question in political rather than economic terms. The SDPP argued that membership in the EC would hasten the consolidation of democracy in Turkey, as it did in other southern European countries. In this respect, the SDPP definition of democracy appears closer to the EC's. However, the SDPP equivocated on the question of economic consequences of EC membership. If the promise of instituting a firm democratic regime able to weather political upheavals without having to undergo military interventions was one of the main election tickets of the SDPP, the other was the question of industrialization. As heir to the banned Republican People's party, the SDPP stressed the need for a largely indigenous industrialization. The likelihood of integration with the EC undermining the comparatively weaker Turkish industry causes much apprehension within the ranks of the SDPP. Therefore, the issue of membership in the EC reveals the difficulties that the party faces in reconciling its political and economic objectives. In this context it is interesting to note that many of the trade unions also see membership in the EC in political rather than economic terms. TÜRK-İŞ, one of the larger confederations of trade unions, supports Turkey's application to the EC on the grounds that such a membership will force the government to apply more rigorously the ILO standards regulating labor relations.

REFLECTIONS ON EUROPEAN RESPONSES TO THE TURKISH APPLICATION

In the years that followed Turkey's formal application for membership, the European Community has activated its normal review and assessment channels. After the Commission prepares a report it is forwarded to the Council of Ministers. Although no formal information was available at the time of preparing this chapter, press leakages indicated that the report would not be favorable. Bearing in mind that the Greek application had met with a similar resistance, Turkish policymakers have not been unduly disturbed by this probable outcome, which puts the onus of the decision on the Council of Ministers.

However, developments within the EC's own process of evolution show that Turkish policymakers have reason to worry. The Turkish application comes at a time when the European Community, having completed its processes of enlargement, is facing problems of consolidation. The addition of new members in the 1970s and 1980s slowed down the pace of European economic and political integration; the process of decision making is also longer and more complicated. A loosely structured European Community alarms its founding members, who believe that only a more consolidated Community can compete successfully against its economic rivals, Japan and the US. The difficulties of small, independent nation-states operating in the world economy prompted the Community toward reforming its constitution (Nicholson and East, 1987: 253-268). These attempts, specifically aimed at creating a more integrated structure, crystallized in the adoption of the Single European Act in 1987. Apart from a number of clauses designed to speed the process of decision making, the Single European Act accepts as a concrete short-term strategy the creation of a single market within Europe by the end of 1992. This strategy has obtained the unreserved support of all the European countries that are working diligently toward the realization of the single market (Wood and Yeşilada, 1991).

It is fairly obvious that the Community will be reluctant at this stage to welcome the application of a new member. Confirmation of this reluctance is obvious from the comments of the head of the Representation of the Commission in Turkey at a roundtable discussion where he stressed that integration will take "priority over all other issues" (Van Rij, 1989:59).[10] Predictably, the Community has tried to postpone Turkey's inclusion as much as possible and offered Turkey solutions other than full membership. Among such offers are the revitalization of the Association Agreement and other forms of economic agreements that would alleviate, to a certain extent, Turkey's difficulties. For Europe, the admission of Turkey seems a question that cannot be considered on its own, but perhaps as part of another, post-1992 enlargement process that would include other countries such as the EFTA members, Malta, and Cyprus. Signs of the consolidation of this policy of delaying Turkey's membership have appeared. For example, the Turkish press in 1989 revealed that the Commission would first submit a preliminary report rather than a final assessment as had been expected, in order to gain more time (Yalçın, 1989a and 1989b). According to the information leaked to the press, an early draft of this report drew a bleak picture of the Turkish economy, putting special emphasis on rising inflation and unemployment as well as the unfavorable prospects of Turkey's export capacity (Sen, 1989).

At that early stage, Turkey's performance in democracy and human rights had not yet been considered by the European Community. This is due to the division of labor between the Commission and the Council of Ministers, whereby mainly the latter deals with political issues . In spite of this, Turkish policy-makers urged the Commission to consider recent efforts at democratization in Turkey rather than simply looking at the economic issues, where Turkey did not appear to be very strong. Nevertheless, the European Parliament will seriously scrutinize Turkish democracy. With the adoption of the Single European Act, the European Parliament obtained the right to ratify the application of new members, and the social democratic views in the European Parliament are sure to make Turkey's case a difficult one to argue.

A second concern of the Turkish policymakers has been to minimize the effects of the Turco-Greek conflict on Turkey's application. The Community has to date tried to stay out of this particular dispute and has avoided any situation in which it would become an arbiter. Nevertheless, prospects of a future Greek veto immediately raised the possibility that Europe is avoiding being drawn into the Turco-Greek conflict by postponing its decision on the Turkish application. It is perhaps with such considerations in mind that the former Turkish prime minister (now president) Turgut Özal tried to create the conditions for a rapprochement with Greece in Davos. However, his efforts to keep the Davos spirit alive were met with innumerable obstacles, as the dispute over salvage operations in the Aegean demonstrated.

At present the Turkish government's view that the Association Agreement is no longer effective is not shared by the European Community. It seems that Turkey has chosen a rather inauspicious time to apply for full membership. Such an application would have been regarded more favorably by Europe had it coincided with the second enlargement process. Nonetheless, it is still very difficult for Europe to reject the Turkish application out of hand. In spite of the fact that Turkey has applied according to Article 237 of the Treaty of Rome, which gives the right of application to any European country, the Ankara Agreement also provides Turkey with the right of an eventual union with Europe. However, the future prospects of the Turkish application should not be evaluated simply in terms of legal prescripts. The various economic and political as well as historical considerations outlined in the preceding pages show that Turkey's membership cannot be dismissed outright, but will certainly take much longer than the applications of Greece, Spain, and Portugal.

CONCLUSION

This chapter has traced the history of the relations between Turkey and the EC to assess the future prospects of Turkey's eventual integration into the Community. Two traditional concerns have largely determined Turkish efforts to become part of Europe. Westernization, the first of these factors, became more problematic in the 1980s as a result of the proliferation of diverse attitudes at home and the tension in European-American relations that constituted the main axis of the Western alliance. This chapter has also argued that the Greek factor, which has always shaped the attitude of Turkish policymakers, has played a crucial role in determining the course of relations with Europe. The present inclusion of Greece in the European Community powerfully reinforces the Turkish determination to apply.

This chapter further suggests that Turkish policymakers turn to Europe when economic and political problems at home urge them to look for new policy alternatives abroad. In contrast, in periods of stability, relations with the EC are accorded secondary importance, while efforts to improve relations with the US gain ascendancy. This pattern occurred in the last years of the Democrat party, and it divided the Motherland party rule. Thus, the issue is raised whether this Turkish habit of turning to Europe only in times of need has an important cost, that of losing sight of the dynamics of European development. This habit also seems to preclude the formulation of a longer-term and sustained policy toward Europe as well as the ability to find viable strategies at the right moment.

NOTES

This chapter was written before the announcement of the decision of the European Community on the application of Turkey for full membership. I believe that the analysis and conclusions offered in this chapter are still valid.

1. Turkey's commitment to the West was so strong that her policymakers felt slighted when Turkey was not included in the Marshall Plan immediately after the war.

2. Similar views seem to have been prevalent in Greece in the same period (Verney, 1987).

3. A second protocol signed in June 1973 envisaged an extension to Turkey over a period of five and a half years of a 195-million-dollar aid package with a further 25 million dollars in European Investment Bank loans (Nicholson and East, 1987:203). Further protocols were to be drawn up during the course of association.

4. The Foundation (IKV in Turkish) was established in 1965 with the specific aim of coordinating the relations of the private sector with the EEC.

5. The fact that the Demirel government needed the outside support of the National Salvation Party, a party that was bitterly opposed to Turkey's admission to the EEC, goes a long way toward explaining the reluctance of the Turkish cabinet to heed its foreign minister (Eralp, 1990). In effect, Erkmen was finally removed from office on September 5, 1980, after a parliamentary no-confidence vote in which the National Salvation party played a key role.

6. I have argued elsewhere (Eralp, 1988b) that the mid-1970s saw a disintegration in the unity of the Western alliance as rivalries between Europe and the US increased. In this climate, Turkish foreign policy makers sought to obtain US credit as well as establish closer collaboration on Middle Eastern issues with the US after the latter had to sever its links with Iran and Lebanon.

7. It must be immediately mentioned that it was not in the 1980s that questions of religion occupied an important place in Turkey's political agenda. The difference between the pre- and post-1980 periods seems to lie in the mode in which demands for an Islamic way of life are articulated.

8. Sezer mentions other points that indicate the growing tensions between Turkey and the US. Among these are the US's refusal to open American markets to Turkish exports to a greater degree and the increased importance accorded by the US Congress to various Armenian claims.

9. Remarks made by one of Özal's foreign policy advisors supports such an interpretation. Minister without Portfolio Kamran Inan, speaking at a meeting of the Turkish Democracy Foundation, argued in favor of the advantages that a multilateral foreign policy would provide in view of the divergence in interests between Turkey and the US and the difficulties experienced by Turkey in dealing with the US on her own.

10. Van Rij (1989:59) explicitly states that the problem raised by Turkey's application is whether the EC and its member states are willing to risk upsetting a new fragile balance by considering new membership applications.

REFERENCES

Birand, M. A. (1985). *Türkiye'nin Ortak Pazar Macerası, 1959-85*. Istanbul: Milliyet Yayınları.

Ceyhan, H. (1988). "Türkiye-Avrupa Toplulugu 25. Ortaklık Yılının Değerlendirilmesi." *İktisadi Kalkınma Vakfı Dergisi*, Ankara Antlaşması 25. Yıl Özel Sayısı. No. 59, pp. 35-41.

Eczacıbaşı, N. (1988). "Ankara Antlaşmasının 25. Yılında Türkiye-AT İlişkileri." *İktisadi Kalkınma Dergisi*, Ankara Antlaşması 25. Yıl Özel Sayısı. No. 59. pp. 31-33.

Eralp, A. (1988a). "The Second Enlargement Process of the European Community and Its Possible Effects on Turkey's External Relations." *Yapı Kredi Economic Review*. Vol. 11. No. 2-3, pp. 3-24.

_____ (1988b). "West European Perspectives on North-South Relations." *Development Studies* (METU). Vol. 15. No. 3-4, pp. 19-46.

_____ (1990). "The Politics of Turkish Development Strategies." In A. Finkel and N. Sirman, eds., *Turkish State, Turkish Society*. London: Routledge.

Gönlübol, M., and H. Ülman (1987). "İkinci Dünya Savaşından Sonra Türk Dış Politikası (1945-1965 Yılları): Genel Durum." In M. Gönlübol, ed., *Olaylarla Türk Dış Politikası*. Ankara: Siyasal Bilgiler Fakültesi Yayınları. 6th edition, pp. 191-334.

IKV (1987). *Avrupa Topluluğu ve Türkiye-AT İlişkileri*. Istanbul: IKV pub. no. 49.

_____ (1989). "İKV Basın Toplantısı." *İktisadi Kalkınma Vakfı Dergisi*. Ankara: no. 64, pp. 6-7.

Koç, V. (1988). "25. Yılında Türkiye-AT Ortaklık İlişkileri." *İktisadi Kalkınma Vakfı Dergisi*, Ankara Antlaşması 25. Yıl Özel Sayısı. No. 59, pp. 24-26.

Mardin, Ş. (1989). "Culture and Religion: Towards the Year 2000." In *Turkey in the Year 2000*. Ankara: Turkish Political Science Association publication, pp. 165-186.

Nicholson, F., and R. East (1987). *From the Six to the Twelve: The Enlargement of the European Communities*. Essex, UK: Longman.

Sander, O. (1979). *Türk Amerikan İlişkileri: 1947-1964*. Ankara: Siyasal Bilgiler Fakültesi Yayınları. No. 427.

Şen, F. (1989). "AT'nin Türkiye Raporu Sevimsiz." *Ekonomik Panorama*. Vol. 2. No. 12, pp. 16-17.

Sezer, D. (1989). "Turkish Foreign Policy in the Year 2000." *In Turkey in the Year 2000*. Ankara: Turkish Political Science Association publication. pp. 63-117.

TOBB (1987). *İktisadi Rapor*. Pub. no. Genel 20, APK-4.

Tsoukalis, L. (1981). *The European Community and Its Mediterranean Enlargement*. London: George Allen and Unwin.

Turan, I. (1988). "Turkish Political Parties and the European Community." *Yapı Kredi Economic Review*. Vol. 3. No. 1, pp. 73-88.

_____(1989). "Turkey and the European Community: Towards the Year 2000." In *Turkey in the Year 2000*. Ankara: Turkish Political Science Association publication, pp. 35-36.

Ülman, H., and O. Sander (1972). "Türk Dış Politikasına Yön Veren Etkenler (1923-1968)." *Siyasal Bilgiler Fakültesi Dergisi*. Vol. 27. No. 1, pp. 1-24.

Van Rij, J. (1989). "Comments on Turkey and the European Community: Towards the Year 2000." In *Turkey in the Year 2000*. Ankara: Turkish Political Science Association publication, pp. 57-59.

Verney, S. (1987). "Greece and the European Community." In K. Featherstone and D. K. Katsoudas, eds., *Political Change in Greece: Before and After the Colonels*. London: Croom Helm.

Wood, David M., and Birol A. Yeşilada (1991). "European Integration in the 1980s and 1990s." *Business in the Contemporary World*. Vol. 3, No. 3 (Spring): 89-101.

Yalçın, N. (1989a). "AT'da Boykot Hazırlığı." *Milliyet*. March 5, 1989.

_____(1989b). "AT Üyeliği 1992'den Önce Hayal." *Milliyet*. March 24, 1989.

Yılmaz, M. (1988). "Ankara Antlaşmasının Siyasi Yönü ve Dış İlişkilerimiz Bakımından Değerlendirilmesi." *İktisadi Kalkınma Vakfı Dergisi*, Ankara Antlaşması 25. Yılı Özel Sayısı. No. 59, pp. 9-11.

10

Turkey and the Western Alliance in the 1980s

Duygu Bazoğlu Sezer

INTRODUCTION

World politics in the 1980s was marked by a wide swing in East-West relations–from confrontation in the first part of the decade to accommodation in the second. The Soviet invasion of Afghanistan at the close of the 1970s, the debacle over the respective nuclear weapons modernization programs of NATO and the Soviet Union/Warsaw Pact (WP), the deepening paralysis over arms control, and the Polish crisis brought East-West relations in the first half of the decade to a state characterized by many as the Second Cold War.

In the mid-1980s a new phase started to unfold. Shortly after Ronald Reagan began his second term as president of the United States, Mikhail Gorbachev gained the leadership of the Soviet Union as the General-Secretary of the Communist party. Soon afterward the search for security through negotiations resumed. In December 1987 the two super powers signed the historic INF treaty. Conventional stability mandate talks began in Vienna in early 1987, and were followed by the negotiations on conventional forces in Europe (CFE) which opened in March 1989. Soviet troops were withdrawn from Afghanistan by February 1989. Finally, the Cold War came to a sudden end with the collapse of the Warsaw Pact and the communist regimes in Eastern Europe and the USSR.

Gorbachev (1987) expounded the conceptual basis of his foreign policy initiatives in what he called the "New Political Thinking," introducing such profoundly significant notions for international relations as the mutuality of national security, reasonable sufficiency as a guide to military doctrine, defense as the organizing concept of military strategy, and international interdependence as a dominant feature of contemporary international life. Gorbachev's truly dramatic, even revolutionary, proposals for change within Soviet society and in the way it related to the outside world led to deep reverberations on the West's perceptions of its own security needs, interests, and corresponding institutional arrangements. Increasing numbers of people began to think in terms of Michael Howard's (1987:487) hypothetical model of a "benign Soviet Union," one which has "rejoined the community of nations and is playing the part which optimists hoped for it in 1945."

As East-West relations went through a new stage of qualitative improvement in the second half of the 1980s, implying perhaps the approach of the final end of the Cold War, transatlantic relations entered a new crisis. The history of the Atlantic Alliance has, in some sense, been the history of managing relations between the United States and the European allies in the face of unfolding challenges to Alliance unity and solidarity. Nevertheless, the Gorbachev challenge has been the most formidable of all for one very simple reason: Gorbachev's system of thought on national and international security, together with his bold peace initiatives, has threatened to reduce the Atlantic Alliance to an irrelevant relic of the past by successfully depriving it of its rationale, that is, the existence of the Soviet threat. Accordingly, the original Western consensus on the objectives and responsibilities of the Atlantic Alliance has been in a greater state of flux and confusion than it has ever been in its forty-year history. Ambassador Jonathan Dean formulated the Alliance problem in 1986 in the following words: "If the Soviet Union is indeed a status quo power in Europe in the military sense and the East-West military confrontation there is in fact on the downgrade, then NATO will have an increasingly political rather than military function," (Dean, 1987:86).

At the more specific level, the ever-present transatlantic tensions over Alliance strategy and the credibility of extended deterrence intensified as it became clearer at Rejkjavik in the Fall of 1986 that the superpowers were intent on moving toward a nuclear disarmed world by the year 2000. The INF treaty became the foremost contractual evidence of their mutual commitment to that goal. On the question of burden sharing, too, the United States became increasingly more adamant. Thus, the changing nature of the security relationship between the United States and Western Europe, underway in fact at least since the dawn of strategic parity, finally forced the Western Europeans to seriously explore their own options to "Europeanize Europe's defense." In this context they had revived the Western European Union (WEU) in 1984, increasingly viewing it in subsequent years as the principal, though unofficial, institutional affiliate of the European Community (EC) in the field of security.

Because Turkey is a member of the Atlantic Alliance and, therefore, structurally tied to the East-West configuration, developments that affected the balance of power among the major players in the East-West and West-West system of interaction drew her into their orbit of influence as well. Turkey is a small power, which by definition implies that in general she is in the position of responding to what happens in the external environment rather than shaping that environment. The nature of and the issues in Turkey's relations with the Alliance in the 1980s provides a useful case study, especially for the theorist working on alliances, of the extent of small power vulnerability to the shifting equilibrium in major geopolitical relationships.

The discussion in the following pages is organized into three sections. The first section reviews the background to Turkey's postwar security policy. The second surveys the course of and the issues in Turkish Alliance relations in the first part of the 1980s. The third focuses on the questions that confront Turkish security at the close of the decade as the international environment undergoes fundamental changes from excessive militarization to moderation against the background of the INF treaty and the "Gorbachev Revolution" within the Soviet Union and Eastern Europe. It should be noted that the analysis in this chapter is confined to the decade of the 1980s and, therefore, does not make any assessment or prediction about Turkey's foreign policy after the collapse of communism in the Soviet Union and Eastern Europe.

TURKISH SECURITY IN THE WESTERN ALLIANCE SINCE 1945

Post-War Political-Military Circumstances

The principal political-military framework of Turkey's security policy of the last four decades was established the unsettling international environment of the immediate postwar years. Uncommitted in its formative years and a neutral in the Second World War, Turkey then chose to join the newly emerging, US-led Western security system as the fundamental tenet of her security policy.

Stalin's daring designs at the close of the war were the most immediate and therefore possibly the most concrete consideration that shaped the desire to seek a security relationship with the US. On March 19, 1945, the Soviet Union had notified Turkey of its intention not to extend the Treaty of Nonaggression of 1925, due to expire in November. Soviet conditions for a new treaty included Soviet bases on the Straits, revision of the Montreux Convention of 1936, which regulated the Straits regime, and the cession of Kars and Ardahan, two provinces in northern Turkey, to the Soviet Union.[1]

There were other considerations as well. Unsettling changes in the surrounding regions, including changes in domestic regimes, were not positive signs for a small and diplomatically isolated country desiring to remain untouched by the repercussions and turbulence of the postwar settlement. Considerations of realpolitik and economic interests led to a favorable view of the US. It was the only world power capable of determining the future of Western Europe and counterbalancing the Soviet Union, which was the single military power on the war-torn continent at the end of the war. Moreover, ideological and domestic socioeconomic choices had crystallized sufficiently to influence the worldviews and foreign policy orientations of Turkish decision makers and other interest groups. By 1945 Turkey was preparing to liberalize its political and economic system. This outlook created a natural affinity with the US, which at the same time seemed to promise to be the most rewarding source of economic and military aid.

Military Integration with the Atlantic Alliance

Turkey's fear of the Soviet Union and the emerging American grand strategy of containment converged by March 1947 to produce the Truman Doctrine. The Korean War further enhanced the strategic value of Turkey for the defense of Western security interests against possible Soviet expansionism in Europe and the Middle East. These calculations finally resulted in Turkey's admission into the North Atlantic Treaty Organization (NATO) in February 1952.

Throughout the 1950s Turkey was an unfliching ally. However, serious strains developed in the 1960s in US-Turkish relations in the context of the Cyprus crisis of 1964. President Johnson's ultimatum in the summer of 1964 directing Turkey not to undertake military action in the island or else to face the Soviets alone was the first stark reminder to Turkey that the US/NATO protection would not cover all national contingencies. The East-West détente in the 1970s and the renewed crisis in Cyprus in 1974 provided further stresses. They culminated in the three-year-long arms embargo by the US to punish Turkey for her intervention in Cyprus in response to the coup d'état against Cypriot President Makarios engineered by the Junta government in Athens.

Turkey pondered for a while in the late 1970s about a national security concept, implying a substantive revision of her Alliance-dominated defense policy (Sezer, 1981:22-29). However, in the late 1970s events moved briskly, domestically and internationally, to destroy whatever chance the idea enjoyed for an intelligent hearing before a final decision. Domestically, political militancy between the right and the left overtook Turkey. Internationally, East-West relations eclipsed into a new round of the Cold War.

THE SECOND COLD WAR AND RETURN TO THE ALLIANCE

As the introduction discussed, East-West relations underwent acute tension in the late 1970s. Situated at the intersection of the outer boundaries of two major international crisis zones, central Europe and southwestern Asia, Turkey keenly sensed in the early 1980s the potential threat to her security due to the volatility of the prevailing situation. The domestic instability and terror in the late 1970s, culminating in the military takeover on September 12, 1980, substantially increased Turkey's exposure to the impact of events outside her borders.

Southwestern Asia

Developments in southwestern Asia, namely the Soviet invasion of Afghanistan, the Iran-Iraq War in the wake of the Iranian Revolution, and Israel's occupation of southern Lebanon, raised questions for Turkish policymakers and military planners in two ways. First, they pointed to an increasing proclivity by states to use force across internationally recognized state boundaries specifically to bring about internal change. Second, no regional power or collectivity existed that shared Turkey's threat perception and worldview, and that was capable of playing a deterrent or defense role against possible local or external threats to regional stability. Anything could have happened at any time.

The Soviet Afghan policy was the single most important event for Turkey, possibly a watershed, in arousing strong suspicions of the return of her great northern neighbor to an interventionist and expansionist foreign policy. Bilateral relations did not suffer much, however. The Soviet Union treated the Turkish military regime as an internal affair. Meanwhile, Turkey settled several thousand Afghan refugees.

The Iranian regime's declared goal of exporting of its Islamic Revolution equally unsettled Turkish domestic politics by 1980, but its influence remained somewhat muted by the exigencies of the Iran-Iraq War. The war presented the most immediate political military complications and dangers. Fear of its possible escalation to a super-power confrontation was the greatest danger, even though an unlikely one. The possibility of American involvement loomed like a more realistic scenario, into which she could drag Turkey, too, through her access to the military bases. Second, maintaining neutrality when both belligerents were border neighbors providing lucrative export markets proved to be a highly controversial task. For example, Turkish military operations against Kurdish insurgents based along border areas in Iraq were often interpreted in Iran as anti-Iranian shows of force. Similarly, Turkey was irritated when Iran suggested the Kerkük-Yumurtalık pipeline as a potential bombing target in August 1983 and several times subsequently. In a prepared statement to the press on August 1, 1983, the Turkish Foreign Minister Ilter Türkmen immediately warned that the war "must not harm the interests of countries in the region" (*Cumhuriyet*, August 2, 1983). Third, Kurdish separatism, unleashed anew under the impact of the war and with a large-scale resort to arms, was vulnerable to exploitation by the belligerents, who hoped to undermine each other's central authority and war plans. Finally, the course of the war occasionally inspired hypothetical scenarios for Turkish intervention in Kerkük and Mosul to prevent the total defeat of Iraq and the subsequent establishment of a radically new regional balance.[2] It also raised the specter of inadvertent Turkish intervention as a result of border incidents in which Iranian aircraft bombed Silop and Habur villages inside Turkey. In retrospect, the Turkish position on the Iran-Iraq War was pragmatic. It did conduct business with both belligerents but stood for the preservation of the existing regional balance, which sometimes translated into a pro-Iraqi stance.

Against this war-ridden, chaotic regional picture, closing ranks with the Western alliance seemed, once again, to be the only reasonable option for Turkish security. Turkey had adhered to the principle of the Islamic Conference in 1952 at Taif which said that coping with regional security issues was the responsibility of regional powers. But the principle lacked credibility, and Turkey, like others, paid only lip service to it. Arguing that the Taif Declaration did not rule out bilateral or multilateral defense cooperation with nonregional parties, Turkey resolved to improve her deterrence and defense capabilities through closer cooperation and consultation with the US and NATO.

Enhanced Alliance Cooperation

Southwesernt Asia was not the sole source of dangers. The fierce nuclear diplomacy between the East and the West, together with the Polish crisis, had already deteriorated the political military scene in Europe. Deep divisions followed not only between the East and the West but also between the US and Western Europe regarding the European nuclear balance, modernization, and arms control.

A number of very important controversies were settled in quick succession. The US-Turkish Defense and Economic Cooperation Agreement (DECA) was swiftly concluded on March 29, 1980, after five years of intermittent negotiations. Turkey retreated from its previous position concerning NATO command and control arrangements in the Aegean in favor of the "Rogers Plan" in order to allow Greece's return to the military structure in October 1980. On November 29, 1982, the US and Turkey signed a Memorandum of Understanding (MOU) for the modernization of close to a dozen airfields in eastern Turkey.

Ample evidence in official statements indicates that the graveness of the external environment in southwestern Asia certainly helped reconfirm for Turkish governments the continuing relevance of NATO, and in particular the special security relationship with the US.[3] Domestic factors added to this view. The conservative philosophy and worldview of the military regime provided strong pro-American and pro-NATO policies. In addition, the developments in southwestern Asia dangerously threatened the interests of the western Alliance. This, in turn, swiftly upgraded the strategic value of Turkey to the Alliance not simply because of its geographical proximity to the region but also because of its stability in the aftermath of the military coup d'état of September 1980. Due to this, the US administration turned favorably to Turkey. During a visit to Ankara in 1982, Secretary of State Alexander Haig affirmed Foreign Minister Türkmen's description of the state of US-Turkish relations as "excellent" (US Department of State, 1982:60). Assistant Secretary of State Richard Burt said in 1983, "A strong and stable Turkey is important to the US and to Turkey's other NATO partners [and therefore] The United States has supported the efforts of the Turkish Government over the past three years to establish tranquility and stable democracy."[4]

Assistant Secretary of Defense Richard N. Perle was even more explicit. Responding in congressional testimony to a question on the strategic importance of Turkey vis-à-vis the Persian Gulf, he said, "In the time that it would take the United States to deliver a division to the upper Gulf in the event of an emergency there, the Soviets could easily deliver 10 divisions. So there is an obvious strategic imbalance in that region that, by virtue of distance, we have no obvious means of overcoming. If Turkey is strong then a Soviet military commander considering a move into a critical region like the Gulf would have to think twice. He would have to think twice because eastern Turkey is within striking distance of those critical Soviet forces based in the Transcaucasus" (US Congress, 1984:20). NATO communiqués in the early 1980s repeatedly urged the affluent allies to extend economic assistance to Turkey and Greece.

The interconnection between Alliance security and the security of eastern Turkey was thus explicitly recognized due to the force of events when the security of the Persian Gulf assumed highest priority among Western concerns. President Carter had responded to the Soviet invasion of Afghanistan by declaring the Gulf region an area of vital interest to the US and by ordering the reinforcement of the Rapid Deployment Joint Task Force (RDJTF). Eastern Turkey was presumably ideally situated to render assistance in contingencies in which the RDJTF would be asked to perform.[5]

Persian Gulf security remained the major external problem for the Atlantic Alliance in the 1980s, as mentioned earlier. The Turkish position on the thorny question of allied responsibility in assisting American efforts regarding Gulf security seemed quite simple at first. It declared it would restrict its cooperation only to obligations emanating from within formal NATO boundaries. In fact, however, its declared position remained largely theoretical as NATO communiqués repeatedly acknowledged the responsibility of the allies, subject to "national decisions," to facilitate external deployments by the US.

The US-Turkish Memorandum of Understanding signed in November 1982 also reflected the blurred distinction that Turkey entertained between strictly NATO obligations and those arising from external contingencies. The agreement envisaged the modernization of ten older airfields and the building of two new ones, one at Mus and one at Batman not far from the Turkish-Soviet and Turkish-Iranian borders. According to Bruce Kuniholm (1983:438-439), "These airfields, once completed would put NATO fighter bombers within 700 miles of Abadan–far closer to the head of the Persian Gulf than any of the 'facilities' to which the Central Command has access." With this very important agreement, then, Turkey became an active ally in the American/NATO plans and preparations for external contingencies in the Gulf region.

Military Assistance

The US demonstrated its resolve to bolster Turkey during widespread instability in southwestern Asia by steadily and generously increasing the total amount of foreign assistance. US assistance to Turkey quadrupled in 1981, only three years after 1978, when the four-year arms embargo was still in force most of the year. Importantly, the US also decided to assist Turkey with her defense industry program and modernization of her ailing air defenses. In 1983 General Dynamics bid for and won the coproduction of 160 F-16 fighter aircraft in Turkey.

The Federal Republic of Germany (FRG), the second biggest source of foreign aid to Turkey, also assumed a bigger role in extending economic and defense assistance. Under a new category entitled Special Armaments Program, she allocated between 600 million DM in grants during 1981-1984, primarily for tank modernization. The rationale for the renewed German interest in Turkey was expressed simply by Foreign Minister Hans Dietrich Genscher of the FRG during a visit to Ankara in 1983: "We want a strong Turkey" (*Milliyet,* March 8, 1984).

Sources of Tension

The impressive improvement in Turkish-American military and political cooperation in the first part of the 1980s did not imply that cooperation was free of complications. In fact, a number of issues threatened to undermine the basic understanding between the two governments. First, Turkey's less-than-explicit and less-than-full commitment concerning American access to bases in Turkey for Gulf and Middle Eastern contingencies seemed to have remained short of American expectations. Jed Snyder (1987:52) expressed skepticism about the Turkish stance: "Despite ([the Turkish Foreign Minister's] supportive public statements, the actual availability of [Turkish] bases in a crisis is open to substantial question." On the Turkish side, the amount of American assistance never seemed sufficient to meet the modernization needs of the armed forces, generally estimated to stand at 1 billion dollars per annum.

Moreover, to the dismay of Turkey, the US continued to respect the 7/10 ratio in determining the amount of aid to Greece and Turkey, respectively. On the other hand, Turkey's objections to the illegal Greek militarization of Lemnos kept it off-limits for NATO exercises–to the consternation of the US. Second, the high-profile crisis diplomacy of the PASOK government under Prime Minister Papandreou toward Turkey succeeded in holding Turkish-American relations hostage to Greek-Turkish relations. Third, the Turkish Cypriots declaration of the Turkish Republic of Northern Cyprus in the fall of 1983, and Turkey's recognition of it, won friends neither in Washington, D.C., nor in Brussels for Turkish diplomacy. Finally, in addition to the Greek lobby, the American-Armenian lobby effectively campaigned against Turkey in the American Congress. These issues stressed political relations but did not substantially militate against military relations.

CHALLENGES OF ADAPTATION TO THE POST-INF ERA

The reduced tension, the accelerating search for expanded areas of political and military accommodation and cooperation, and hence the growing stability between the East and the West since roughly the mid-1980s, as discussed briefly above, have drastically altered the agenda of Turkey's security concerns. The issues for Turkey center on the question of how to maximize military security through the alliance framework in a period of East-West confrontation and regional turbulence. The fundamental challenge in the closing years of the 1980s has been twofold: to determine the essential change in East-West relations, and depending on the direction of that assessment, either to continue with the status quo with some modifications, or to devise radically new policies responsive to the evolving security environment. The East-West momentum toward security in negotiated disarmament rather than in armaments was the critical factor, at first, in the framing of these tasks. The quick disintegration of the Eastern bloc in the second part of 1989 provided the second critical impetus to the foreign and security policy community.

Needless to say, not only Turkey but also the full membership of NATO as well as the Warsaw Pact and their respective leaders, confronted this twin challenge. In fact, it was the single most important challenge facing all of Europe as the 1990s neared. While, on the one hand, progress in arms control negotiations in Europe since 1987 undermined the rationale behind the East-West military alliances, on the other, political developments in the East, culminating in momentous popular developments in the second half of 1989, carved large holes in the ideological and physical division of Europe. In short, history was remade in Europe, and it seemed highly plausible that the new historical stage could, in the not--too-distant future, seal the end of the alliance structures erected in the Cold War era. What happened then, to Turkish security policy?

Turkish views changed as East-West interaction proceeded from one new stage to yet another, especially in the area of arms control and of dramatic popular reform movements in the East which totally discredited the postwar communist regimes. However, because of the very dynamic and complex process of change and attendant fluidity, vagueness and caution characterized Turkish assessments all along.

The First Shock: The INF Treaty

The historic INF treaty on the elimination of Soviet and American medium- and short-range nuclear forces was a watershed event for Turkish security perceptions,[6] as it was for everyone else. Turkey reacted to the INF treaty cautiously, not euphorically. She acknowledged the vital contribution of the treaty to East-West relations, but, at the same time, carefully indicated where she thought corrections and adjustments were necessary to preserve the Alliance's deterrence credibility.

More specifically, in the Turkish view, the elimination of land-based INFs made the conventional superiority of Warsaw Pact (WP) forces over NATO forces even more pronounced. With the conventional imbalance having thus gained in prominence and significance as a negative input to deterrence, it was argued, the post-INF period could breed, paradoxically, more insecurity than security especially in regions like the southeastern flank. To remedy this situation, the argument went, NATO needed to enhance its conventional capabilities, particularly in exposed areas such as Turkey where disparities were most acute. It was presumed that such a policy would induce the WP to be more forthcoming at the prospective conventional stability negotiations. Turkey did not substantially revise this view immediately after Gorbachev announced at the United Nations in December 1988 a promise for substantial unilateral reductions in Soviet forces.

Conversely, according to Turkey, remedies did not need to began with the modernization of short-range nuclear forces. It is important to note that Turkey is the only frontline country, other than the FRG, with short-range nuclear weapons on its soil. Until recently, Turkish decisionmakers publicly assigned deterrence power to these obsolete nuclear systems, deployed initially in the 1950s, and which included Honest John rockets and nuclear artillery and bombs. Turkey had opposed the earlier Bulgarian and Greek proposals for a nuclear-weapons-free zone in the Balkans. Furthermore, the absence of a public debate had kept any public questioning about the weapons themselves and their highly questionable military value to a minimum. Opposition to modernization intentions enunciated at the Montebello meeting in 1983 by the Nuclear

Planning Group was restricted to a small section of the informed public. The post-INF Alliance debate on the issue triggered a more open and clear official stance. Firm opposition was expressed to modernization as a way to compensate for the elimination of the INFs and to reconfirm the validity of the flexible response strategy. The Soviet Union signaled her pleasure at the Turkish stand. The alternative, in the Turkish view, was conventional force improvements. Interestingly, Turkey still did not call for the elimination of these obsolete nuclear systems, apparently continuing to retain her confidence in their deterrent value.

The Core Question: How Much Systemic Change in the Military Environment?

Turkey based her views of the immediate post-INF era of East-West relations on the answer or answers to what she saw as the critical question: How are the evolving changes in the military resources a threat to one's security? To the West's security?

Until about mid-1989, the answer in official circles was, "not much, yet." Apparently they believed that the external security environment had not undergone sufficiently deep and durable systemic change as to warrant a radical revision or total repudiation of existing security frameworks and approaches. They argued that the declared changes in Soviet/Warsaw Pact military doctrine in favor of "defensive defense" was a goal whose realization would be dependent on the successful completion of a long-term complex process. They were particularly apprehensive about the superior Warsaw Pact forces facing Turkey, which continued to be offensively manned, equipped, and deployed.

By mid-1989, Turkish assessments of the nature of evolving change in the Soviet threat (i.e., Soviet military doctrine and the NATO/Warsaw Pact conventional forces balance) relaxed. It appears that perceptions and the official stance were adjusted in line with the whirlwind speed of and progress achieved at the CFE negotiations in Vienna in March 1989. At year's end, Turkey seemed to entertain a sense of ambivalent optimism in anticipation of further substantive progress in the CFE negotiations, which offered the prospect of an enhanced security relationship with the "North."

Transatlantic Trends: "Fortress America" and "Fortress Europe"

In the immediate post-INF period, Turkey was a strong proponent of the view that the preservation of the Atlantic Alliance was, without reservation, the most important security task of the West over the medium term. The collective political military potency and strategic integrity of the Alliance and continued

American leadership were seen, in turn, as the essential elements of a strong, credible Alliance. The remedy to transatlantic discord lay in burden sharing, not in devolution or American disengagement.

The view that American leadership continued to be indispensible for European, and therefore Turkish, security in the post-INF period posed a basic dilemma for Turkey's Alliance diplomacy. While she advocated a closing of ranks within the Alliance in those times of fluidity, centrifugal forces and tendencies on both sides of the Atlantic were pulling the Alliance apart.

The more important of these forces fall into three categories. First, American skepticism about the continued merits of her security commitment to Europe increased. Second, the Western European publics grew reluctant to support defense expenditures particularly within the Alliance framework. And third, several West European countries increasingly tended to improve the coordination and cooperation of their security policies in institutions and channels outside the Alliance, that is, in the Western European Union (WEU) and some European Community (EC) chambers such as the European Political Cooperation (EPC). Even though the EPC's specific mandate was foreign policy coordination, it helped form a "European Pillar" to give greater energy and more substance to the process generally referred to as "the Europeanization of Europe's defense."

All three tendencies were mutually causative and reinforcing, of course. What was most disconcerting for Turkey was the long-term eventuality that these trends and exploratory moves could some day actually culminate in a Europe without the United States and a European security community, a kind of "Fortress Europe" built around the EC and the WEU, but without Turkey. The year 1992 loomed conspicuously in everyone's calculations.

In short, therefore, it was the inward-looking pull among the Western Europeans against the background of an inward-looking America that clearly posed the greatest challenge to Turkey's security planners. The likelihood of Turkey's admission into either the EC or the WEU seemed, and still seems, to be almost nil in the medium term, notwithstanding her application in 1987 for membership the EC and her declaration of accession to the WEU Platform soon after its proclamation in October 1987. The Independent European Program Group (IEPG) is one important all-European security entity, not strictly part of NATO because of the French membership, where Turkey seemed to have the opportunity to partake in the process of the Europeanization of defense. She participated in two joint projects and assumed the chairmanship of the IEPG in 1991 for a two-year term. Turkey's interest in the IEPG is probably equally motivated by her desire to attract foreign investment and technology transfer to help build the incipient defense industry.

Another trend troubling to Turkey was the fashionable strand of opinion in some Alliance circles in favor of a regional approach to defense concepts, strategies, and preparations. Apparently, this group was particularly interested in concentrating on the security and defense of the core countries located in the center of NATO Europe. Turkish official circles defended a more holistic view of security and defense, subscribing to the concept of "indivisibility" of Alliance security. It was only logical, then, that they rejected cente-oriented regional approaches, arguing that the outcome would be the creation of different zones at different levels of security within the Alliance, contrary to the philosophy of common defense.

The implications of regional approaches to Alliance defense was more unnerving to a flank country when joined with another hypothetical scenario: the convergence or overlap of the focus on the center with the evolving European pillar, in which the dominant tendency would also emphasize the center to the exclusion of the flanks. This could be forestalled, in the Turkish view, if the European pillar defined its boundaries from the outset to include the southern flank.

Liberalization in Europe and West European Security

The security debate in the West reached a dramatically new stage within the two brief years after the signing of the INF treaty in December 1987. Neither the speed of the progress at the CFE negotiations in Vienna through 1989, nor the extent and the pace of the movement of liberalization that swept over Eastern Europe in the second part of 1989 were envisaged in 1987 or even in 1988.

The developments in Eastern Europe, in particular, mobilized an entirely new political mood in the West, creating the prospect for the reunion of Eastern and Western Europe. The force of events pressed Western European integrationists into a new debate on how to reconcile the prospects of a liberal and liberated Eastern Europe with their ultimate vision of a compact, integrated Western Europe closed within itself. Thus, the vision of a reunited and integrated Europe, a vision regenerated and reinforced by the momentous changes in Eastern Europe, has rivaled the vision of an integrated Western Europe, pressuring it to expand its boundaries to include Eastern Europe into its fold. Could this be the beginning of a "Fortress Europe" on an all-European scale, instead of the Western portion only? The next logical but extremely formidable unknown would be the U.S. response. How would the US greet an all-European economic entity? Security entity?

The new phase of the political mood in the West, dominated by a sense of extreme fluidity and flux but of an optimistic hue, has inevitably spread to the security domain as well. Just as Western European integrationists have had to comprehend the implications of the political and economic changes in Eastern Europe throughout 1989, and since, so those Western European security communities contemplating a "Western European Pillar" have had to allow for the new developments in their plans and deliberations. Security in Europe has been transformed into an all-European concern.

Reordering the Threat Perception

If the receding Soviet threat was a long-overdue positive development in Turkey's security environment in the north, an adverse overall situation prevailed to her south. Generally speaking, southwestern Asia presents a precarious regional picture for long-term peace and stability. More specifically, at a time when certain categories of the Soviet's military force were officially declared to be the target of reduction, the military muscle of Iran, Iraq, and Syria was growing. The proliferation of ballistic missile technology, in particular, greatly increased Turkey's vulnerability in the southeast where she had a colossal irrigation and power-generation complex under construction. Moreover, Iran's tendency to interfere in Turkish secularism, and the regional intricacies of the Kurdish problem, for example, the role of Syria as sanctuary and training ground for anti-Turkey Kurdish separatists, had already created serious discord in Turkey's bilateral diplomacy with these countries.

Southeastern Turkey has been kept outside the zone of application of both the confidence-building provisions of the Conference on Security and Cooperation in Europe (CSCE) and of the CFE negotiations in Vienna. This is the context of the new round of the arms race in the region in which Turkey has explained her recent commitment to upgrade her defense industry and modernize her armed forces.[7] As is all too well-known, the Greek-Turkish conflict is another security problem for Turkey. The Davos initiative of winter 1988 helped reduce mutual tensions but not the underlying suspicion and mistrust. It is not inconceivable that with the Soviet threat receding into the background, the Greek threat will gain greater prominence in Turkish security concerns.

CONCLUSION

In conclusion, Turkish security on the East-West front and relations with the NATO/US alliance in the 1980s reflected the general flux, fluidity and optimism that characterized East-West and intra-Alliance relations in Europe. However, her optimism was somewhat more guarded, and conservative and her pro-Alliance stand more definitive. As the Cold War came to a close, the Soviet Union was gradually and cautiously being viewed as a credible candidate for recognition as a status quo member of the international community with scaled-down, nonaggressive, and nonoffensive political military ambitions. Threats, especially from southwesernt Asia and to some extent from Greece, were upgraded in importance and urgency. In these times of change, the future of Turkey's alliance relations with NATO and the US is likely to be heavily influenced by the course of developments external to her, for example, by evolving policies in Washington and Brussels, and less as a matter of her individual choice and initiative.

NOTES

1. For this critical period see Harry N. Howard, *Turkey, the Straits and U.S. Policy* (Baltimore: Johns Hopkins University Press, 1974), Chapter 7; Bruce R. Kuniholm, *The Origins of the Cold War in the Near East: Great Power Conflict and Diplomacy in Iran, Turkey, and Greece* (Princeton: Princeton University Press, 1980), pp. 260-269.

2. For the highlights of the debate see *Milliyet* (October 5, 1986); and *Hürriyet* (November 7, 1986). On November 5, the Turkish Foreign Ministry issued a statement rejecting as irresponsible and baseless the speculation in some foreign presses about Turkey's presumable intention to invade Kerkük if and when Iraq lost control of this region (*Hürriyet*, November 7, 1986).

3. *Turkish Republic Consultative Assembly Minutes*, 39th Session, Vol. 2 (January 20, 1982), pp. 367-369; 21st Session, Vol. 12 (November 22, 1982), pp. 250-253; 175th Session, Vol. 23 (October 11, 1983), pp. 139-141; and *Turkish Grand National Assembly Minutes*, 44th Session (December 16, 1984), pp. 37-43.

4. Richard Burt, speech at AHEPA, Chicago. August 12, 1983. USICA Fax print, Ankara. O.T.-83-18/12, p. 4.

5. In an interview with a Turkish daily on April 24, 1983, Assistant Secretary of State Richard Burt and Assistant Secretary of Defense Richard N. Perle rejected suggestions that the US administration's recently revived strategic interest in Turkey stemmed from a desire to turn it into the policeman of the Middle East, and denied that they were contemplating utilizing eastern Turkey as a suitable basing areas for the RDJTF (*Milliyet*, April 24, 1983, p. 4).

6. These views have been obtained from: Biren Işık (admiral, Turkish Navy. retired), "NATO's Security in the Mediterranean," *Turkish Review*, 2:10 (Winter 1987):11-17; Diplomatic Pulse (Abstract of *Turkish Daily Press*) Antalya, March 14, 1989; Vahit Halefoğlu (then minister of foreign affairs, "Allies and Partners," *NATO Review*, 34:1 (February 1986):1-6; Ministry of Foreign Affairs, *Budget Report*, Fiscal Year 1988; Turkish Grand National Assembly, Office of Minutes, Ankara, November 3, 1988 (in Turkish); Ministry of Foreign Affairs, Press Release, Ankara, December 9, 1988; Özal, Turgut (then prime minister), "Turkey in the Southern Flank," *Defense Yearbook 1989*, London: Brassey's Defense Publishers, 1989, pp. 3-9; Ercan Vuralhan (then minister of Defense), Statement before the Commission on the Plan and the Budget of the Grand National Assembly of Turkey, Ankara, November 18, 1988, Mimeographed Records (in Turkish); Ercan Vuralhan. Opening Statement, Eurogroup Round Table Meeting, Washington, D.C., November 28, 1988; Mesut Yılmaz (minister of foreign affairs). "Burden-Sharing from Turkey's Perspective," *NATO Review*, (October-November 1988):1-3.

7. For the military view see General Necip Torumtay (Turkish chief of general staff), "Turkish-US Relations: New Era, New Vision." *Newspot: Turkish Digest*, Ankara, November 18, 1989, p. 2.

REFERENCES

Cumhuriyet. August 2, 1983.

Dean, J. (1987). *Watershed in Europe: Dismantling the East-West Military Confrontation.* Lexington, Mass.: Lexington Books.

Gorbachev, M. (1987). *Perestroika: New Thinking for Our Country and the World.* New York: Harper and Row.

Howard, M. (1987). "The Gorbachev Challenge and the Defense of the West." *Survival.* Vol. 30, No. 6 (November/December):487.

Kuniholm, B. (1983). *The Origins of the Cold War in the Near East: Great Power Conflict and Diplomacy in Iran, Turkey, and Greece.* Princeton: Princeton University Press.

Milliyet. March 8, 1984.

Sezer, D. B. (1981). *Turkey's Security Policies.* London: The International Institute for Strategic Studies. Adelphi Paper 164.

Snyder, J. C. (1987). *Defending the Fringe: NATO, the Mediterranean and the Persian Gulf.* Boulder: Westview Press.

US Department of State (1982). *Department of State Bulletin.* 82:2065. Washington: D.C.

Epilogue

Atila Eralp, Muharrem Tünay,
and Birol A. Yeşilada

The 1980s were a difficult decade for Turkey. As the authors in this volume demonstrate, new right-wing governments embarked on a series of policies following the September 1980 coup that were designed to completely transform the socioeconomic and political structures of Turkey. These governments of the NSC and Özal's MP represented what Tünay calls the "new right," which had the financial and political support of the IMF, World Bank, and US administrations. As the country moved into the 1990s, however, developments show that the new right's efforts to transform Turkey had limited success in each policy area. Among the topics that are crucial for this transformation, women's issues and ethnic problems hold important place. However, the editors acknowledge that they were unable to incorporate these issues into this volume. Based on the analyses in this book, and in the light of recent developments in Turkey, one could nevertheless ask whether stabilization was worth it. To answer this question, this epilogue assesses this volume's findings and relevant developments since 1989.

In domestic politics, Muharrem Tünay explained the new right's attempt at hegemony, while Ayşe Ayata discussed the nature of the post-1980 political parties. Tünay's analysis suggests that the new rightist coalition of Turgut Özal, composed of elements from the fundamentalist, nationalist, and liberal groups, did not have the capacity to overcome differences in the individual preferences of these factions. Thus, this new coalition not only lacked organizational solidarity but also had internal contradictions. Ayata, on the other hand, argued that Özal's coalition presented a pragmatic solution to Turkey's political problems in a new era. Nonetheless, her findings also indicated that the organizational strength of the MP was much weaker than that of its challengers, the TPP and SDPP, each representing pre-1980 political forces. In essence, the MP's organizational stability depended on the ability of one man, Turgut Özal, to keep a balance between the three major factions of the party. Özal tried to mediate between the opposing elements of his coalition and temporarily supported the Holy Alliance of the fundamentalists and nationalists. Even so, when Özal became president of Turkey and resigned his seat in the MP, leaders of the three opposing groups jockeyed to replace him as party leader. Eventually, the liberals, led by former Foreign Minister Mesut Yılmaz, prevailed. In the end, the political cost of internal rivalries proved too costly. The TPP of Süleyman Demirel won the national elections in November 1991 and formed a coalition government with its archrival, the SDPP. Ironically, one could point out that had Demirel and the then leader of the RPP, Bülent Ecevit, agreed to form a similar national coalition in 1979, the country could have been spared a military coup.

Similarly, the coup coalition's attempts to transform the Turkish political system backfired. As Ayata, Şenses, and Tünay explained, the NSC tried to institutionalize new political parties and interest group associations under the control of an authoritarian state. The NSC replaced the liberal constitution of 1961 with an authoritarian document that allowed for limited pluralism in political party and interest association activity. Various restrictions on labor relations, which Şenses outlined, led to the formation of a limited number of political parties and controlled transition to civilian rule in 1983. Ayata and Tünay discussed this, and the resurgence of Islamic fundamentalist groups that Sencer Ayata analyzed are examples of the new right's attempts to establish hegemony in Turkey. In essence, the new right tried to establish what Bianchi (1986) and Stepan (1978) called an exclusionary form of state corporatism. However, developments in recent years has cast doubt on the success of their efforts. The outcome was neither a corporatist or truly pluralist political system. Rather, as Yeşilada (1988:373) explained, the new political order in Turkey satisfies the requirements of a heterogeneous form of interest representation:

In specific terms, the new constitution of Turkey includes articles and clauses that impose state control over the activities of citizens, interest groups, and political parties much like practices observed in other state corporatistic systems. Furthermore, the internal tensions and contradictions of the new political system meet Stepan's propositions concerning the future stability of state corporatist systems. Yet, despite the state corporatist nature of the new constitution, daily political life has steady moved toward pluralist tendencies . . . Such dramatic changes in party coalitions and the reemergence of pre-coup political groups are indicative of a volatile political atmosphere. It seems that the real showdown between these forces is yet to come.

The analyses in chapters 1-3 and 5 clearly outline the nature of these internal tensions and contradictions. Turgut Özal's efforts to maintain a balance between his party's three ideologically hostile factions indicate one such potentially dangerous contradiction. As explained above, once Özal left the party, this tenuous alliance promptly collapsed.

Furthermore, with regard to the new right's goal of reshaping Turkey's political future, coup leaders' attempts to exclude precoup political elites from the new political order proved a complete failure by 1991. Not only did these pre-1980 political leaders return to political life by 1987, but they also managed to win the national elections in November 1991 and form a coalition government between the True Path party and Social Democratic Populist party under the premiership of Süleyman Demirel. The new coalition government has promised that it will reverse the corporatistic legislations of the NSC and Özal governments and bring back liberal pluralist democracy.

In economic restructuring, export-led policies integrated the Turkish economy with the capitalist world market, as the chapters by Aydın, Balkır, Şenses, and Türel indicate. All these efforts received the support of the IMF and World Bank. Despite the claims of these international organizations that the Turkish experience is a model for other middle-income countries to follow, the results of economic stabilization are mixed as Turkey prepares to enter the twenty-first century.

On the positive side, Turkey did manage to implement an export-led growth model which included more realistic exchange rates and export promotion policies. Export earnings increased significantly and the current account balance came out of a deficit by 1990. Furthermore, industrial products' share in total exports increased from 36 percent to 78 percent, and the share of total trade in GNP doubled between 1980 and 1989. Finally, liberalization of investment laws attracted direct foreign investment in most sectors of the economy. On the down-side, the Stabilization Program resulted in a major redistribution of national income. In chapter 4, Türel found that lack of a rational industrial policy resulted in a transfer of profits away from industrial pursuits to rentiers and traders. The magnitude of this income redistribution, however, is substantially greater. According to Yeşilada and Fisunoğlu (1992:200), "The net result has been a regression in income distribution from popular sectors (agriculture, wages, and salaries) to profits, rents, and interest income. Factor shares as percent of national incomes for agriculture (farmers' income) declined from 26.7 in 1980 to 13.2 in 1988. During the same period, the share of wages and salaries fell from 23.9 to 15.8 percent. On the other hand, the share of rents, profits, and interest income increased from 49.5 percent in 1980 to 71 percent in 1988." Other negative outcomes include (1) failure to eliminate Turkey's trade deficit which is currently running around $2.6-4.0 billion annually; (2) a steady increase in the money supply (M2) which reached 33 percent of GNP by the end of 1980s; (3) high inflation rate–around 65 percent in 1992; (4) a serious decline in the real wages of workers and civil servants; and (5) a very large external debt resulting from the excessive borrowing of the Özal governments. At the end of 1991, Turkey's external debt (included undisbursed) was $45 billion. In the form of a debt service ratio, foreign debt obliterated more than one third of the country's annual export earnings.

One major outcome of the new right's political and economic policies was the entry of Islamic capital into the country. As Yeşilada explains, this capital provides the economic support for Islamic fundamentalism. Interestingly enough, members of Özal's family were active participants in establishing these financial ties. Furthermore, as Sencer Ayata describes, Islam appeals increasingly to all segments of society. Its influence is pervasive and becoming highly politicized, as is evident in the activities of the *tarikats*. Not everyone in the country welcomed this new financial relationship, however. Turkish secularists feared that influxes of Arab capital were an Islamic plot to undermine the Kemalist principles of Turkey and to drag the country backward and away from Europe (Henry, 1992:2). In addition, the various *tarikats* greatly suspect each other, and thus create internal obstacles for a union between the various factions. As long as they remain divided, their direct threat to the secular state is limited. Nonetheless, as Ayata points out, uneven economic development, rapid urbanization, and poor income distribution will continue to add to the appeal of Islam among the masses. If the current political leaders fail to improve socioeconomic conditions in the peripheral regions, Islamic fundamentalism will become an even greater force in Turkish socioeconomic and political life. In this regard one could argue that the jury is still out in the case of "Islamic revival in Turkish politics" and that the rest of the 1990s presents the most serious period for the contest between the secular and religious forces in the country.

Turkey's economic ties to the Arab world are part of her foreign policy toward this region. During the 1980s, Turkey's foreign policy profile became highly personalized under General Evren and Turgut Özal. As Sezer and Yeşilada explain, Turkish-American relations entered a new age of cooperation with agreements on military assistance and improved commercial ties. This rapprochement in US-Turkish relations culminated in Turkey's support of the American efforts in the Iraq-Kuwait crisis. This crisis once again highlighted Turkey's strategic significance for Western interests in the region. Furthermore, the collapse of the Soviet Union further reinforced this reality. Yet, with Özal out of office, the new Turkish government of Demirel has chosen to pursue a more moderate foreign policy toward the United States and the Arab world. Demirel's government aims to have Turkey accepted as a friend of the Arab states. The reasons for the policy shift are clear. The Gulf War undermined precoup Turkish governmental efforts to understand the country's heritage and security needs in the region as a friend of the Arab world. While the governments of those Arab states that supported the US coalition during the war may look favorably on Turkey's stand in the conflict, the image of Turks as mere proponents of Western imperialism in the Middle East has once again been brought to the minds of the Arab masses. Thus, the Demirel government is engaged in high-level diplomatic discussions to reestablish Turkish-Iraqi relations, improve relations with the PLO, and ease the concerns of its southern neighbors over the water problem caused by the Southeastern Anatolian Project.

With regard to the collapse of the Soviet Union, the rise of the newly independent Turkic states has shifted attention in Turkey toward the east. Suddenly, promotion of socioeconomic, cultural, and political ties with Azerbaijan, Kazakhistan, Kyrgyzstan, Uzbekistan, and Turkmenistan centers policy. Whether or not Turkey will succeed in this endeavor depends on a competition that is emerging between Turkey, Iran, and Saudi Arabia in this region. However, Turkey seems to have some advantages over the other two countries. First, there are linguistic, cultural, ethnic, and historical ties between the Turks and their cousins in the Turkic states. Second, Turkey presents a working democracy, in spite of three coups in three decades, that could serve as a secular political model for the Turkic states. And third, the Turkish economic model seems to be attractive to the Turkic states as they attempt to restructure their economies and establish ties to Western markets. It is also clear that the US and other Western countries support Turkey's efforts in this regard.

As to Turkey's relations with the EC, Eralp's findings are valid in the light of recent developments. The EC Commission decided on December 17, 1989 that it was impossible for the Community to enter into membership talks with Turkey. The Commission's decision was based on the following reasons. First, Turkey's economy was not compatible with the EC members' economies. Thus, it would be very costly for the EC to absorb the Turkish economy. Second, the Community could not absorb Turkey's large population and unemployment. Third, serious cultural differences exist between the EC and Turkey. Fourth, Turkish democracy still showed weaknesses in human rights areas. And fifth, though unspecified in the report, problems existed between Turkey and Greece over the Aegean and Cyprus (Commission of the EC, 1989). These problems still remain in EC-Turkish relations. Furthermore, the internal problems in the Community over the Maastricht treaty and exchange rate fluctuations are bound to postpone any immediate warming of ties between the two parties. In spite of all this, the above-mentioned developments in the Middle East and Central Asia have poised Turkey for regional supremacy, a fact not unnoticed by EC officials. Under the current presidency of the United Kingdom, EC officials drafted a report calling for improved relations with Turkey. The seriousness of this issue was best summed up by the *Economist* (September 12, 1992: 18):

The damage [in Turkish-EC relations] needs to be repaired, and more decisively than by the EC's usual bureaucratic fiddling. As a start, Britain should be aiming to get three things done by the end of the year. On the economic side, the EC aid for Turkey long blocked by Greece should be released, and the modest benefits to Turkey of the customs union due by 1996 should be accelerated. On the military side, Turkey deserves to be in the Western European Union with no strings attached. On the wider Euro-development front, Turkish ministers ought to be invited to all EC council meetings on subjects that affect Turkey. The Greeks will resist all these three things, but Greeks cannot forever be allowed to dictate relationships that transcend them.

Regardless of these realities, EC-Turkish relations do not show any prospects for improvement in the near future. In its November 1992 meeting of the WEU, the EC accepted the full membership of Greece in this organization, whereas Turkey remained an associate member. On the economic front, problems presented by the Greek veto still remain in effect. Given these difficulties, it is probable that Turkish leaders will attempt to advance their relations with the Turkic states while maintaining cordiality with the EC.

REFERENCES

Bianchi, R. (1986). "Interest Group Politics in the Third World." *Third World Quarterly*. Vol. 8. No. 2 (April).

Commission of the EC. (1989). *Commission Opinion on Turkey's Request for Accession to the Community*. Sec (89) 2290. Brussels, December 18.

The Economist. September 12, 1992.

Henry, C. M. (1992). "The Turkish Opening to Arab-Islamic Capital." Paper presented at the 1992 Annual Conference of the Middle East Studies Association. Portland, Oregon. October 10-14.

Stepan, A. (1978). *The State and Society: Peru in Comparative Perspective*. Princeton: Princeton University Press.

Yeşilada, B. A., and M. Fisunoğlu (1992). "Assessing the January 24, 1980 Economic Stabilization Program in Turkey." In Henri J. Barkey, ed., *The Politics of Economic Reform in the Middle East*. New York: St. Martin's Press, pp. 183-212.

Yeşilada, B. A. (1988). "Problems of Political Development in the Third Turkish Republic." *Polity*. Vol. 21. No. 2 (Winter):345-372.

Index

About the Editors and Contributors

Ayşe Ayata, Associate Professor of Political Science
Department of Public Administration
Middle East Technical University, Turkey

Sencer Ayata, Associate Professor of Sociology
Department of Sociology
Middle East Technical University, Turkey

Zülküf Aydın, Lecturer in Sociology
Department of Sociology
Leeds University, United Kingdom

Canan Balkır, Professor of Economics
Department of Economics
Dokuz Eylül University, Turkey

Atila Eralp, Associate Professor of International Relations
Department of International Relations
Middle East Technical University, Turkey

Duygu Bazoğlu Sezer, Professor of International Relations
Department of International Relations
Bilkent University, Turkey

Fikret Şenses, Professor of Economics
Department of Economics
Middle East Technical University, Turkey

Muharrem Tünay, Associate Professor of Political Science
Department of Public Administration
Middle East Technical University, Turkey

Oktar Türel, Professor of Economics
Department of Economics
Middle East Technical University, Turkey

Birol A. Yeşilada, Associate Professor of Political Science
Department of Political Science
University of Missouri-Columbia, US